CONTENTS

EDITOR'S WELCOME

Welcome to HomeDesigns for Sloping Lots. This exciting book illustrates modern home plans with the latest features and ideas for unusual sites. These unique homes take full advantage of views while economizing construction.

To create this book, we studied more than 4,000 home plans from 35 of America's leading residential designers. We also carefully reviewed plan sales statistics from the past five years to select only the most popular designs for sloping or hillside lots.

At HomeStyles "SOURCE 1" Designers' Network, we not only design home plans, we build dreams. For 45 years (since 1946), we've supplied more than 175,000 home plans to professional builders, home owners, and do-it-yourselfers. All have shared the common goal of building their dream home. The tremendous variety of designs represented in this book allows you to choose the home that best suits your lifestyle, budget, and building site.

Keep in mind that the most important part of a home design is the floor plan — the layout and flow of the rooms. If the floor plan excites you, minor changes are easily made by qualified professionals. Also, exterior styling and appearance can be easily modified. Wood siding can be changed to shakes or even to stucco, for example. Window and trim styles can also be changed. The only limits to creative customizing are your own taste and ingenuity.

As you let your dreams run wild, you'll discover one of the most exciting aspects about this book is the tremendous savings that our home plans give to you. Custom designs cost thousands of dollars, usually 5% to 15% of the cost of construction. The design costs for a $100,000 home, for example, can range from $5,000 to $15,000.

A "SOURCE 1" plan costs only $190 to $420 depending on the size of the home and the number of sets of blueprints that you order. When you order a "SOURCE 1" plan, you save the money you need to truly build your dream — to add a deck, swimming pool, beautiful kitchen, elegant master bedroom, luxurious bathroom, or other extras.

You can be assured of the quality of "SOURCE 1" plans. All of the blueprints are designed by licensed architects or members of the AIBD (American Institute of Building Designers). Each plan is designed to meet the nationally recognized building codes in effect, at the time and place that they were drawn.

Please note that all "SOURCE 1" plans are designed to meet the specifications of seismic zones I or II. Because the United States has such a wide variety of geography and climate, each county and municipality will have its own codes, ordinances, zoning requirements, and building regulations.

Therefore, depending on where you live, your plan may need to be modified to comply with your local building requirements — snow loads, energy codes, seismic zones, etc. If you need information or have questions regarding your specific requirements, call your local contractor, municipal building department, lumber yard, or the American Institute of Building Designers (AIBD 1-800-366-2423). You may also call the National Association of Home Builders (NAHB) (1-800-368-5242) to get the number of your local Home Builders Association, who can recommend a quality member builder in your area.

Building a home is truly the American dream. This book includes articles on how to select the right home design, offers money-saving tips on cutting construction costs, and most importantly, contains over 200 new, up-to-date and best-selling home designs.

"SOURCE 1" doesn't just design homes, we build dreams! We hope that this book brings you one step closer to building yours.

CHOOSING THE DESIGN THAT'S RIGHT FOR YOU

For most of us, our home is the largest investment we will ever make. As a result, the style and type of home that we build is largely an economic decision. But of equal importance are issues of lifestyle, personal taste, and self-expression. Inevitably, our home is both our castle and our captor. We invest in it with the incomes that we earn from our weekday labor, and on the weekends, we invest in it with our saws, hammers, paintbrushes, and lawn tools. Our homes are truly an all-consuming labor of love.

Recognizing that love is in the eyes of the beholder, the following is a helpful guide to follow as you search for your dream home.

BUDGET

As a general rule, building a home costs between $60 and $100 per square foot of living space. However, as with most rules, the exceptions are greater than the rule. The greatest variables are land costs, labor and material costs, and individual tastes and style. The best bet is to contact your local builders association, lumberyard, or contractor.

Once you have an idea of what you can afford, determine any changes that you foresee in your income over the next five to ten years. For many, the future holds a greater income and therefore the possibility of a larger house. For others — young parents considering part-time work or empty-nesters soon to retire, the future may hold a reduction in income. Keep these considerations in mind as you evaluate your home plan needs.

LIFESTYLE

Just as your income may change, so too may your lifestyle. Select a plan that is flexible, versatile and adaptable. Young families may need a design that allows for expansion or flexibility in the floor plan. A 10′ x 10′ nursery may be adequate for a young child but will be terribly cramped for a teenager. On the other hand, a nursery today may become a den tomorrow.

For empty-nesters, there are other considerations. Children leave but they also return with friends, spouses, and grandchildren. The flexibility of the home design is a major consideration in dealing with these changes.

Your final lifestyle consideration is "aging." As we get older stairs become more difficult, doors are harder to open, and kitchens and bathrooms become more difficult to manage (especially in a wheelchair). If you plan on aging with your home, be sure to design your home so that it ages with you. Wider hallways, reinforced bathrooms for handgrips and railings, and gradual slopes in stairways are easy and less expensive to install at the time of construction. Renovating your home for wheelchair accessibility or handicapped living can be extremely costly down the line.

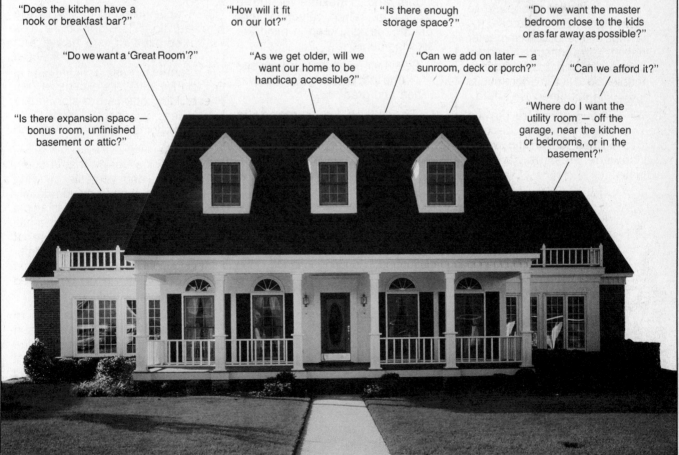

"Does the kitchen have a nook or breakfast bar?"

"Do we want a 'Great Room'?"

"How will it fit on our lot?"

"As we get older, will we want our home to be handicap accessible?"

"Is there enough storage space?"

"Can we add on later — a sunroom, deck or porch?"

"Do we want the master bedroom close to the kids or as far away as possible?"

"Can we afford it?"

"Is there expansion space — bonus room, unfinished basement or attic?"

"Where do I want the utility room — off the garage, near the kitchen or bedrooms, or in the basement?"

COST-SAVING TIPS FOR BUILDING A HOME IN THE 90's

With construction costs and land values on the rise, record numbers of home builders are looking for money-saving ideas to build an affordable "dream home." Real estate, design costs, building materials, and contracting are the four areas that offer the greatest savings potential for new home buyers.

REAL ESTATE TIPS

The cost of land will vary depending on its location, whether or not it is developed or undeveloped, and whether the site poses any problems such as a difficult terrain, complicated configuration, or local zoning requirements.

1. When evaluating the land you wish to buy, keep in mind that undeveloped land is generally cheaper than developed land. It also has greater potential for appreciation as the surrounding area develops.

2. Despite potential problems, a difficult site can be a blessing in disguise. Although additional expenses may be required to excavate or provide access, the savings on the lot can be greater than the extra construction costs. Also, buying a problem site may enable you to live in a community you could not otherwise afford.

NOTE: Although unimproved and problem sites are cheaper, the costs of road access, electricity, water, and sewage must be carefully evaluated.

Photo courtesy of Piercy & Barclay Designers   Plan P-7659

DESIGN TIPS

Once you have your lot, you must select a design that fits both your site and your lifestyle.

Identify your family's current and future needs and income. As a general rule, it is much safer to select a design that is within your budget and is flexible for future expansion. When selecting your "dream" design, keep in mind the following items:

1. Select a design that fits your site — one that will minimize excavation and grading.

2. There can be tremendous savings using predesigned blueprints from "SOURCE 1" or other reputable stock blueprint companies. Architects' fees for custom drawn blueprints will range from 5% to 15% of the cost of building your home. Design costs for a $100,000 home, for example, can range from $5,000 to $15,000. However, complete construction blueprints are available from most stock design companies for $190-$490.

3. A rectangular design with simple roof lines is significantly less expensive than a home with numerous angles, nooks and crannies. Also, building up is significantly less expensive than building out. (A two-story home is less expensive than a one-story home with the same living space).

4. Look for a design that is open, flexible, and versatile allowing rooms to change as your family grows. Built-in furniture is a cost effective way of utilizing small spaces. It gives a sense of greater volume in a small home. Look for a home with unfinished space such as an unfinished basement or attic.

5. Decks, patios, screened in porches, greenhouses, and sun rooms add tremendously to the comfort and pleasure that you'll have in living in your home. They also translate to increased value for resale!

6. Design your home for energy efficiency. 2x6 construction of the walls may be more expensive

Plan R-1028   Photo courtesy of Barclay Home Designs

4

Plan H-930

Photos by Bob Hallinen

in the short run, but these minimal costs will be paid back in energy savings.

Site your house correctly. A southern exposure in colder climates and a northern exposure in warmer climates will have a surprising effect on your fuel bills.

MATERIAL TIPS

The materials used to build your home are the most expensive costs of construction. Don't compromise on materials to save money! Savings can be made in using pre-manufactured materials and standard sizes.

1. Limit custom work! As attractive as elaborate detailing can be, the cost is often exorbitant. Look for mass produced detailing wherever possible.

2. Areas such as the kitchen and the bathroom are often very expensive to build due to the number of appliances, cabinets and features. Your builder and local supplier can design the kitchen and bathroom to take advantage of pre-designed cabinetry and counters.

CONTRACTING TIPS

Cutting construction costs (i.e. labor and materials) requires experience, time, and organizational skills.

As a home builder you have four options:

1. A construction company;

2. A general contractor (carpenter/ builder);

3. Act as your own general contractor;

4. Build your own home.

In all of these cases, the contractor is responsible for coordinating the work of all "trades" — electricians, plumbers, painters, builders, etc., securing permits, handling finances and ensuring quality. There are advantages and disadvantages to each option:

1. A general construction company may offer some cost savings because your project will be consolidated with a number of other concurrent projects and there may be labor savings with sub-contractors. However, your house is one of many and you will not have much personal contact with your builder.

2. The general contractor can provide more personalized attention than a construction company. However, you will have to spend more time reviewing and comparing competitive bids and possibly specifying materials. A general contractor usually works on a "cost-plus" basis — the costs of materials and sub-contractors' charges plus the contract fee. This can either be a fixed cost or a percentage of the cost.

3. Acting as your own general contractor significantly reduces costs but also significantly increases the time and responsibility you must commit to the project. In this role, you have the responsibility of hiring, supervising, securing permits, and getting materials. This requires knowledge of local building codes and means working with construction specialists. Although the savings are significant, you must weigh the extensive commitment and time involved against having the work done by a professional.

4. The most cost efficient approach is to act as your own contractor and builder. In this case you eliminate all the costs except for materials. This option can be rewarding but requires a tremendous commitment of time — first in educating yourself, and then in doing it.

Photo by Gil Ford

Plan E-2208

5

10 Most Popular Elements of a Good Home Design

1. Eye-Catching Exterior

Your house is a form of self-expression. Whether simple or subdued, stately or elegant, the exterior creates the first impression of your home. Does the exterior appearance of the home suit your tastes? If not, will changing the exterior materials or the color help?

2. Entryway Warmth

An inviting entryway sets the tone and atmosphere of your home. Does the entry have ample closet storage? Are the entrances covered or sheltered from rain or snow?

3. Zoning

There are three major zones in each home: working zones — kitchen, utility room, garage, bathrooms, and entryways; living zones — the living room, dining room, nook, family room, and/or Great Room; quiet zones — master bedroom, secondary bedrooms, library, den, and study.

As you look at your home plan, keep in mind that a good plan buffers the quiet zones from working zones by physically separating them on different levels or by placing living areas between them.

4. Traffic Flow

Another issue to consider is how people will travel between rooms and between zones. This is called traffic flow. You may wish to analyze the floor plan by asking: Is there a convenient path between the garage and the kitchen for carrying groceries and other supplies? How does traffic pass between the kitchen and other eating areas? Are bathrooms easily accessible to bedrooms and the family and recreation areas? Do I want the master bedroom close to or separate from the other bedrooms? Do I want the utility area in the basement, near the kitchen or near the bedrooms?

5. Openness, Flexibility, and Versatility

Look for a design that is open and airy and has rooms with multiple uses to change with your family's

Photo courtesy of Piercy & Barclay Designers

Plan P-6563

needs. For example, the "Great Room" concept has become increasingly popular. In this idea, the kitchen, breakfast room, and family room work together as one large area yet function as separate spaces with their own identities. Also, ask yourself, can a nursery or spare bedroom be converted into a study, library, or parlour? Could the kitchen or Great Room be expanded by adding a sun room or sliding door for a future deck or screened porch?

6. Atmosphere

Atmosphere is created by the use of natural light, heightened ceilings, skylights, clerestory windows, and creative use of built-in artificial lights. Heightened ceilings create a greater sense of space and volume without increasing the actual dimensions of the room. A ceiling can also change the entire atmosphere of a room — vaulted and cathedral ceilings provide a contemporary "feel," trayed ceilings are more formal and elegant, and beamed ceilings create a casual and homey atmosphere.

7. Master Suites and Luxurious Master Bathrooms

A spacious, refreshing, and relaxing private bedroom retreat is highly popular. Walk-in closets, dual vanities, skylights, a separate shower and tub are added luxuries in high demand.

8. Kitchens

The kitchen has become a social center often incorporated with a breakfast nook and Great Room. A large, open kitchen with plenty of counter space, an island or peninsula counter, and a breakfast bar are highly desirable features.

9. Storage, Built-ins, and Utility Rooms

Creative use of alcoves, built-in bookshelves, nooks, and wet bars are both popular and cost effective. These small elements can create a larger sense of space in an otherwise small or medium-sized design.

Storage spaces are in high demand. Does the home you are looking for have an unfinished attic, basement, bonus room, or expandable garage? Do the bedrooms have adequate closet space? Does the kitchen have a pantry and sufficient cupboards? Does the utility room have extra storage and sufficient space?

10. Inside/Outside

To bring the outdoors in, new home designs are incorporating sun rooms, solariums, and greenhouses, as well as decks, patios, and porches. Creative window shapes and energy-efficient glass doors allow your home design to capture the beauty and freshness of the outdoors. If your home does not have a backyard deck or patio, could these be added without major expense?

Photo by: Karl Bischoff

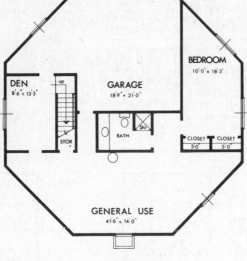

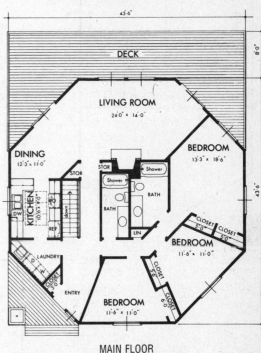

DEN
8'-6" x 13'-3"

up

GARAGE
18'-9" x 21'-0"

BEDROOM
10'-0" x 18'-3"

STOR

BATH

Shr.

CLOSET
5'-0"

CLOSET
5'-0"

GENERAL USE
41'-6" x 14'-0"

BASEMENT

1/16" = 1'
0 1 2 3 4 5 6 7 8 9 10

DECK

43'-6"

8'-0"

LIVING ROOM
24'-0" x 14'-0"

DINING
12'-3" x 11'-0"

STOR

Shower

STOR

Shower

BEDROOM
13'-3" x 18'-6"

KITCHEN
10'-6" x 9'-0"

down

BATH

BATH

CLOSET
5'-0"

CLOSET
5'-0"

43'-6"

DW

REF

LIN

BEDROOM
11'-6" x 11'-0"

LAUNDRY

D W

CLOSET

ENTRY

CLOSET
5'-6"

CLOSET
6'-0"

BEDROOM
11'-6" x 11'-0"

MAIN FLOOR

Unique Octagon Design

- Irregularly shaped rooms are oriented around an entrance hall paralleling the octagonal exterior.
- Short directional hallways eliminate cross-room traffic and provide independent room access to the front door.
- Spacious living and dining rooms form a continuous area more than 38' wide.
- Oversized bathroom serves a large master suite which features a deck view and dual closets.
- This plan is also available with a stucco exterior (Plans H-942-2, with daylight basement, and H-942-2A, without basement).

Plans H-942-1, -1A & -2A

Bedrooms: 3-4	Baths: 2-3
Space:	
Main floor:	1,564 sq. ft.
Basement:	approx. 1,170 sq. ft.
Total with basement:	2,734 sq. ft.
Garage:	394 sq. ft.
Exterior Wall Framing:	2x6

Foundation options:
Daylight basement (Plans H-942-1 & -2).
Crawlspace (Plans H-942-1A & -2A).
(Foundation & framing conversion diagram available — see order form.)

Blueprint Price Code:
Without basement:	B
With basement:	D

Plans H-942-1/1A & -2/2A

***TO ORDER THIS BLUEPRINT,
CALL TOLL-FREE 1-800-547-5570***
(Prices and details on pp. 12-15.)

7

Photo by Bob Hallinen

Soaring Design
Lifts the Human Spirit

- Suitable for level or sloping lots, this versatile design can be expanded or finished as time and budget allow.
- Surrounding deck accessible from all main living areas.
- Great living room enhanced by vaulted ceilings, second-floor balcony, skylights and dramatic window wall.
- Rear entrance has convenient access to full bath and laundry room.
- Two additional bedrooms on upper level share second bath and balcony room.

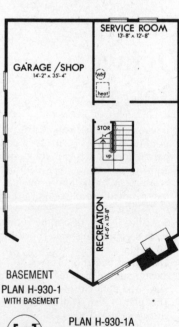

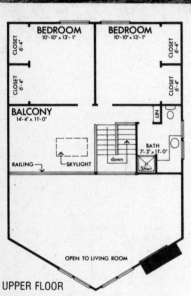

UPPER FLOOR

Plans H-930-1 & -1A

Bedrooms: 3	Baths: 2

Space:

Upper floor:	710 sq. ft.
Main floor:	1,210 sq. ft.
Total living area:	**1,920 sq. ft.**
Basement:	1,210 sq. ft.
Garage:	(Included in basement).

Exterior Wall Framing:	2x6

Foundation options:
Daylight basement (Plan H-930-1).
Crawlspace (Plan H-930-1A).
(Foundation & framing conversion diagram available — see order form.)

Blueprint Price Code:

Without finished basement:	B
With finished basement:	D

Plans H-930-1 & -1A

Popular Plan for Any Setting

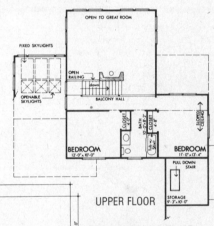

Photo by Kevin Robinson

- City, country, or casual living is possible in this versatile two-story design.
- A spa room and sunning area lie between the master suite and Great Room, all encased in an extended eating and viewing deck.
- U-shaped kitchen, nook, and dining area fulfill your entertaining and dining needs.
- Two additional bedrooms and a balcony hall are located on the second level.
- Daylight basement option provides a fourth bedroom, shop, and recreation area.

UPPER FLOOR

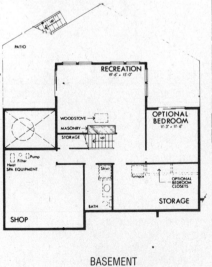

BASEMENT

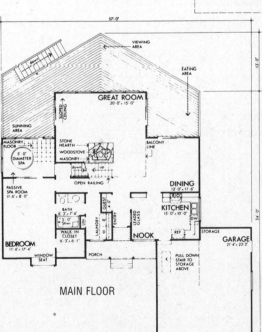

MAIN FLOOR

Plans H-952-1A & -1B

Bedrooms: 3-4	Baths: 2-3

Space:

Upper floor:	470 sq. ft.
Main floor:	1,207 sq. ft.
Passive spa room:	102 sq. ft.
Total living area:	**1,779 sq. ft.**
Basement:	1,105 sq. ft.
Garage:	496 sq. ft.

Exterior Wall Framing:	**2x6**

Foundation options:
Daylight basement (Plan H-952-1B).
Crawlspace (Plan H-952-1A).
(Foundation & framing conversion diagram available — see order form.)

Blueprint Price Code:

Without finished basement:	B
With finished basement:	D

TO ORDER THIS BLUEPRINT, CALL TOLL-FREE 1-800-547-5570
(Prices and details on pp. 12-15.)

Plans H-952-1A & -1B

Dramatic Interior Makes a Best-Seller

- An incredible master suite takes up the entire 705 sq. ft. second floor, and includes deluxe bath, huge closet and skylighted balcony.
- Main floor design utilizes angles and shapes to create dramatic interior.
- Extra-spacious kitchen features large island, sunny windows and plenty of counter space.
- Sunken living room focuses on massive fireplace and stone hearth.
- Impressive two-level foyer is lit by skylights high above.

Photo by Karlis Grants

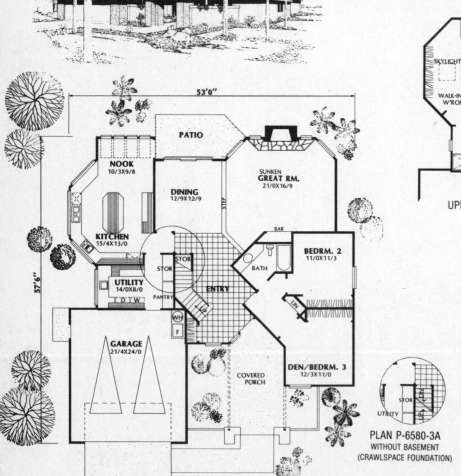

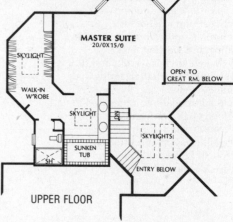

UPPER FLOOR

MAIN FLOOR

PLAN P-6580-3A
WITHOUT BASEMENT
(CRAWLSPACE FOUNDATION)

Plans P-6580-3A & -3D

Bedrooms: 2-3	Baths: 2
Space:	
Upper floor:	705 sq. ft.
Main floor:	1,738 sq. ft.
Total living area:	2,443 sq. ft.
Basement:	1,738 sq. ft.
Garage:	512 sq. ft.
Exterior Wall Framing:	2x4

Foundation options:
Daylight basement (Plan P-6580-3D).
Crawlspace (Plan P-6580-3A).
(Foundation & framing conversion diagram available — see order form.)

Blueprint Price Code:	C

TO ORDER THIS BLUEPRINT,
CALL TOLL-FREE 1-800-547-5570
(Prices and details on pp. 12-15.)

Plans P-6580-3A & -3D

Photo by Carren Strock

Proven Plan Features Passive Sun Room

- A passive sun room, energy-efficient wood stove, and a panorama of windows make this design highly economical.
- Open living/dining room features attractive balcony railing, stone hearth, and adjoining sun room with durable stone floor.
- Well-equipped kitchen is separated from dining area by a convenient breakfast bar.
- Second level sleeping areas border a hallway and balcony.
- Optional basement plan provides extra space for entertaining or work.

Plans H-855-3A & -3B

Bedrooms: 3	Baths: 2-3
Space:	
Upper floor:	586 sq. ft.
Main floor:	1,192 sq. ft.
Sun room:	132 sq. ft.
Total living area:	1,910 sq. ft.
Basement:	approx. 1,192 sq. ft.
Garage:	520 sq. ft.
Exterior Wall Framing:	2x6

Foundation options:
Daylight basement (Plan H-855-3B).
Crawlspace (Plan H-855-3A).
(Foundation & framing conversion diagram available — see order form.)

Blueprint Price Code:
Without basement	B
With basement	E

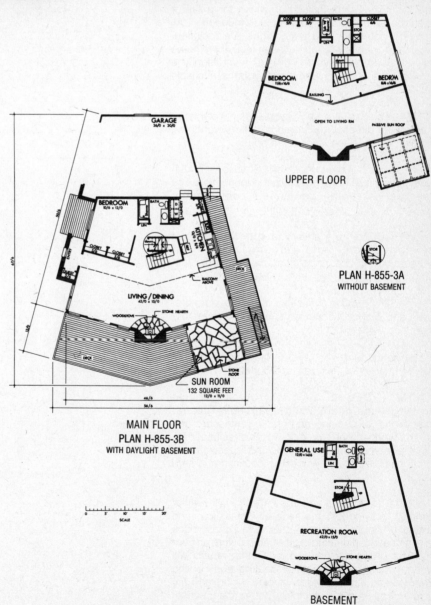

UPPER FLOOR

PLAN H-855-3A
WITHOUT BASEMENT

MAIN FLOOR
PLAN H-855-3B
WITH DAYLIGHT BASEMENT

BASEMENT

THE "SOURCE 1" PLANS PACKAGE — COMPLETE

WHAT OUR PLANS INCLUDE

"SOURCE 1" construction blueprints are detailed, clear and concise. All blueprints are designed by licensed architects or members of the A.I.B.D. (American Institute of Building Designers), and each plan is designed to meet the nationally recognized building codes (either the Uniform Building Code, Standard Building Code or Basic Building Code) at the time and place they were drawn.

Although blueprints will vary depending on the size and complexity of the home and on the individual designer's style, each set will include the following elements:

1. **Exterior Elevations** show the front, rear, and the sides of the house including exterior materials, details, and measurements.

2. **Foundation Plans** include drawings for a full or daylight basement, crawlspace, or slab foundation. All necessary notations and dimensions are included. (Foundation options will vary for each plan. If the home you want does not have the type of foundation you desire, a foundation conversion diagram is available from "SOURCE 1".)

3. **Detailed Floor Plans** show the placement of interior walls and the dimensions for rooms, doors, windows, stairways, etc. of each level of the house.

4. **Cross Sections** show details of the house as though it were cut in slices from the roof to the foundation. The cross sections detail the home's construction, insulation, flooring and roofing details.

5. **Interior Elevations** show the specific details of cabinets (kitchen, bathroom, and utility room) fireplaces, built-in units, and other special interior features.

6. **Roof Plans** provide the layout of rafters, dormers, gables, and other roof elements including clerestory windows and skylights.

7. **Schematic Electrical Layouts** show the suggested location for switches, fixtures, and outlets.

8. **General Specifications** provide general instructions and information regarding structural specifications, excavating and grading, masonry and concrete work, carpentry and wood specifications, thermal and moisture protection, and specifications about drywall, tile, flooring, glazing, caulking and sealants.

NOTE: Due to regional variations, local availability of materials, local codes, methods of installation, and individual preferences, it is impossible to include much detail on heating, plumbing, and electrical work on your plans. The duct work, venting, and other details will vary depending on the type of heating and cooling system (forced air, hot water, electric, solar) and the type of energy (gas, oil, electricity, solar) that you use. These details and specifications are easily obtained from your builder, contractor, and/or local suppliers.

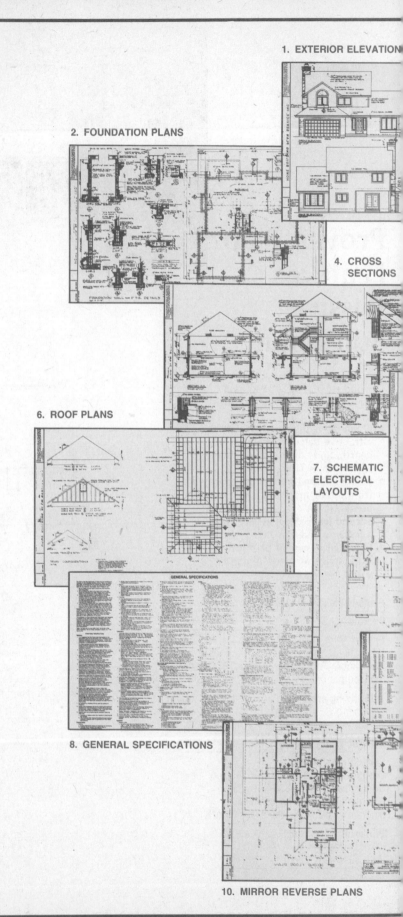

1. EXTERIOR ELEVATION

2. FOUNDATION PLANS

4. CROSS SECTIONS

6. ROOF PLANS

7. SCHEMATIC ELECTRICAL LAYOUTS

8. GENERAL SPECIFICATIONS

10. MIRROR REVERSE PLANS

CONSTRUCTION BLUEPRINTS TO BUILD YOUR HOME

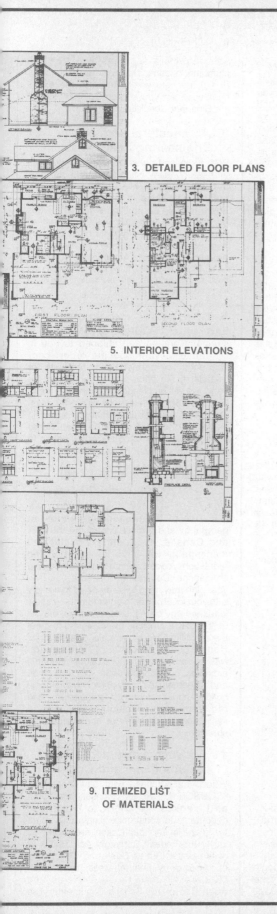

3. DETAILED FLOOR PLANS

5. INTERIOR ELEVATIONS

9. ITEMIZED LIST OF MATERIALS

11. HELPFUL "HOW-TO" DIAGRAMS

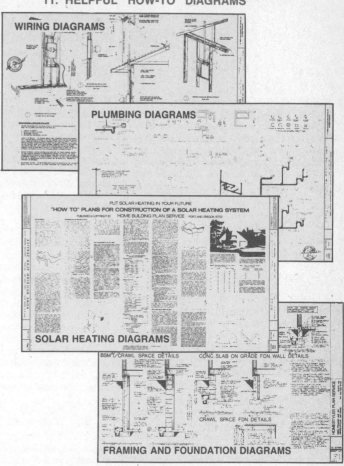

WIRING DIAGRAMS

PLUMBING DIAGRAMS

SOLAR HEATING DIAGRAMS

FRAMING AND FOUNDATION DIAGRAMS

Important Extras and Helpful Building Aids
(Sold Separately)

Every set of plans that you order will contain all the details that your builder will need. However, "Source 1" provides additional guides and information as follows:

9. **Itemized List of Materials** details the quantity, type, and size of materials needed to build your home. (This list is extremely helpful in acquiring an accurate construction estimate. It is not intended for use to order materials.)

10. **Mirror Reverse Plans** are useful if you want to build your home in the reverse of the plan that is shown. Reverse plans are available for an additional charge. However, since the lettering and dimensions will read backwards, we recommend that you order at least one regular-reading set of blueprints.

11. **Helpful "How-To" Diagrams — Plumbing, Wiring, Solar Heating, and Framing and Foundation Conversion Diagrams**

Each of these diagrams details the basic tools and techniques needed to plumb, wire, and install a solar heating system, convert plans with 2 x 4 exterior walls to 2 x 6 (or vice versa), or adapt a plan for a basement, crawlspace, or slab foundation.

WHAT YOU NEED TO KNOW
BEFORE YOU ORDER

1. HomeStyles "SOURCE 1" Designers' Network

"SOURCE 1" is a consortium of 35 of America's leading residential designers. All the plans presented in this book are designed by licensed architects or members of the A.I.B.D. (American Institute of Building Designers), and each plan is designed to meet the nationally recognized building codes (either the Uniform Building Code, Standard Building Code or Basic Building Code) in effect at the time and place that they were drawn.

2. Blueprint Price Schedule

Our sales volume allows us to offer quality blueprints at a fraction of the cost it takes to develop them. Custom designs cost thousands of dollars, usually 5 to 15 percent of the cost of construction. Design costs for a $100,000 home, for example, can range from $5,000 to $15,000. A HomeStyles "SOURCE 1" plan costs only $190 to $490 depending on the size of the home and the number of sets of blueprints that you order. By ordering a "SOURCE 1" plan, you save enough money to add a deck, swimming pool, beautiful kitchen, luxurious master bedroom, elegant bathroom, or other extras.

The "SOURCE 1" pricing schedule is based on "total finished living space." When we calculate "living space" we do not include garages, porches, decks, unfinished space or unfinished basements. The schedule below outlines the value and savings you get from ordering "SOURCE 1" plans and multiple sets:

NUMBER OF SETS	PRICE CODE GROUP BY SQUARE FEET						
	A Under 1,500	B 1,500-1,999	C 2,000-2,499	D 2,500-2,999	E 3,000-3,499	F 3,500-3,999	G 4,000 & Up
7	$265	$315	$350	$385	$420	$455	$490
4	$235	$275	$305	$340	$375	$410	$445
1	$190	$225	$255	$285	$320	$355	$390

*Prices guaranteed to December 31, 1991.

3. Revisions, Modifications, and Customizing

The tremendous variety of designs available through "SOURCE 1" allows you to choose the home that best suits your lifestyle, budget and building site. Your home can be easily customized through your choice of siding, roof, trim, decorating, color, and other non-structural alterations and materials.

Most "SOURCE 1" plans are easily modified by qualified professionals. Minor changes and material substitutions can be made by any professional builder without the need for expensive blueprint revisions. However, if you are considering making major changes to your design, we strongly recommend that you seek the services of an architect or professional designer to assist you.

Also, every state, county, and municipality has its own codes, zoning requirements, ordinances, and building regulations. Modifications may be necessary to comply with your specific requirements — snow loads, energy codes, seismic zones, etc.

4. Estimating Building Costs

Building costs vary widely depending on style and size, the type of finishing materials you select, and the local rates for labor and building materials. With an average cost per square foot of construction, you can multiply this figure by the total living area of your home and derive a rough estimate. More accurate estimates will require a professional review of the working blueprints and the types of materials you choose. To get a rough estimate, call a local contractor, your state or local Builders Association, the National Association of Home Builders (NAHB), or the AIBD.

5. Foundation Options and Exterior Construction

Depending on your specific geography and climate, your home will be built with either a slab, crawlspace, or basement type foundation and the exterior walls will either be 2 x 4 or 2 x 6. Most professional contractors and builders can easily adapt a home to meet the foundation and exterior wall requirements that you desire. If the specific home that you select does not meet your foundation or exterior wall requirements, "SOURCE 1" has a foundation and framing conversion diagram available.

6. "SOURCE 1" Service Policy and Blueprint Delivery

"SOURCE 1" service representatives are available to answer questions and assist you in placing your blueprint order. All telephone orders are entered directly into our computer. Mail orders are entered upon receipt. We try to process and ship every order within 48 hours. For regular mailing (US First Class Mail or UPS Second Day Air) you should receive your blueprints within 4 to 5 working days. For express mail (UPS Next Day Air or Federal Express) please expect 1 to 2 days for delivery.

7. How Many Blueprints Should I Order?

```
BLUEPRINT CHECKLIST
____  OWNER'S SET(S)
____  BUILDER (usually requires at least
      three sets: one for legal document,
      one for inspections, and a minimum
      of one set for subcontractors.)
____  BUILDING PERMIT DEPARTMENT
      (at least one set; check with your
      local governing body for number of
      sets required.)
____  LENDING INSTITUTION (usually
      one set for conventional mortgage;
      three sets for FHA or VA loans.)
____  TOTAL NUMBER OF SETS NEEDED
```

A single set of blueprints is sufficient to study and review a home in greater detail. However, if you are planning to get cost estimates or are planning to build, you will need a minimum of 4 sets and more likely 7 sets — sometimes more. Once you begin the process of building your home, everyone seems to need a set. As the owner, you will want to retain a set (1), your lending institution (2), the local building authorities (3), your builder/contractor (4), and of course,

subcontractors — foundation, framing, plumbing, heating, electrical, insulation, etc. (5-10) To help you determine the exact number of sets you will need, please refer to the Blueprint Checklist.

8. Architectural and Engineering Seals

With increased concern over energy costs and safety, many cities and states are now requiring that an architect or engineer review and "seal" a blueprint prior to construction. There may be an additional charge for this service. Please contact your local lumber yard, municipal building department, Builders Association, or local chapters of the AIBD or American Institute of Architecture (AIA).
Note: (Plans for homes to be built in Nevada may have to be re-drawn and sealed by a Nevada-licensed design professional.)

9. Returns and Exchanges

Each set of "SOURCE 1" blueprints is specially printed and shipped to you in response to your specific order; consequently, we cannot honor requests for refunds. If the prints you order cannot be used, we will be pleased to exchange them. Please return all sets to us within 30 days. For the new set of plans that you select in exchange, there will simply be a flat charge of $50 (plus $5 for each additional set up to the original number of sets ordered).

10. Compliance With Local Codes and Building Regulations

Because of the tremendous variety of geography and climate throughout the U.S. and Canada, every state, county, and municipality will have its own building regulations, codes, zoning requirements and ordinances. Depending on where you live, your plan may need to be modified to comply with your local building requirements — snow loads, energy codes, seismic zones, etc. All of "SOURCE 1" plans are designed to meet the specifications of seismic zones I or II. HomeStyles "SOURCE 1" Designers' Network authorizes the use of our blueprints expressly conditioned upon your obligation and agreement to strictly comply with all local building codes, ordinances, regulations, and requirements — including permits and inspections at the time of and during construction.

11. License Agreement, Copy Restrictions, and Copyright

When you purchase your blueprints from "SOURCE 1," we, as Licensor, grant you, as Licensee, the right to use these documents to construct a single unit. All of the plans in this publication are protected under the Federal Copyright Act, Title XVII of the United States Code and Chapter 37 of the Code of Federal Regulations. Each "Source 1" designer retains title and ownership of the original documents. The blueprints licensed to you cannot be used, resold to any other person, copied or reproduced by any means.

How to Order Your Blueprints

Ordering blueprints is fast and easy. You can order by mail, by fax (use our International Fax number 1-612-338-1626) or call our toll free number **1-800-547-5570.** When ordering by phone, please have your credit card ready. Thank you for your order. Good luck building your dream home.

★ "Source 1" Home Photo Contest — Win $1000 ★

When you build your "Source 1" home, we'd like to give you national recognition. We are always looking for cover photos of finished homes for our home plan magazines. Even if you've made modifications, we would love to see your pictures. Send us snapshots of your finished homes. Photos need not be professionally taken. If we use your home as a cover or inside feature, you will win $250. If we select your home for our Annual cover, you will win $1,000. Please send all photos along with your name, address, phone number and the plan number to the attention of Ms. Pam Tasler, Ass't Editor.

------ BLUEPRINT ORDER FORM -----------

Mail to:
HomeStyles "Source 1"
275 Market St., Suite 521
Minneapolis, MN 55405

For Faster Service
Call Toll-Free
1-800-547-5570

Please send me the following:

Plan Number _____ **Price Code** _____

Foundation _____
(Please review your plan carefully for foundation options — basement, crawlspace, or slab. Many plans offer all three options, others offer only one.)

Number of Sets	A	B	C	D	E	F	G	Amount
☐ 7	$265	$315	$350	$385	$420	$455	$490	$ _____
☐ 4	$235	$275	$305	$340	$375	$410	$445	$ _____
☐ 1	$190	$225	$255	$285	$320	$355	$390	$ _____

Blueprint Price Codes

*Prices guaranteed to December 31, 1991.

☐ **Additional Sets** of this plan, $25 now; $35 later, each. (Number of sets _____) $ _____

☐ **Itemized List of Materials,** $30, each additional set $10.
Lists are available only for plans with prefix letters AH, AM*, AX, B, C, CDG*, CPS, DD*, DG, E, H, I, J, K, N, NW*, P, R, S, SD, U, W
*Please ask when ordering, not available on all plans $ _____

☐ **Description of Materials:** Two sets $25
(For use in obtaining FHA or VA financing)
(Only available for Plans with prefix letters C, E, H, J, K, N, P, U) $ _____

☐ **Mirror Reverse Surcharge,** $25.
(Number of sets to be reversed _____.)
*The writing on Mirror Reverse plans will be backwards. Order at least one regular set. $ _____

☐ **Typical How-To Diagrams** $ _____
☐ Plumbing ☐ Wiring ☐ Solar Heating
☐ Framing & Foundation Conversion
One set @ $12.50, any two @ $23.00, any three @ $30.00, all four only $35.

☐ **Sales Tax** (MN Residents, please add 6%) $ _____

Please Add Postage Charges (Check One)

☐ First-Class Priority or UPS Blue Label (U.S. only), $10.50 $ _____
Allow 4-5 working days for delivery. *Must have street address for UPS delivery.
☐ First-Class Priority (Canada only) $10.50 $ _____
Allow 2-3 weeks for delivery.
☐ Overnight Express Delivery (U.S. only) $25.00 $ _____
Allow 1-2 working days for delivery. *Must have street address.
☐ Express Delivery (Canada only) $40.00 $ _____
Allow 4-5 working days for delivery. *Must have street address.
☐ Overseas Airmail Delivery $40.00 $ _____
Allow approx. 7 working days.

Payment   TOTAL ORDER $ _____
☐ Check/money order enclosed (in U.S. funds)
☐ VISA ☐ MasterCard ☐ AmEx ☐ Discover   Exp. Date_____

Card Number _____

Signature _____

Name _____

Street _____

City _____ State ____ Zip_____

Daytime Telephone (____) _____

☐ Builder-Contractor ☐ Home Owner ☐ Renter   PG-19

------ BLUEPRINT ORDER FORM --------

Mail to:
HomeStyles "Source 1"
275 Market St., Suite 521
Minneapolis, MN 55405

For Faster Service
Call Toll-Free
1-800-547-5570

Please send me the following:

Plan Number _____ **Price Code** _____

Foundation _____
(Please review your plan carefully for foundation options — basement, crawlspace, or slab. Many plans offer all three options, others offer only one.)

Number of Sets	A	B	C	D	E	F	G	Amount
☐ 7	$265	$315	$350	$385	$420	$455	$490	$ _____
☐ 4	$235	$275	$305	$340	$375	$410	$445	$ _____
☐ 1	$190	$225	$255	$285	$320	$355	$390	$ _____

Blueprint Price Codes

*Prices guaranteed to December 31, 1991.

☐ **Additional Sets** of this plan, $25 now; $35 later, each. (Number of sets _____) $ _____

☐ **Itemized List of Materials,** $30, each additional set $10.
Lists are available only for plans with prefix letters AH, AM*, AX, B, C, CDG*, CPS, DD*, DG, E, H, I, J, K, N, NW*, P, R, S, SD, U, W
*Please ask when ordering, not available on all plans $ _____

☐ **Description of Materials:** Two sets $25
(For use in obtaining FHA or VA financing)
(Only available for Plans with prefix letters C, E, H, J, K, N, P, U) $ _____

☐ **Mirror Reverse Surcharge,** $25.
(Number of sets to be reversed _____.)
*The writing on Mirror Reverse plans will be backwards. Order at least one regular set. $ _____

☐ **Typical How-To Diagrams** $ _____
☐ Plumbing ☐ Wiring ☐ Solar Heating
☐ Framing & Foundation Conversion
One set @ $12.50, any two @ $23.00, any three @ $30.00, all four only $35.

☐ **Sales Tax** (MN Residents, please add 6%) $ _____

Please Add Postage Charges (Check One)

☐ First-Class Priority or UPS Blue Label (U.S. only), $10.50 $ _____
Allow 4-5 working days for delivery. *Must have street address for UPS delivery.
☐ First-Class Priority (Canada only) $10.50 $ _____
Allow 2-3 weeks for delivery.
☐ Overnight Express Delivery (U.S. only) $25.00 $ _____
Allow 1-2 working days for delivery. *Must have street address.
☐ Express Delivery (Canada only) $40.00 $ _____
Allow 4-5 working days for delivery. *Must have street address.
☐ Overseas Airmail Delivery $40.00 $ _____
Allow approx. 7 working days.

Payment   TOTAL ORDER $ _____
☐ Check/money order enclosed (in U.S. funds)
☐ VISA ☐ MasterCard ☐ AmEx ☐ Discover   Exp. Date_____

Card Number _____

Signature _____

Name _____

Street _____

City _____ State ____ Zip_____

Daytime Telephone (____) _____

☐ Builder-Contractor ☐ Home Owner ☐ Renter   PG-19

Photo by Kevin Haslip

Convenience and Luxury

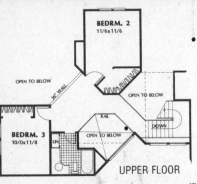

UPPER FLOOR

- Large roof planes and a modest exterior enclose a thoroughly modern, open floor plan.
- Entry hall, living/dining area and family room all have vaulted ceilings.
- Living room has floor-to-ceiling windows, fireplace and wall-length stone hearth.

- A sun room next to the spacious, angular kitchen offers passive solar heating and a bright look to the area.
- Main floor master suite includes a raised tub and separate shower, plus a large walk-in wardrobe.
- Upstairs, a bridge hallway overlooks the rooms below.
- The daylight basement version includes another 2,025 square feet of versatile space.

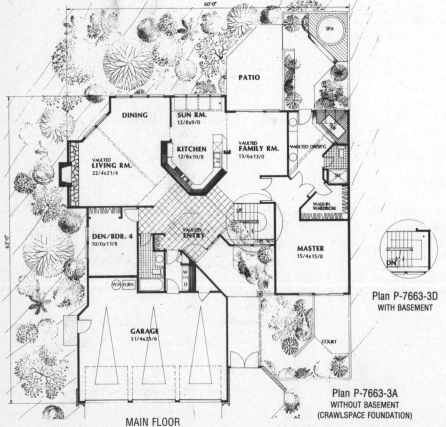

Plan P-7663-3D
WITH BASEMENT

Plan P-7663-3A
WITHOUT BASEMENT
(CRAWLSPACE FOUNDATION)

MAIN FLOOR

Plans P-7663-3A & -3D	
Bedrooms: 3-4	**Baths:** 3
Space:	
Upper floor:	470 sq. ft.
Main floor:	2,025 sq. ft.
Total living area:	**2,495 sq. ft.**
Basement:	2,025 sq. ft.
Garage:	799 sq. ft.
Exterior Wall Framing:	2x4
Foundation options:	
Daylight basement (Plan P-7663-3D). Crawlspace (Plan P-7663-3A). (Foundation & framing conversion diagram available — see order form.)	
Blueprint Price Code:	C

Plans P-7663-3A & -3D

Crisp Contemporary Styling

- Contemporary split-level is designed for lots that slope down from the front.
- Daylight basement in rear adds extra living space.
- Angled wall and railing offer unique character to living room.
- Dining area overlooks living room through railings on either side of the fireplace.

- Living room also looks into family room below.
- Spacious kitchen/dining area provides plenty of space for casual dining.
- Master suite includes private bath and large walk-in closet.
- Lower level includes ample laundry and utility areas, plus a third bedroom and another full bath.

Plan CPS-1132-S

Bedrooms: 3	Baths: 3
Space:	
Main floor:	1,185 sq. ft.
Lower level:	858 sq. ft.
Total living area:	2,043 sq. ft.
Garage:	494 sq. ft.
Exterior Wall Framing:	2x6

Foundation options:
Daylight basement only.
(Foundation & framing conversion diagram available — see order form.)

Blueprint Price Code:	C

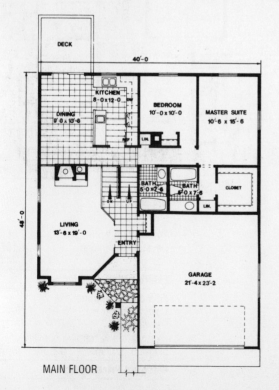

MAIN FLOOR

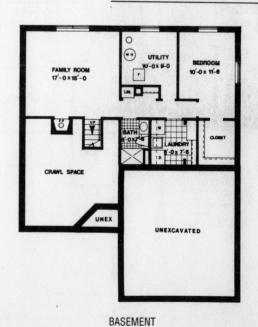

BASEMENT

Plan CPS-1132-S

Unique, Family Living

- This smart-looking, narrow, transitional design displays an exterior accented by half-windows, pillars and brick trim.
- A lovely vaulted parlor or study off the entry is entered through double doors and can also function as a guest room.
- Adjoining the parlor is the formal dining room with coffered ceiling and sliders that access the rear covered patio.
- The merging peninsula kitchen features a unique angled eating bar

and vaulted nook illuminated by skylights.
- Open to the kitchen is the spacious family room with dramatic corner fireplace and sliding glass doors to view the patio to the rear.
- Upstairs, the vaulted master suite has an elegant double-door entrance and a private bath with dressing area, skylit spa, and huge walk-in closet.
- The vaulted secondary bedrooms each have independent access to the bath between them, featuring separate vanities.

UPPER FLOOR

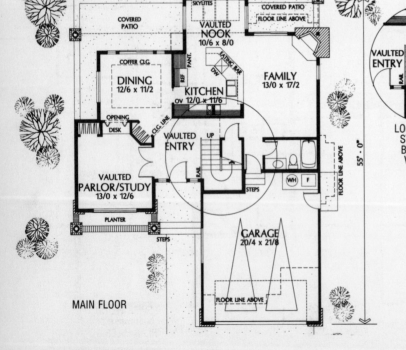

LOCATION OF STAIRS IN BASEMENT VERSION.

MAIN FLOOR

Plans P-7733-4A & P-7733-4D

Bedrooms: 3-4	Baths: 3

Space:	
Upper floor:	960 sq. ft.
Main floor:	1,107 sq. ft.

Total living area:	**2,067 sq. ft.**
Daylight basement:	1,107 sq. ft.
Garage:	441 sq. ft.

Exterior Wall Framing:	2x6

Foundation options:
Daylight basement.   (P-7733-4D)
Crawlspace.   (P-7733-4A)
(Foundation & framing conversion diagram available — see order form.)

Blueprint Price Code: C

Plans P-7733-4A & -4D

Simple, Spacious, Easy to Build

For a simple, spacious, easy-to-construct home away from home, you should definitely consider this plan.

Entrance to the home is by way of the lower level or the side door to the living room, or both, where grade levels permit. This has the advantage of elevating the second floor to take advantage of a view that otherwise may be blocked out by surrounding buildings.

The living area, consisting of the living room, dining room and kitchen, occupies 565 sq. ft. of the main floor. The open room arrangement allows the cook to remain part of the family even when occupied with necessary chores.

The design's basically simple rectangular shape allows for easy construction, and the home could be built by any moderately experienced do-it-yourselfer. All you have to do is order the plan that fits your setting.

Plan H-833-5 has the garage entry to the street side. H-833-6 puts the garage under the view-side deck.

Upper floor:	1,200 sq. ft.
Lower level:	876 sq. ft.
Total living area: (Not counting garage)	2,076 sq. ft.

UPPER FLOOR
1200 SQUARE FEET

LOWER FLOOR
876 SQUARE FEET
PLAN H-833-5

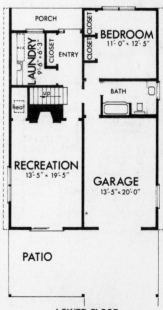

LOWER FLOOR
876 SQUARE FEET
PLAN H-833-6

Blueprint Price Code C

Plans H-833-5 & -6

TO ORDER THIS BLUEPRINT, CALL TOLL-FREE 1-800-547-5570 (Prices and details on pp. 12-15.)

Open Living in a Modern Design

Spacious open living areas plus window-walls and wood decks are carefully combined in this contemporary home for both indoor and outdoor family activities and entertaining. Roof setbacks, skylights and windows over the high entry hall and strong fascia boards add interesting relief to the long slope of the gable roof.

In contrast, the rear wall of the home is obviously planned for enjoyment of a view, with a window-wall covering the five-sided, two-story extension of the Great Room. Sliding glass doors open onto the wide wood deck from the Great Room, dining room and master bedroom. Smaller viewing decks open off two second-floor rooms. The full-window treatment repeats in the daylight basement version of the plan.

All floors have open areas in this 2,089 sq. ft. home. The entry hall opens directly into the Great Room, including a free-standing fireplace, the dining area and the U-shaped kitchen. Adjoining this area are a three-quarters bathroom and the utility room. On the other side of the main floor is the master bedroom, including a walk-in wardrobe and a private bath with a window seat.

Open stairs lead off the entry hall to the 824 sq. ft. upper floor, which includes a large loft room overlooking the Great Room and warmed by a woodstove. A study, storage area, bathroom and two bedrooms are also included on the second floor.

The 1,210 sq. ft. daylight basement has a large recreation room with a wood stove, a fourth bedroom with walk-in closet, a full bath and an unfinished area that could become a workshop, crafts area or a guest room.

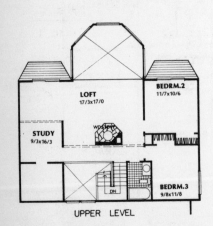

UPPER LEVEL

Main floor:	1,265 sq. ft.
Second floor:	824 sq. ft.
Total living area: (Not counting basement or garage)	2,089 sq. ft.
Daylight basement:	1,210 sq. ft.
Total with basement:	3,299 sq. ft.

***TO ORDER THIS BLUEPRINT,
CALL TOLL-FREE 1-800-547-5570***
(Prices and details on pp. 12-15.)

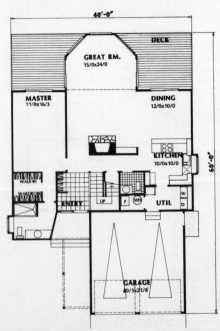

Blueprint Price Code D With Basement
Blueprint Price Code C Without Basement

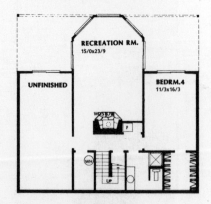

PLAN P-533-2D
WITH DAYLIGHT BASEMENT

PLAN P-533-2A
WITHOUT BASEMENT
(CRAWLSPACE FOUNDATION)

Plans P-533-2A & P-533-2D

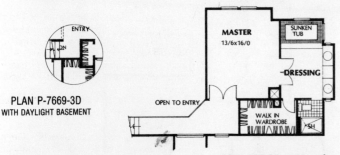

PLAN P-7669-3D
WITH DAYLIGHT BASEMENT

MASTER
13/6x16/0

SUNKEN TUB

DRESSING

OPEN TO ENTRY

WALK IN WARDROBE

SH

UPPER FLOOR 550 sq.ft.

"Adult Retreat" in Upstairs Master Suite

First floor:	1,545 sq. ft.
Second floor:	550 sq. ft.
Total living area:	2,095 sq. ft.
(Not counting basement or garage)	
Basement level:	1,102 sq. ft.

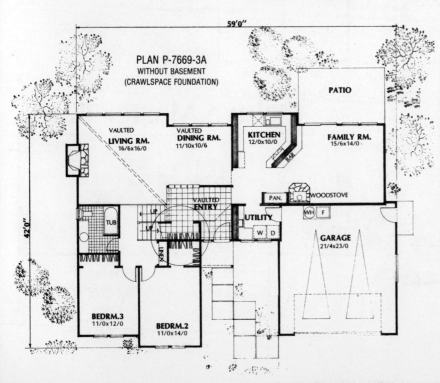

59'0"

PLAN P-7669-3A
WITHOUT BASEMENT
(CRAWLSPACE FOUNDATION)

PATIO

VAULTED LIVING RM.
16/6x16/0

VAULTED DINING RM.
11/10x10/6

KITCHEN
12/0x10/0

FAMILY RM.
15/6x14/0

BAR

TUB

VAULTED ENTRY

UP

UP

UTILITY

PAN.

WOODSTOVE

WH   F

W   D

GARAGE
21/4x23/0

42'0"

BEDRM.3
11/0x12/0

BEDRM.2
11/0x14/0

Blueprint Price Code C

Plans P-7669-3A & -3D

**TO ORDER THIS BLUEPRINT,
CALL TOLL-FREE 1-800-547-5570**
(Prices and details on pp. 12-15.)

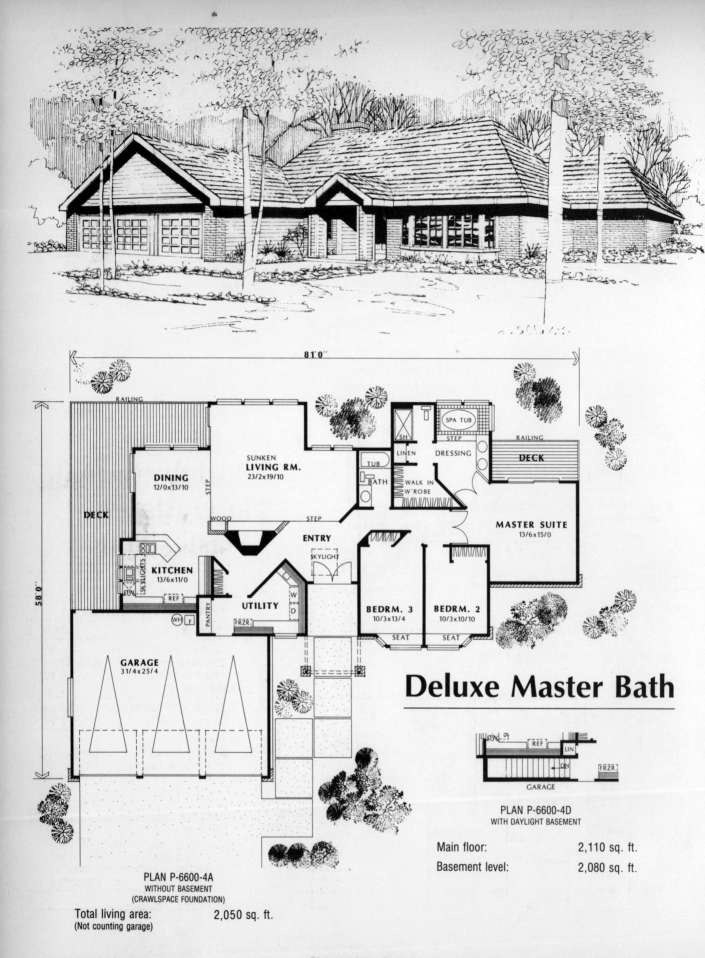

81'0"

58'0"

RAILING

DECK

DINING
12/0x13/10

STEP

SUNKEN
LIVING RM.
23/2x19/10

WOOD   STEP

KITCHEN
13/6x11/0

SKYLIGHTS

DW

REF

WH   F

PANTRY

FRZR

UTILITY

ENTRY

SKYLIGHT

W
D

SH

TUB
BATH

LINEN

SPA TUB

STEP

DRESSING

WALK IN
W'ROBE

RAILING

DECK

MASTER SUITE
13/6x15/0

BEDRM. 3
10/3x13/4

BEDRM. 2
10/3x10/10

SEAT   SEAT

GARAGE
31/4x25/4

Deluxe Master Bath

DW SH

REF

LIN

DN

FRZR

GARAGE

PLAN P-6600-4D
WITH DAYLIGHT BASEMENT

Main floor: 2,110 sq. ft.

Basement level: 2,080 sq. ft.

PLAN P-6600-4A
WITHOUT BASEMENT
(CRAWLSPACE FOUNDATION)

Total living area: 2,050 sq. ft.
(Not counting garage)

TO ORDER THIS BLUEPRINT,
CALL TOLL-FREE 1-800-547-5570
(Prices and details on pp. 12-15.)

22

Blueprint Price Code C

Plans P-6600-4A & -4D

Spacious One-Story with Optional Daylight Basement

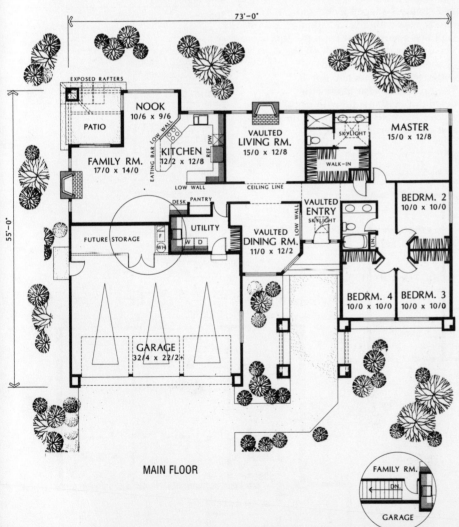

73'-0"

55'-0"

EXPOSED RAFTERS

NOOK
10/6 x 9/6

PATIO

VAULTED
LIVING RM.
15/0 x 12/8

SKYLIGHT

MASTER
15/0 x 12/8

WALK-IN

FAMILY RM.
17/0 x 14/0

EATING BAR LOW WALL

KITCHEN
12/2 x 12/8

REF. DW

LOW WALL

CEILING LINE

DESK PANTRY

FUTURE STORAGE

UTILITY

F WH

W D

VAULTED
DINING RM.
11/0 x 12/2

VAULTED
ENTRY
SKYLIGHT

LOW WALL

BEDRM. 2
10/0 x 10/0

LIN.

BEDRM. 4
10/0 x 10/0

BEDRM. 3
10/0 x 10/0

GARAGE
32/4 x 22/2+

MAIN FLOOR

FAMILY RM.

DN.

GARAGE

PLAN 7736-3D
WITH DAYLIGHT BASEMENT

Plans P-7736-3A & P-7736-3D

Bedrooms: 4	Baths: 2

Finished space:

Main floor: (non-basement)	2,121 sq. ft.
Main floor:	2,177 sq. ft.
Basement:	2,197 sq. ft.

Total with basement:	4,374 sq. ft.
Garage: (three-car)	716 sq. ft.

Features:
Columns define covered entryway.
Roomy family/nook/kitchen area.
Vaulted ceilings in living and
   dining rooms.

Exterior Wall Framing:	2x4

Foundation options: (Specify)
Daylight basement: Plan P-7736-3D
Crawlspace: Plan P-7736-3A
(Foundation & framing conversion
diagram available — see order form.)

Blueprint Price Code:	C

Plans P-7736-3A & P-7736-3D

TO ORDER THIS BLUEPRINT,
CALL TOLL-FREE 1-800-547-5570
(Prices and details on pp. 12-15.)

23

Built for All Seasons

- Spectacular rear viewing is yours in this exciting, yet homey design that provides comfort in all seasons.
- The heat-absorbing wall in the lower level and the fireplace-to-furnace "tie-in" circulation system help balance mild and cold days during the heating season.
- Two secondary bedrooms and extra storage space are also offered on the lower level.

- The main level features a bright and cheery L-shaped living and dining area with a brick column wall that absorbs heat from the sun.
- The upper side patio deck off the kitchen can be roofed and converted to a screened porch.
- The main level also houses the delightful master suite with dressing alcove and bath with step-up tub and corner mirrored wall.

Plan CPS-1045-SE	
Bedrooms: 3	Baths: 2½
Space:	
Lower floor:	1,095 sq. ft.
Main floor:	1,040 sq. ft.
Total living area:	2,135 sq. ft.
Garage:	624 sq. ft.
Exterior Wall Framing:	2x6
Foundation options: Daylight basement. (Foundation & framing conversion diagram available — see order form.)	
Blueprint Price Code:	C

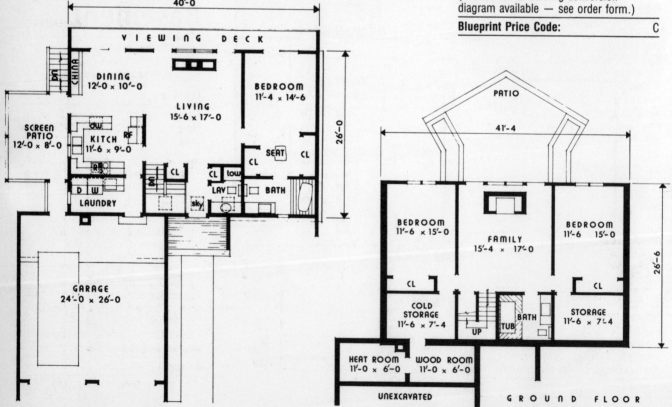

Plan CPS-1045-SE

Country Charm

- Two story bay windows, a wrap-around porch and a half-round window theme adds up to country charm.
- Interior charm begins with a two-story entry at the stairwell, with a view into the living/dining room with fireplace, bay windows and sliders to the side porch.
- The kitchen serves the formal dining room and the breakfast bay, and enjoys the family room fireplace.
- There are four large bedrooms upstairs, including a master suite that features a walk-in closet and private bath.

Plans P-7748-2A & -2D

Bedrooms: 4	Baths: 2½
Space:	
Upper floor:	1,010 sq. ft.
Main floor:	1,157 sq. ft.
Total living area:	**2,167 sq. ft.**
Basement:	1,157 sq. ft.
Garage:	498 sq. ft.
Exterior Wall Framing:	2x6

Foundation options:
Daylight basement.   (P-7748-2D)
Crawlspace.   (P-7748-2A)
(Foundation & framing conversion diagram available — see order form.)

Blueprint Price Code: C

UPPER FLOOR

BASEMENT

MAIN FLOOR

Plans P-7748-2A & -2D

Year-Round Vacation Home

- This rustic multi-level cabin offers the flexibility of an optional basement for building on a sloping lot; the basement may be omitted if you have a level lot.
- A massive country kitchen and Great Room, each with a fireplace, share the main level with the master bedroom; an impressive deck wraps the Great Room, accessible from sliding glass doors on three sides.
- Two additional bedrooms are located on the upper level; a rec room with fireplace and sliders to an outdoor patio and a garage or boat storage area are found in the optional lower level.

Plan AX-7944-A

Bedrooms: 3	Baths: 2-3
Space:	
Upper floor:	457 sq. ft.
Main floor:	1,191 sq. ft.
Total living area:	1,648 sq. ft.
(without basement)	
Optional basement:	809 sq. ft.
Total living area:	2,457 sq. ft.
(with basement)	
Garage:	382 sq. ft.

Exterior Wall Framing:	2x4

Foundation options:
Daylight basement.
Slab.
(Foundation & framing conversion diagram available — see order form.)

Blueprint Price Code:
Without basement:	B
With basement:	C

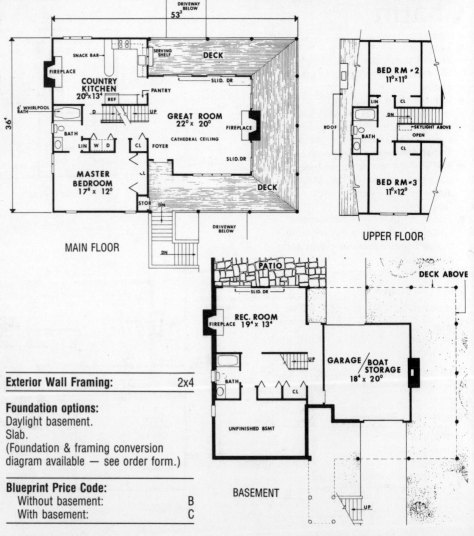

MAIN FLOOR

UPPER FLOOR

BASEMENT

Plan AX-7944-A

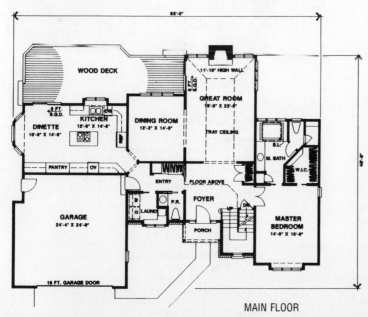

BEDROOM 3
12'-8" X 14'-0"

GREAT ROOM BELOW

RAILING

BALCONY

FOYER BELOW

BEDROOM 2
14'-0" X 13'-0"

BATH

DN

TC

UPPER FLOOR

68'-0"

WOOD DECK

3'1"-10" HIGH WALL

6 FT. S.G.D.

GREAT ROOM
16'-0" X 22'-0"

TRAY CEILING

KITCHEN
12'-0" X 14'-0"

DINING ROOM
12'-3" X 14'-0"

M. BATH

W.I.C.

DINETTE
10'-0" X 14'-0"

PANTRY

OV

ENTRY

FLOOR ABOVE

ENTRY

P.R.

FOYER

LAUND

UP DN

GARAGE
24'-4" X 24'-0"

PORCH

MASTER BEDROOM
14'-0" X 16'-0"

16 FT. GARAGE DOOR

MAIN FLOOR

Transitional Traditional

- A secluded first floor master suite is a major attraction to you if you're looking for privacy; it offers dual vanities, separate shower and commode area and large bath with skylight.
- Central to the home is a large combination Great Room and dining area, both offering access to the adjoining rear deck.
- The kitchen is ideal, with a central work island, pantry, abundant counter space and an attached dinette with bay window.
- A balcony reaches across the second floor overlooking the foyer and Great Room and connecting the two secondary bedrooms.

Plan A-628-R

Bedrooms: 3	Baths: 2½

Space:

Upper floor:	665 sq. ft.
Main floor:	1,542 sq. ft.

Total living area:	2,207 sq. ft.
Garage:	576 sq. ft.

Exterior Wall Framing:	2x6

Foundation options:
Standard basement.
(Foundation & framing conversion diagram available — see order form.)

Blueprint Price Code:	C

Plan A-628-R

TO ORDER THIS BLUEPRINT, CALL TOLL-FREE 1-800-547-5570
(Prices and details on pp. 12-15.)

Designed for Moderate Side-to-Side Slope

- Tri-level design puts all four bedrooms in quiet upper level.
- Main level includes spacious dining/living room area to accommodate large gatherings.
- Lower level includes large family room with fireplace and adjacent half-bath, utility area and garage entry.
- Kitchen/nook combination is great for casual family meals.
- Three-car garage offers abundant vehicle space.

MAIN FLOOR

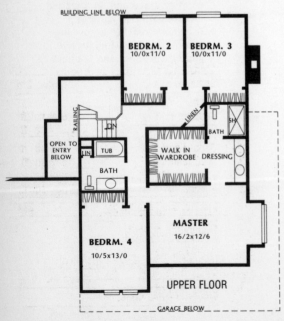

UPPER FLOOR

Plan P-7687-3A

Bedrooms: 4	Baths: 2½

Space:

Upper floor:	1,029 sq. ft.
Two main levels:	1,204 sq. ft.
Total living area:	**2,233 sq. ft.**
Garage:	772 sq. ft.

Exterior Wall Framing: 2x6

Foundation options:
Crawlspace only.
(Foundation & framing conversion diagram available — see order form.)

Blueprint Price Code: C

Plan P-7687-3A

Old-Fashioned Charm

- A trio of dormers add old-fashioned charm to this modern design.
- Living and dining rooms both offer vaulted ceilings and flow together for feeling of spaciousness.
- The open kitchen/nook/family room arrangement features a sunny alcove, walk-in pantry and a wood stove.
- Master suite includes walk-in closet and deluxe bath with spa tub and shower.

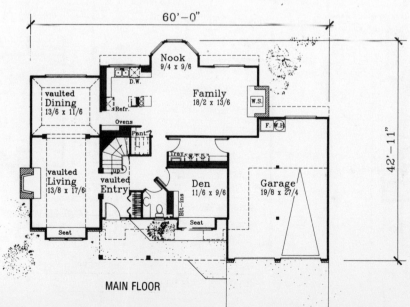

UPPER FLOOR

MAIN FLOOR

Plan CDG-2004

Bedrooms: 3	Baths: 2½

Space:

Upper floor:	928 sq. ft.
Main floor:	1,317 sq. ft.
Total living area:	**2,245 sq. ft.**
Bonus area:	192 sq. ft.
Basement:	882 sq. ft.
Garage:	537 sq. ft.

Exterior Wall Framing:	2x4

Foundation options:
  Daylight basement.
  Crawlspace.
(Foundation & framing conversion diagram available — see order form.)

Blueprint Price Code:	C

Plan CDG-2004

Sun Nook Brightens Split-Level Contemporary

A breakfast nook splashed with sunlight through a glass roof and windows on two walls serve as passive solar collectors in this spacious four-bedroom, split-level contemporary home.

Traffic is directed along a central hall, turning right at the top of the stairs to the sun nook and kitchen, or straight ahead to the vaulted-ceiling living room.

Clerestory windows at one end and a sliding glass door and window at the other end lighten the living room, warmed by a corner fireplace.

A wide wood deck extends along the back of the home, with sliding glass doors off the living room and master bedroom. The two other bedrooms have window seats and share the second bath.

Exterior walls are framed with 2x6 studs for energy efficiency.

Main floor:	1,408 sq. ft.
Lower level:	855 sq. ft.
Total living area:	2,263 sq. ft.
(Not counting garage)	

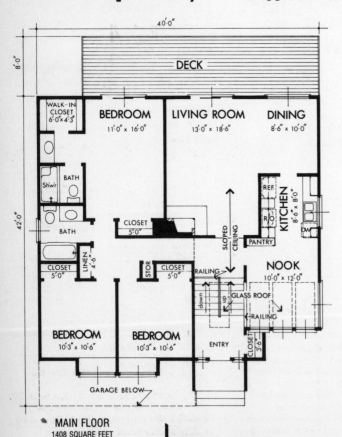

MAIN FLOOR
1408 SQUARE FEET

CLERESTORY WINDOWS OVER LIV. RM.

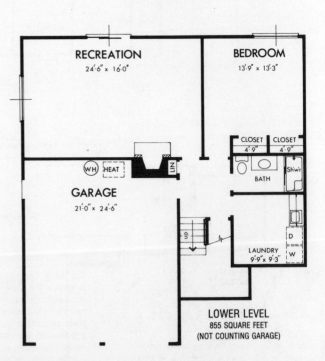

LOWER LEVEL
855 SQUARE FEET
(NOT COUNTING GARAGE)

Blueprint Price Code C
Plan H-2106-1

(Prices and details on pp. 12-15.)

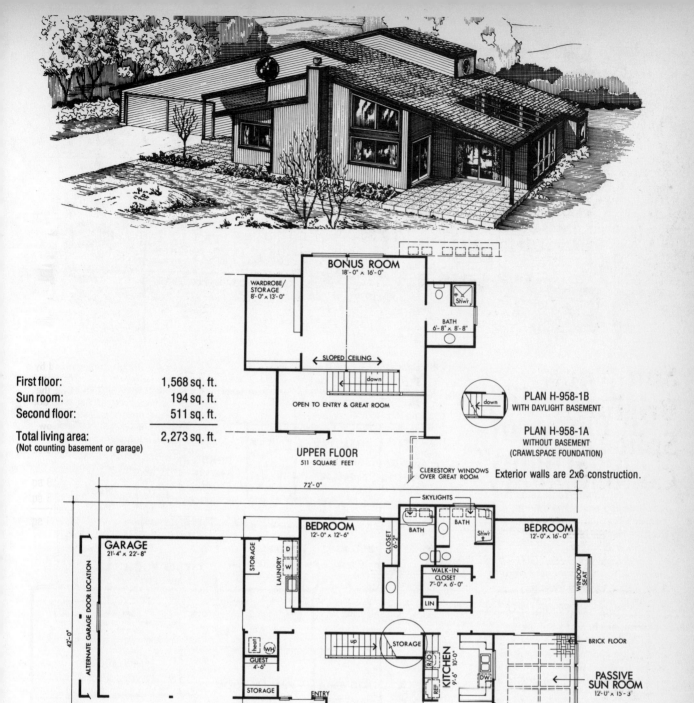

First floor: 1,568 sq. ft.
Sun room: 194 sq. ft.
Second floor: 511 sq. ft.

Total living area: 2,273 sq. ft.
(Not counting basement or garage)

BONUS ROOM
18'- 0" x 16'- 0"

WARDROBE/
STORAGE
8'- 0" x 13'- 0"

BATH
6'- 8" x 8'- 8"
Shwr

SLOPED CEILING

down

OPEN TO ENTRY & GREAT ROOM

UPPER FLOOR
511 SQUARE FEET

down

PLAN H-958-1B
WITH DAYLIGHT BASEMENT

PLAN H-958-1A
WITHOUT BASEMENT
(CRAWLSPACE FOUNDATION)

CLERESTORY WINDOWS
OVER GREAT ROOM

Exterior walls are 2x6 construction.

72'- 0"

GARAGE
21'- 4" x 22'- 8"

STORAGE

LAUNDRY
D
W

BEDROOM
12'- 0" x 12'- 6"

SKYLIGHTS

BATH

CLOSET
6'- 2"

BATH
Shwr

BEDROOM
12'- 0" x 16'- 0"

WINDOW
SEAT

WALK-IN
CLOSET
7'- 0" x 6'- 0"

LIN

42'- 0"

ALTERNATE GARAGE DOOR LOCATION

heat WH

GUEST
4'- 6"

STORAGE

ENTRY

up

STORAGE

KITCHEN
9'- 6" 10'- 0"
R/O
REF
DW

BRICK FLOOR

PASSIVE
SUN ROOM
12'- 0" x 15'- 3"

PASSIVE SUN ROOF

MAIN FLOOR

SLOPED CEILING

GREAT ROOM
24'- 6" x 19'- 0"

DECK OR PATIO

Spacious Contemporary

Because of the many internal amenities to be found in this spacious home, it is ideally suited for a piece of property where an outward focus would not be appropriate.

A decorative stairway graces one end of the living room and a large masonry-faced fireplace the other. Dining space is conveniently near the living room and an excellent U-shaped kitchen adjoins. The main attraction in this part of the home is the passive sun room. This glass enclosed space can serve as a breakfast room, a family room, or an arboretum while at the same time collecting and redistributing the sun's heat throughout the home. Two large bedrooms, two complete bathrooms and a convenient laundry room complete the main floor.

On the second floor one finds a huge 18' x 16' room overlooking the entry and stairway. Although this room is flanked by a full bathroom and a huge walk-in wardrobe it can be used in many ways other than as a bedroom.

Blueprint Price Code C

Plans H-958-1A & H-958-1B

Small Package with Plenty of "Good Things"

- The modest square footage of this ranch design offers maximum affordability, while plenty of exciting design features offer maximum livability.
- Covered main and secondary entries, a bay window, and stone accent give exterior charm.
- The foyer opens to dramatic views into the living room to the right and straight ahead to the dining room and beyond to the rear yard.
- The dining room has sliding door access to the expansive rear deck, which wraps around the side to a front portico.
- The central kitchen serves the formal dining room and overlooks the sunny breakfast eating area, which also has sliders to the deck.
- The left wing of the plan incorporates three bedrooms and two full bathrooms. The master bedroom offers his and her walk-in closets, a cozy window seat and a dressing area just outside the private bath.
- The plan shows a handy two-car tuck-under garage for sites which would allow it. The optional lower level floor plan can be finished into a walk-out family room with fireplace, a fourth bedroom and a third full bath. There is also plenty of storage in the lower level.

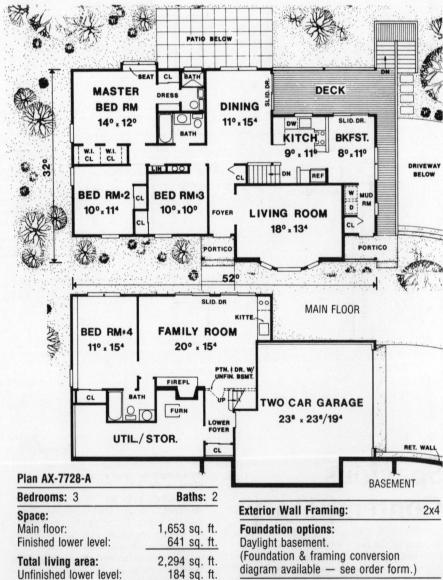

Plan AX-7728-A

Bedrooms: 3	Baths: 2

Space:

Main floor:	1,653 sq. ft.
Finished lower level:	641 sq. ft.
Total living area:	**2,294 sq. ft.**
Unfinished lower level:	184 sq. ft.
Garage:	approx. 500 sq. ft.

Exterior Wall Framing: 2x4

Foundation options:
Daylight basement.
(Foundation & framing conversion diagram available — see order form.)

Blueprint Price Code: C

TO ORDER THIS BLUEPRINT, CALL TOLL-FREE 1-800-547-5570

(Prices and details on pp. 12-15.)

Plan AX-7728-A

Soaring Spaces under Vaulted Ceilings

- A dignified exterior and a gracious, spacious interior combine to make this an outstanding plan for today's families.
- The living, dining, family rooms and breakfast nook all feature soaring vaulted ceilings.
- An interior atrium provides an extra touch of elegance, with its sunny space for growing plants and sunbathing.
- The master suite is first class all the way, with a spacious sleeping area, opulent bath, large skylight and enormous walk-in closet.
- A gorgeous kitchen includes a large work/cooktop island, corner sink with large corner windows and plenty of counter space.

Plans P-7697-4A & -4D

Bedrooms: 3	Baths: 2

Space:

Main floor (crawlspace version):	2,003 sq. ft.
Main floor (basement version):	2,030 sq. ft.
Basement:	2,015 sq. ft.
Garage:	647 sq. ft.

Exterior Wall Framing:	2x4

Foundation options:
Daylight basement (Plan P-7697-4D).
Crawlspace (Plan P-7697-4A).
(Foundation & framing conversion diagram available — see order form.)

Blueprint Price Code:	C

Floor plan labels

63'0"

PATIO

COVERED PATIO

SUNKEN TUB

DRESSING

SKYLIGHT

STEP

WALK IN W'ROBE

SKYLHT

SHWR

MASTER 12/0x15/0

VAULTED FAMILY RM. 21/6x16/10

WOODSTOVE

VAULTED NOOK

D.W.

KITCHEN 10/0x14/8

REF

DESK

ATRIUM

VAULTED DINING RM. 12/0x10/0

BEDRM. 2 10/8x11/0

LIN

LIN

SEAT

SEAT

STEP

BEDRM. 3 11/8x10/0

UTILITY

BATH

W D

F

TUB

WH

VAULTED ENTRY

STEP

VAULTED SUNKEN LIVING RM. 13/4x17/0

61'0"

GARAGE 31/4 x 20/8

RAILING

DN

BATH

W D

VAULTED ENTRY

PLAN P-7697-4D
WITH DAYLIGHT BASEMENT

Plans P-7697-4A & -4D

A Glorious Blend of New and Old

This three-bedroom, two and one-half-bath home is a glorious blend of contemporary and traditional lines. Inside, its 2,035 sq. ft. are wisely distributed among amply proportioned, practically appointed rooms. A vaulted entry gives way to a second reception area bordering on a broad, vaulted living room nearly 20' long.

With its walls of windows overlooking the back yard, this grand room's centerpiece is a massive woodstove, whose central location contributes extra energy efficiency to the home — upstairs as well as down. The dining room offers quiet separation from the living room, while still enjoying the warmth from its woodstove. Its sliding door accesses a large wraparound covered patio to create a cool, shady refuge.

For sun-seeking, another wraparound patio at the front is fenced but uncovered, and elegantly accessed by double doors from a well-lighted, vaulted nook.

Placed conveniently between the two dining areas is a kitchen with all the trimmings: pantry, large sink window, and an expansive breakfast bar.

A stylish upstairs landing overlooks the living room on one side and the entry on the other, and leads to a master suite that rambles over fully half of the second floor.

Adjacent to the huge bedroom area is a spacious dressing area bordered by an abundance of closet space and a double-sink bath area. Unusual extras include walk-in wardrobe in the third bedroom and the long double-sink counter in the second upstairs bath.

Note also the exceptional abundance of closet space on both floors, and the separate utility room that also serves as a clean-up room connecting with the garage.

Main floor:	950 sq. ft.
Upper floor:	1,085 sq. ft.
Total living area: (Not counting basement or garage)	2,035 sq. ft.

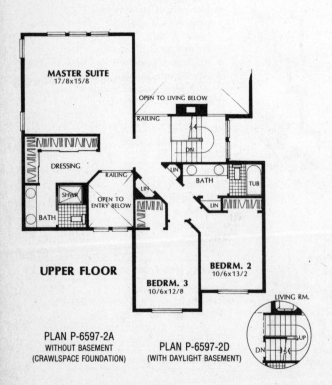

PLAN P-6597-2A
WITHOUT BASEMENT
(CRAWLSPACE FOUNDATION)

PLAN P-6597-2D
(WITH DAYLIGHT BASEMENT)

Blueprint Price Code C

Plans P-6597-2A & P-6597-2D

Grand Indoor/ Outdoor Living

- At the center of attention in this contemporary cottage is a dramatic Grand room with an all-glass end wall, volume ceilings and three outdoor attached decks.
- The owner suite overlooks a private deck and has its own bath with walk-in shower and closet.
- The kitchen features a countertop bar, pantry, space for a stacked washer/dryer and a pass-thru to the attached dining deck.
- A second bedroom or guest room has a convenient bath and closet.
- The lower level offers its own foyer, plus room for two additional bedrooms, guest rooms or recreation areas, and a third bath.

MAIN FLOOR

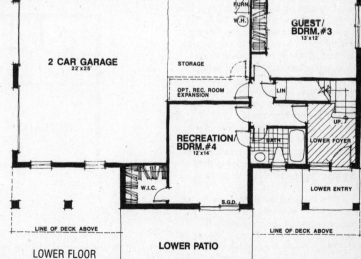

LOWER FLOOR

Plan EOP-45	
Bedrooms: 4	Baths: 3

Space:

Main floor:	1,448 sq. ft.
Lower floor:	673 sq. ft.
Total living area:	**2,121 sq. ft.**
Garage:	550 sq. ft.
Storage:	approx. 150 sq. ft.
Exterior Wall Framing:	**2x4**

Foundation options:
Daylight basement.
(Foundation & framing conversion diagram available — see order form.)

Blueprint Price Code:	**C**

Plan EOF-45

TO ORDER THIS BLUEPRINT, CALL TOLL-FREE 1-800-547-5570
(Prices and details on pp. 12-15.)

FRONT VIEW

Home Designed for Sloping Site

Here's a home that takes advantage of the natural contours of a sloping site. Besides the car storage and children's play area, the lower level of the home has a utility room, recreation area and a half-bath. Also notice the workshop complete with bench and overhead cabinets.

An abundance of storage is provided throughout in the form of a closet flanking the central hall and a storage area under the staircase. The full length of the daylight basement is used for a recreation room that also measures almost 14' wide. The latter room also includes a wet bar and fireplace.

The kitchen is convenient to the dining area as well as to the hall leading to the front entry. The generously sized living room connects with the dining area so that dining space may be expanded if needed. The gable wall includes sliding glass doors opening to the covered deck.

Bedrooms are placed to the rear in the quiet zone of the home. There, you will also find two complete bathrooms. One of the bathrooms is designed to serve the master bedroom, which also features a walk-in closet.

Overall size of the main floor area is 48' in length by 27' in depth. To this, add 9' for the extension of the covered deck. Living area of the main plan is 1,296 sq. ft.

An attractive exterior is achieved with the use of cedar for both the exterior siding and the shake roofing. A brick planter wall bordering the approach to the front porch

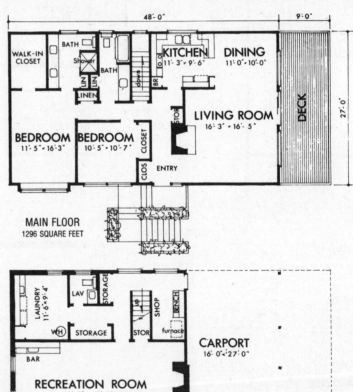

MAIN FLOOR
1296 SQUARE FEET

BASEMENT
829 SQUARE FEET

matches the masonry of the fireplace. Brick is also used to trim the pilaster supporting the front end of the dwelling.

Total living area: 2,125 sq. ft.

Blueprint Price Code C

Plan H-2015-6

High Style in A Moderate Design

Sweeping roof lines amplify the clean exterior of this wood-finished contemporary home.

Majority of glass is positioned at rear of home for maximum solar benefit. A sunspace may also be added if desired.

Interior of home is designed around the "open plan concept," allowing free movement of air while visually borrowing space from the adjacent areas.

The vaulted entry features a clerestory located over the second-floor balcony, which overlooks the first floor spaces.

Kitchen, family and breakfast nook areas may be zoned off from the more formal areas of the home.

A large master bedroom features a walk-in closet, master bath, shower, tub and a deck to the rear of the home.

Living room of home is vaulted to the balcony level.

Total square footage of this residence is 2,139. Building dimensions are 50' wide by 52' deep. Please specify type of basement version desired.

Total living area: 2,139 sq. ft.
(Not counting basement or garage)

Exterior walls are 2x6 construction.

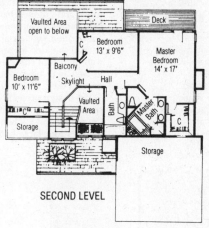

SECOND LEVEL

PLAN S-2001
WITHOUT BASEMENT
(CRAWLSPACE FOUNDATION)

PLAN S-2001-FB
FULL BASEMENT VERSION

PLAN S-2001-DB
DAYLIGHT BASEMENT VERSION

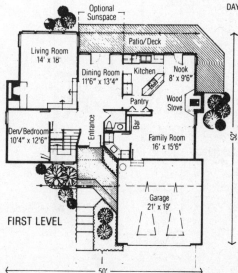

FIRST LEVEL

REAR VIEW

A Striking Contemporary

A multiplicity of decks and outcroppings along with unusual window arrangements combine to establish this striking contemporary as a classic type of architecture. To adapt to the sloping terrain, the structure has three levels of living space on the downhill side. As one moves around the house from the entry to the various rooms and living areas, both the appearance and function of the different spaces change, as do the angular forms and cutouts that define the floor plan arrangement. Almost all the rooms are flooded with an abundance of daylight, yet are shielded by projections of wing walls and roof surfaces to assure privacy as well as to block undesirable direct rays of sunshine.

The design projects open planning of a spacious living room that connects with the dining and kitchen area. The home features four large bedrooms, two of which have walk-in closets and private baths. The remaining two bedrooms also have an abundance of wardrobe space, and the rooms are of generous proportions.

For energy efficiency, exterior walls are framed with 2x6 studs.

First floor:	1,216 sq. ft.
Second floor:	958 sq. ft.
Total living area: (Not counting basement or garage)	2,174 sq. ft.
Basement:	1,019 sq. ft.

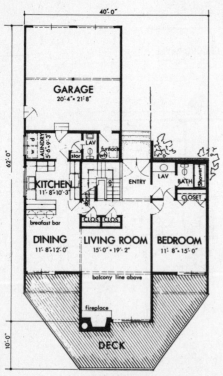

FIRST FLOOR
1216 SQUARE FEET

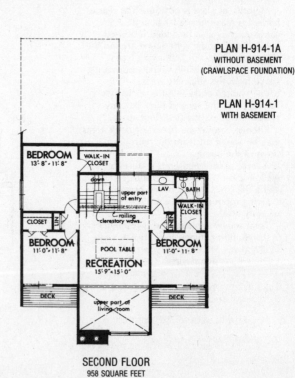

PLAN H-914-1A
WITHOUT BASEMENT
(CRAWLSPACE FOUNDATION)

PLAN H-914-1
WITH BASEMENT

SECOND FLOOR
958 SQUARE FEET

Blueprint Price Code C
Plans H-914-1 & H-914-1A

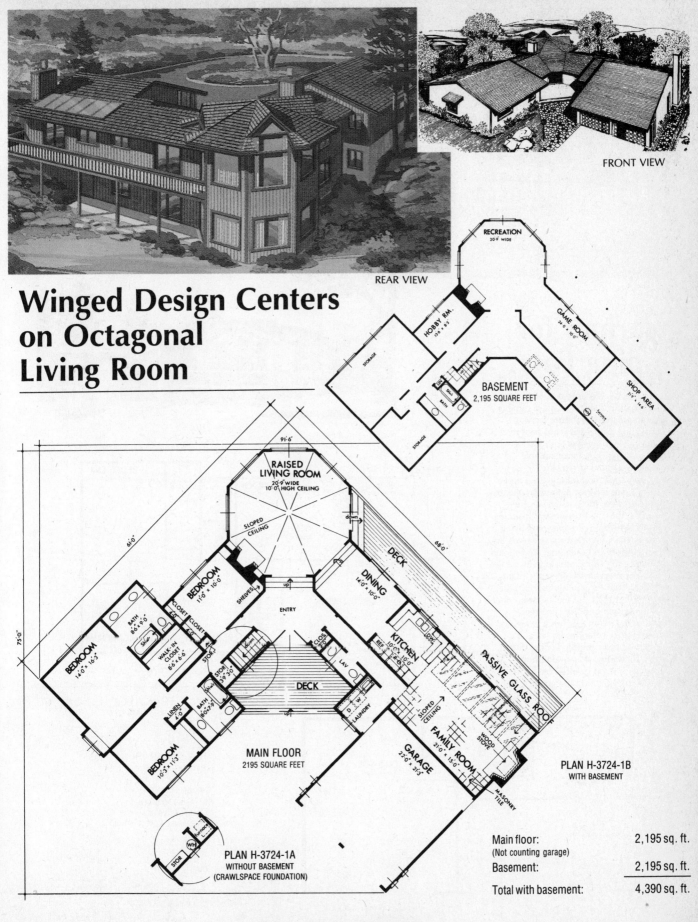

REAR VIEW

FRONT VIEW

Winged Design Centers on Octagonal Living Room

RECREATION
20'9" WIDE

HOBBY RM.
13'6" x 8'3"

GAME ROOM
24'0" x 10'0"

STORAGE

BASEMENT
2,195 SQUARE FEET

SHOP AREA
21'9" x 14'6"

BATH

STORAGE

91'6"

RAISED
LIVING ROOM
20'9" WIDE
10'0" HIGH CEILING

SLOPED
CEILING

64'0"

DECK

68'0"

DINING
14'0" x 10'0"

BEDROOM
11'0" x 10'0"

CLOSET CLOSET

SHELVES

down

up

KITCHEN
10'0" x 10'0"

ENTRY

BATH
8'6" x 9'0"

BEDROOM
14'0" x 16'3"

WALK-IN
CLOSET
8'6" x 6'6"

REF.

PASSIVE GLASS ROOM

75'0"

STOR.
3'9" x 3'0"

LAV.

DECK

LINEN

BATH
8'6" x 9'2"

D.W.

LAUNDRY

FAMILY ROOM
21'0" x 15'0"

WOOD STOVE

BEDROOM
10'3" x 11'3"

up

MAIN FLOOR
2195 SQUARE FEET

GARAGE
22'0" x 21'3"

PLAN H-3724-1B
WITH BASEMENT

MASONRY
TILE

furnace

WH

STOR

PLAN H-3724-1A
WITHOUT BASEMENT
(CRAWLSPACE FOUNDATION)

Main floor: (Not counting garage)	2,195 sq. ft.
Basement:	2,195 sq. ft.
Total with basement:	4,390 sq. ft.

Blueprint Price Code G With Basement
Blueprint Price Code C Without Basement

Plans H-3724-1A & -1B

TO ORDER THIS BLUEPRINT,
CALL TOLL-FREE 1-800-547-5570
(Prices and details on pp. 12-15.)

PLAN H-2107-1B

Solarium for Sloping Lots

This plan is available in two versions. Plan H-2107-1B, shown above, is most suitable for a lot sloping upward from front to rear, providing a daylight front for the lower floor. The other version, Plan H-2107-1 (at right), is more suitable for a lot that slopes from side to side.

Either way, this moderately sized home has a number of interesting and imaginative features. Of these, the passive sun room will provoke the most comment. Spanning two floors between recreation and living rooms, this glass-enclosed space serves the practical purpose of collecting, storing and redistributing the sun's natural heat, while acting as a conservatory for exotic plants, an exercise room, or any number of other uses. A link between the formal atmosphere of the living room and the carefree activities of the recreation area is created by this two-story solarium by way of an open balcony railing. Living, dining, and entry blend together in one huge space made to seem even larger by the vaulted ceiling spanning the entire complex of rooms.

PLAN H-2107-1

MAIN FLOOR
1505 SQUARE FEET

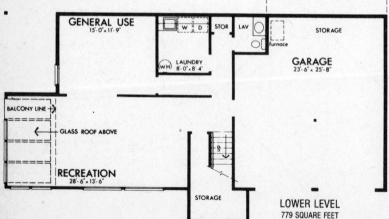

LOWER LEVEL
779 SQUARE FEET

PLAN H-2107-1B
DAYLIGHT BASEMENT

PLAN H-2107-1
WITH STANDARD BASEMENT
(BOTH VERSIONS INCLUDE
2X6 EXTERIOR WALL CONSTRUCTION)

Main floor:	1,505 sq. ft.
Lower level:	779 sq. ft.
Total living area: (Not counting garage)	2,284 sq. ft.

Blueprint Price Code C

**TO ORDER THIS BLUEPRINT,
CALL TOLL-FREE 1-800-547-5570**
(Prices and details on pp. 12-15.)

Plans H-2107-1 & H-2107-1B

Luxury Home with Outdoor Orientation

- Courtyards, patios and a sun room orient this multi-level home to the outdoors.
- Interior design is carefully zoned for informal family living and formal entertaining.
- Expansive kitchen includes large island and plenty of counter space, and a sunny nook adjoins the kitchen.
- Soaring entry area leads visitors to the vaulted living room with fireplace, or to the more casual family room.
- An optional fourth bedroom off the foyer would make an ideal home office.
- Upstairs master suite includes luxury bath and big walk-in closet.
- Daylight basement version adds nearly 1,500 more square feet of space.

Plans P-7659-3A & P-7659-3D

Bedrooms: 3-4	Baths: 3

Space:	
Upper floor:	1,050 sq. ft.
Main floor:	1,498 sq. ft.
Total living area:	**2,548 sq. ft.**
Basement:	1,490 sq. ft.
Garage:	583 sq. ft.

Exterior Wall Framing:	2x4

Foundation options:
Daylight basement, Plan P-7659-3D.
Crawlspace, Plan P-7659-3A.
(Foundation & framing conversion diagram available — see order form.)

Blueprint Price Code:	D

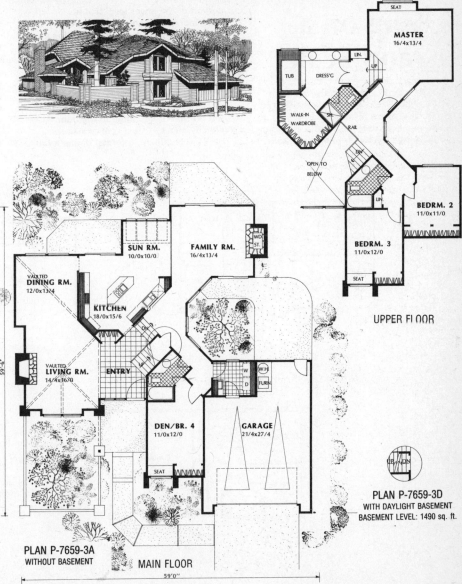

MASTER
16/4x13/4

SEAT

TUB   DRESS'G   LIN.   UP

WALK-IN WARDROBE

OPEN TO BELOW

RAIL

BEDRM. 2
11/0x11/0

BEDRM. 3
11/0x12/0

SEAT

UPPER FLOOR

SUN RM.
10/0x10/0

FAMILY RM.
16/4x13/4

WD ST.

VAULTED DINING RM.
12/0x13/4

KITCHEN
18/0x15/6

VAULTED LIVING RM.
14/4x16/0

ENTRY

W W.H. D FURN

DEN/BR. 4
11/0x12/0

GARAGE
21/4x27/4

SEAT

59'-6"

PLAN P-7659-3A
WITHOUT BASEMENT

MAIN FLOOR

59'0"

PLAN P-7659-3D
WITH DAYLIGHT BASEMENT
BASEMENT LEVEL: 1490 sq. ft.

Plans P-7659-3A & -3D

TO ORDER THIS BLUEPRINT,
CALL TOLL-FREE 1-800-547-5570
(Prices and details on pp. 12-15.)

Gracious Living on a Grand Scale

Well suited to either a gently sloping or flat building site, this home is also geared to a conservative building budget. First, it saves money through the partial enclosure of the lower level with foundation walls. A portion of the lower level that is surrounded by concrete walls is devoted to a 15'-10" x 13'-0" bedroom or optional den with wardrobe closet, a spacious recreation room with fireplace, and a third complete bathroom along with an abundance of storage space.

The balance of the area at this level is devoted to a two-car garage. Access from this portion of the home to the floor directly above is via a central staircase.

In Plan H-2082-2, a formal dining room and large kitchen provide two places for family eating.

Plan H-2082-1 includes a combination family room and U-shaped kitchen in one open area. Spatial continuity is further extended into the cantilevered deck that projects over the garage driveway below and is accessible through sliding glass doors off the family room.

This system of multi-level planning offers economy in building where grading would otherwise be required.

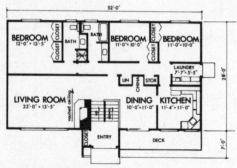

PLAN H-2082-2
MAIN FLOOR
1500 SQUARE FEET

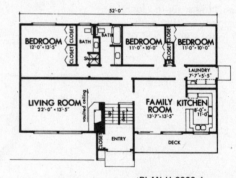

PLAN H-2082-1
MAIN FLOOR
1500 SQUARE FEET

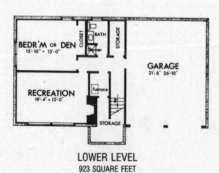

LOWER LEVEL
923 SQUARE FEET

Main floor:	1,500 sq. ft.
Lower level:	923 sq. ft.
Total living area: (Not counting garage)	2,423 sq. ft.

TO ORDER THIS BLUEPRINT,
CALL TOLL-FREE 1-800-547-5570
(Prices and details on pp. 12-15.)

Blueprint Price Code C
Plans H-2082-1 & -2

Ultimate in Luxury and Livability

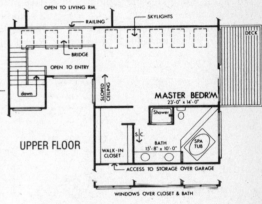

- This popular design is loaded with features for families of the 90's.
- Entire second floor of 735 sq. ft. is devoted to a sumptuous master suite with luxurious bath, large closet and skylights.
- Sunken living room is large and includes a fireplace.
- Roomy family room adjoins handy computer room and large kitchen.
- Kitchen includes a large walk-in pantry and work island.

UPPER FLOOR

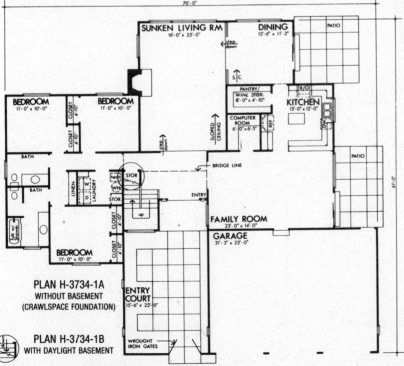

PLAN H-3734-1A
WITHOUT BASEMENT
(CRAWLSPACE FOUNDATION)

PLAN H-3734-1B
WITH DAYLIGHT BASEMENT

MAIN FLOOR

Plans H-3734-1A & -1B

Bedrooms: 4	Baths: 2½

Space:

Upper floor:	735 sq. ft.
Main floor:	2,024 sq. ft.
Total living area:	**2,759 sq. ft.**
Basement:	2,024 sq. ft.
Garage:	687 sq. ft.
Exterior Wall Framing:	**2x6**

Foundation options:
Daylight basement, Plan H-3734-1B.
Crawlspace, Plan H-3734-1A.
(Foundation & framing conversion diagram available — see order form.)

Blueprint Price Code:	D

Plans H-3734-1A & -1B

Gracious Open-Concept Floor Plan

- A striking and luxurious contemporary, this home offers great space and modern styling.
- A covered entry leads to a spacious foyer which flows into the sunken dining and stunning Great Room area.
- A spectacular two-story high fireplace dominates the vaulted Great Room.
- A bright nook adjoins the open kitchen, which includes a corner window above the sink.
- The den, which may be an optional guest bedroom, also opens onto the expansive deck.
- The majestic master bedroom on the second floor offers a 10' high coved ceiling, splendid bath, large closet and a private deck.
- Two other upstairs bedrooms share a second bath and a balcony hallway overlooking the Great Room and entry below.

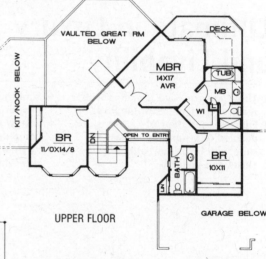

UPPER FLOOR

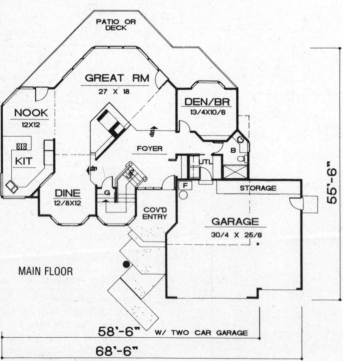

MAIN FLOOR

58'-6" W/ TWO CAR GARAGE

68'-6"

55'-6"

Plan S-41587	
Bedrooms: 3-4	Baths: 3

Space:
Upper floor:	1,001 sq. ft.
Main floor:	1,550 sq. ft.
Total living area:	**2,551 sq. ft.**
Basement:	1,550 sq. ft.
Garage (triple):	773 sq. ft.
Exterior Wall Framing:	2x6

Foundation options:
Daylight basement.
Standard basement.
Crawlspace.
(Foundation & framing conversion diagram available — see order form.)

Blueprint Price Code:	D

Plan S-41587

Dramatic Contemporary Takes Advantage of Slope

- Popular plan puts problem building site to work by taking advantage of the slope to create a dramatic and pleasant home.
- Spacious vaulted living/dining area is bathed in natural light from cathedral windows facing the front and clerestory windows at the peak.
- Big kitchen includes pantry and abundant counter space.
- Three main-level bedrooms are isolated for more peace and quiet.
- Lower level includes large recreation room, a fourth bedroom, third bath, laundry area and extra space for a multitude of other uses.

Photo courtesy of HomeStyles Plan Service

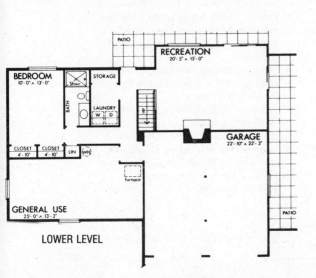

LOWER LEVEL

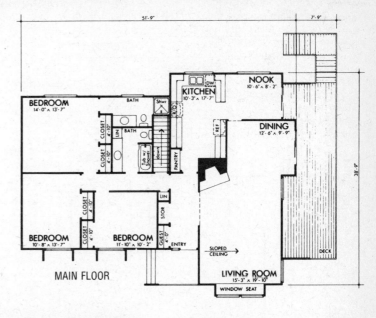

MAIN FLOOR

Plan H-2045-5

Bedrooms: 4	**Baths:** 3

Space:

Main floor:	1,602 sq. ft.
Lower floor:	1,133 sq. ft.
Total living area:	**2,735 sq. ft.**
Garage:	508 sq. ft.

Exterior Wall Framing:	2x4

Foundation options:
Daylight basement only.
(Foundation & framing conversion diagram available — see order form.)

Blueprint Price Code:	D

Plans H-2045-5

TO ORDER THIS BLUEPRINT, CALL TOLL-FREE 1-800-547-5570 (Prices and details on pp. 12-15.)

PLAN H-2114-1B REAR VIEW

Designed for Outdoor Living

- Dining room, living room, and spa are oriented toward the full-width deck extending across the rear of the home.
- Floor-to-ceiling windows, vaulted ceilings, and a fireplace are featured in the living room.
- Spa room has tile floor, operable skylights, and private access through connecting master suite.
- Upper level offers two bedrooms, spacious bathroom, and a balcony view of the living room and scenery beyond.

MAIN FLOOR

DECK

LIVING ROOM
23/0 x 13/10

SPA ROOM
13/6 x 10/0

SPA

SKYLIGHTS ABOVE

DINING
14/0 x 14/0

KITCHEN
11/0 x 11/0

PANTRY

STORAGE

BATH

REF.

NOOK
12/0 x 11/0

ENTRY

GUEST

LAV

LINEN

GARAGE
23/4 x 21/4

WALK-IN CLOSET
8/0 x 7/6

BEDROOM
13/6 x 20/6

SEAT

70'-2"

STORAGE

LAUNDRY ROOM
FOR PLAN W/O BSMT.

W D

PLAN H-2114-1A
WITHOUT BASEMENT

Plans H-2114-1A & -1B

Bedrooms: 3-4	Baths: 2½-3½

Space:	
Upper floor:	732 sq. ft.
Main floor:	1,682 sq. ft.
Sun room:	147 sq. ft.

Total living area:	2,561 sq. ft.
Basement:	approx. 1,386 sq. ft.
Garage:	547 sq. ft.

Exterior Wall Framing:	2x6

Foundation options:
Daylight basement (Plan H-2114-1B).
Crawlspace (Plan H-2114-1A).
(Foundation & framing conversion diagram available — see order form.)

Blueprint Price Code:
Without basement: D
With basement: F

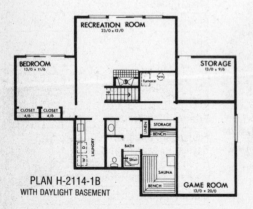

RECREATION ROOM
23/0 x 12/0

BEDROOM
13/0 x 11/0

STORAGE
13/0 x 9/6

CLOSET
4/6

CLOSET
4/6

furnace

STORAGE

LINEN

BENCH

LAUNDRY

BATH

SAUNA

BENCH

GAME ROOM
13/0 x 20/0

PLAN H-2114-1B
WITH DAYLIGHT BASEMENT

OPEN TO LIVING ROOM

CLOSET
6/6

CLOSET
6/6

RAIL

BATH

LINEN

CLOSET
8/6

BEDROOM
13/6 x 16/0

BEDROOM
12/0 x 11/0

UPPER FLOOR

***TO ORDER THIS BLUEPRINT,
CALL TOLL-FREE 1-800-547-5570***
(Prices and details on pp. 12-15.)

Plans H-2114-1A & -1B

Tudor-Inspired Hillside Design

- The vaulted entry opens to a stunning living room with a high ceiling and massive fireplace.
- The dining room, five steps higher, overlooks the living room for a dramatic effect.
- Double doors lead into the informal family area, which consists of a beautifully integrated kitchen, nook and family room.
- The magnificent master suite, isolated downstairs, includes a sumptuous bath, enormous wardrobe and double-door entry.
- The upstairs consists of three more bedrooms, a bath and balcony hallway open to the entry below.
- Three-car garage is tucked under the family room/dining room area.

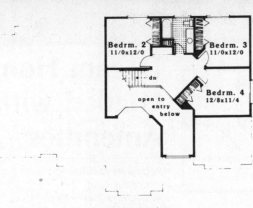

UPPER FLOOR

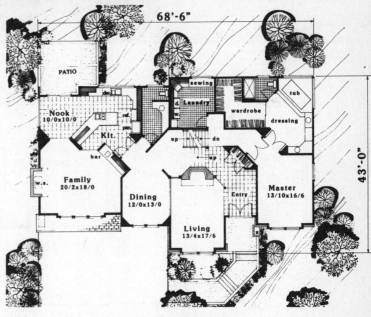

MAIN FLOOR

Plan R-4001

Bedrooms: 4	Baths: 2½

Space:	
Upper floor:	709 sq. ft.
Main floor:	2,388 sq. ft.
Total living area:	**3,097 sq. ft.**
Garage:	906 sq. ft.
Exterior Wall Framing:	2x4

Foundation options:
Crawlspace only.
(Foundation & framing conversion diagram available — see order form)

Blueprint Price Code:	E

PLAN R-4001
WITHOUT BASEMENT
(CRAWLSPACE FOUNDATION)

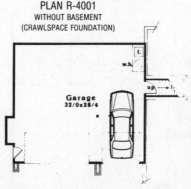

Plan R-4001

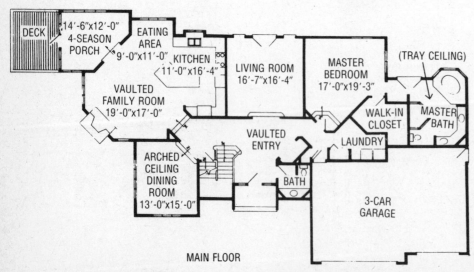

BEDROOM
12'-0"x12'-4"

BATH

BEDROOM
11'-7"x11'-0"

LOFT

OPEN TO ENTRY
BELOW

BEDROOM
15'-8"x13'-7"

UPPER FLOOR

Dream Home Loaded with Amenities

- Unique family room with vaulted ceiling.
- Large vaulted entry.
- Luxurious master suite.
- Large island kitchen.
- Striking design inside and out.

Plan AH-3230

Bedrooms: 4	Baths: 2½
Space:	
Upper floor:	890 sq. ft.
Main floor:	2,340 sq. ft.
Total living area:	3,230 sq. ft.
Basement:	2,214 sq. ft.
Garage:	693 sq. ft.
Exterior Wall Framing:	2x6
Ceiling Heights:	
Upper floor:	8'
Main floor:	9'

Foundation options:
Basement only.
(Foundation & framing conversion diagram available — see order form.)

Blueprint Price Code:	E

DECK

14'-6"x12'-0"
4-SEASON
PORCH

EATING
AREA
9'-0"x11'-0"

KITCHEN
11'-0"x16'-4"

LIVING ROOM
16'-7"x16'-4"

MASTER
BEDROOM
17'-0"x19'-3"

(TRAY CEILING)

VAULTED
FAMILY ROOM
19'-0"x17'-0"

WALK-IN
CLOSET

MASTER
BATH

VAULTED
ENTRY

LAUNDRY

ARCHED
CEILING
DINING
ROOM
13'-0"x15'-0"

BATH

3-CAR
GARAGE

MAIN FLOOR

Plan AH-3230

Four-Bedroom Contemporary Style

Steeply pitched, multi-level gable rooflines accented by diagonal board siding and tall windows add imposing height to this contemporary, 2,289 sq. ft. home. With most of the 1,389 sq. ft. main floor devoted to the living, dining and family rooms, and a long patio or wood deck accessible off the nook, the home lends itself ideally to family activities and gracious entertaining.

Directly off the spacious foyer is the vaulted-ceiling living room and dining area, brightened with high windows and warmed by a log-sized fireplace. The wide U-shaped kitchen, nook and family room, with wood stove, join and extend across the back half of the main floor. With doors off the nook and utility room leading to a large patio, this area combines for large, informal activities. Also off the front entry hall is a full bathroom, a den or fourth bedroom, and the open stairway, brightened by a skylight, leading to the upper floor.

The master bedroom suite, occupying about half of the upper floor, has a wide picture window, walk-in dressing room/ wardrobe, and a skylighted bathroom with sunken tub and separate shower. The other two bedrooms share the hall bathroom. A daylight basement version of the plan further expands the family living and recreation areas of this home.

Main floor:	1,389 sq. ft.
Upper floor:	900 sq. ft.
Total living area:	2,289 sq. ft.
(Not counting basement or garage)	
Basement level:	1,389 sq. ft.

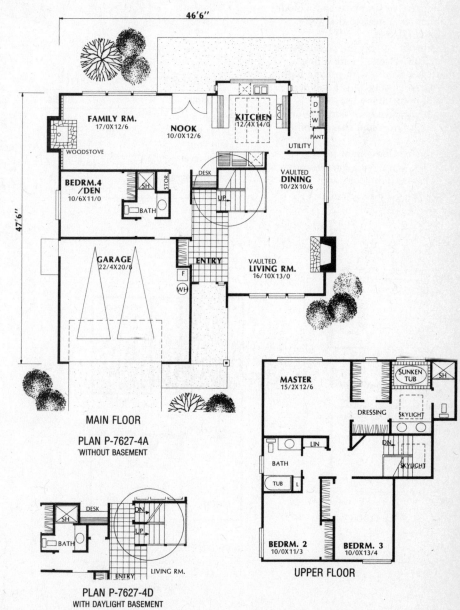

MAIN FLOOR

PLAN P-7627-4A
WITHOUT BASEMENT

PLAN P-7627-4D
WITH DAYLIGHT BASEMENT

UPPER FLOOR

Blueprint Price Code C

Plans P-7627-4A & P-7627-4D

TO ORDER THIS BLUEPRINT, CALL TOLL-FREE 1-800-547-5570 (Prices and details on pp. 12-15.)

Chalet Style for Town or Country

- The exterior features exposed beams, board siding and viewing decks with cut-out railings to give this home the look of a mountain chalet.
- Inside, the design lends itself equally well to year-round family living or part-time recreational enjoyment.
- An expansive Great Room features an impressive fireplace and includes a dining area next to the well-planned kitchen.
- The upstairs offers the possibility of an "adult retreat," with a fine master bedroom with private bath and large closets, plus a loft area available for many uses.
- Two secondary bedrooms are on the main floor, and share another bath.
- The daylight basement level provides space for a garage and large recreation room with fireplace.

Plan P-531-2D

Bedrooms: 3	Baths: 2

Space:

Upper floor:	573 sq. ft.
Main floor:	1,120 sq. ft.
Lower level:	532 sq. ft.

Total living area:	2,225 sq. ft.
Garage:	approx. 588 sq. ft.

Exterior Wall Framing: 2x4

Foundation options:
Daylight basement only.
(Foundation & framing conversion diagram available — see order form.)

Blueprint Price Code: C

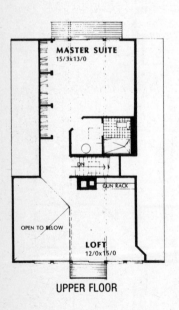

UPPER FLOOR

MASTER SUITE 15/3x13/0

DN

GUN RACK

OPEN TO BELOW

LOFT 12/0x15/0

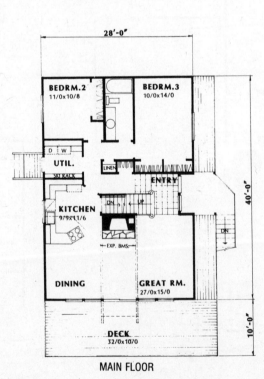

MAIN FLOOR

28'-0"

BEDRM. 2 11/0x10/8

BEDRM. 3 10/0x14/0

D W

UTIL.

SKI RACK

LINEN

ENTRY

KITCHEN 9/9x11/6

DN UP

EXP. BMS.

DN

40'-0"

10'-0"

DINING

GREAT RM. 27/0x15/0

DECK 32/0x10/0

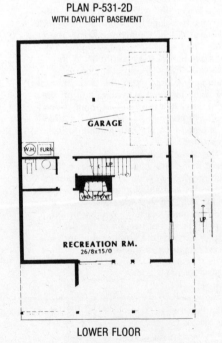

PLAN P-531-2D
WITH DAYLIGHT BASEMENT

GARAGE

W.H. FURN

W.D. STOVE

UP

RECREATION RM. 26/8x15/0

UP

LOWER FLOOR

TO ORDER THIS BLUEPRINT,
CALL TOLL-FREE 1-800-547-5570
(Prices and details on pp. 12-15.)

Plan P-531-2D

Designed for Rear-Sloping Lot

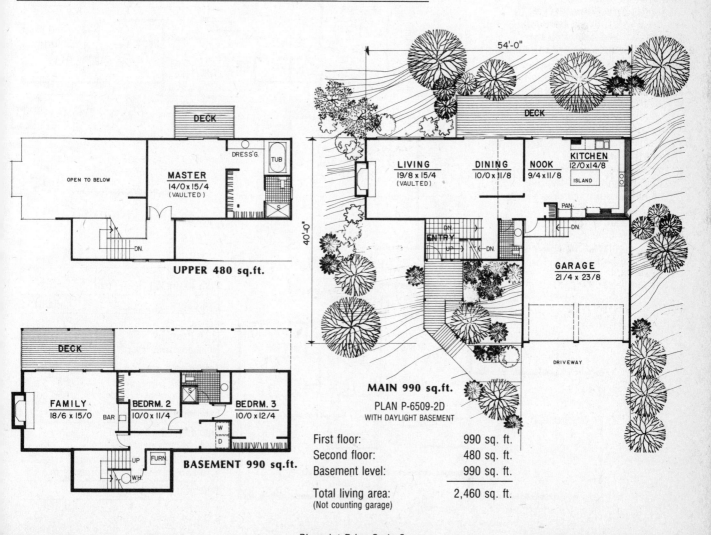

DECK

DRESS'G.

TUB

OPEN TO BELOW

MASTER
14/0 x 15/4
(VAULTED)

DN.

UPPER 480 sq.ft.

DECK

FAMILY
18/6 x 15/0

BAR

BEDRM. 2
10/0 x 11/4

BEDRM. 3
10/0 x 12/4

W
D

UP

FURN

WH

BASEMENT 990 sq.ft.

54'-0"

DECK

LIVING
19/8 x 15/4
(VAULTED)

DINING
10/0 x 11/8

NOOK
9/4 x 11/8

KITCHEN
12/0 x 14/8

ISLAND

PAN.

DN.

40'-0"

ENTRY

UP

DN.

GARAGE
21/4 x 23/8

DRIVEWAY

MAIN 990 sq.ft.

PLAN P-6509-2D
WITH DAYLIGHT BASEMENT

First floor: 990 sq. ft.
Second floor: 480 sq. ft.
Basement level: 990 sq. ft.
———————————————————
Total living area: 2,460 sq. ft.
(Not counting garage)

Blueprint Price Code C

Plan P-6509-2D

TO ORDER THIS BLUEPRINT,
CALL TOLL-FREE 1-800-547-5570
(Prices and details on pp. 12-15.)

Rustic Ranch Appeal

- Multiple gables, wood siding and shingles, and trapezoid windows with heavy beam details give this ranch a rustic, yet contemporary appeal.
- The dramatic entry foyer is sunbathed from the transom windows, and overlooks the vaulted living room with fireplace and open stairwell.
- The island kitchen opens to the breakfast room and beyond to the rear deck where the optional solar greenhouse may be positioned.
- The formal dining room also has deck access and is mere steps away from the kitchen.
- The sleeping wing incorporates three bedrooms and two full baths. The master suite features sliding doors to a private balcony, a window seat, and a walk-in closet.
- The lower floor can be finished into a wonderful rec room plus two additional bedrooms and storage galore.

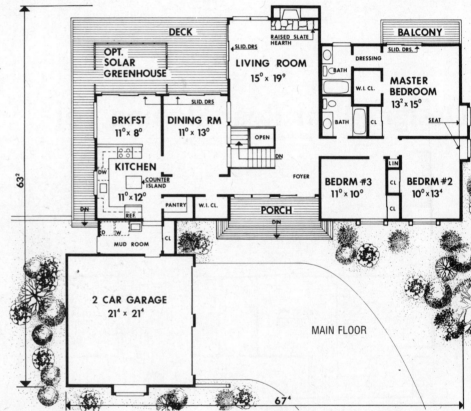

MAIN FLOOR

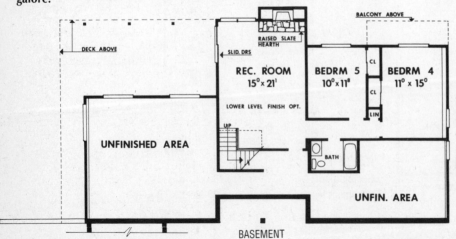

BASEMENT

Plan AX-98053

Bedrooms: 3	Baths: 2

Space:

Main floor:	1,724 sq. ft.
Finished lower level:	766 sq. ft.
Total living area:	**2,490 sq. ft.**
Unfinished lower level:	881 sq. ft.
Garage:	455 sq. ft.

Exterior Wall Framing: 2x4

Foundation options:
Daylight basement.
(Foundation & framing conversion diagram available — see order form.)

Blueprint Price Code: C

Plan AX-98053

Full of Surprises

- While dignified and reserved on the outside, this plan presents delightful surprises throughout the interior.
- Interesting angles, vaulted ceilings, surprising spaces and bright windows abound everywhere you look in this home.
- The elegant, vaulted living room is off the expansive foyer, and includes an imposing fireplace and large windows areas.
- The delightful kitchen includes a handy island and large corner windows in front of the sink.
- The nook is brightened not only by large windows, but also by a skylight.
- The vaulted family room includes a corner wood stove area plus easy access to the outdoors.
- A superb master suite includes an exquisite bath with a skylighted dressing area and large walk-in closet.
- Three secondary bedrooms share another full bath, and the large laundry room is conveniently positioned near the bedrooms.

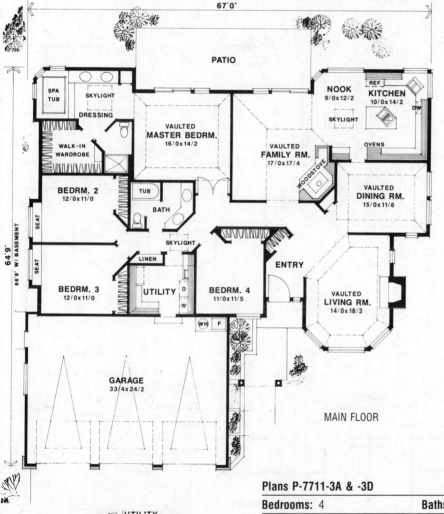

MAIN FLOOR

GARAGE
PLAN P-7711-3D
WITH DAYLIGHT BASEMENT

Plans P-7711-3A & -3D

Bedrooms: 4   Baths: 2

Space:
Main floor (non-basement
version):   2,510 sq. ft.
Main floor (basement version): 2,580 sq. ft.
Basement: 2,635 sq. ft.
Garage: 806 sq. ft.

Exterior Wall Framing: 2x6

Foundation options:
Daylight basement (Plan P-7711-3D).
Crawlspace (Plan P-7711-3A).
(Foundation & framing conversion diagram available — see order form.)

Blueprint Price Code: D

Plans P-7711-3A & -3D

TO ORDER THIS BLUEPRINT,
CALL TOLL-FREE 1-800-547-5570
(Prices and details on pp. 12-15.)

Hill-Hugging Design

- This angled ranch plan, with expandable daylight basement, makes the most of a rear-sloping hillside site.
- Strong angles, trapezoid windows and diagonal wood siding create a contemporary appeal.
- A grand entry foyer awaits visitors, with light streaming in from trapezoid transom windows above the front door and open rails over the staircase leading to the lower level.
- Ahead of the foyer unfolds a dynamic Great Room with 12-foot walls, corner transom windows and a central fireplace.
- The island kitchen serves the adjacent skylit dinette with deck access and the formal dining room with transom window.
- The main-floor master bedroom includes a large walk-in closet and private bath with spa tub under a skylight. Thre is also a nearby den/guest/reading room.
- The partially finished lower-level offers two more bedrooms and a full bath. There is plenty of room for later finishing into a rec room or additional bedrooms.

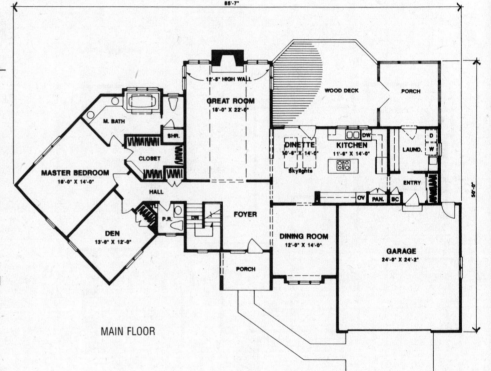

MAIN FLOOR

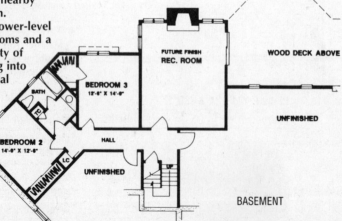

BASEMENT

Plan A-691-R

Bedrooms: 3	Baths: 2½

Space:

Main floor:	1,947 sq. ft.
Lower floor (finished):	587 sq. ft.

Total living area:	2,534 sq. ft.
Lower level (unfinished):	1,360 sq. ft.
Garage:	580 sq. ft.

Exterior Wall Framing:	2x6

Foundation options:
Daylight basement.
Standard basement.
(Foundation & framing conversion diagram available — see order form.)

Blueprint Price Code:	D

Plan A-691-R

Traditional Design for Sloping Lot

A striking traditional design, this residence offers 2,562 square feet of gracious living space. The high arched windows and elaborately glassed front door give this home an exceptional curb appeal for any high-income neighborhood.

The high vaulted entry lends further traditional atmosphere to the interior of the home, with double curved stairs leading to the upper level. Passing through the foyer, you enter the formal living and dining areas. These rooms are view-oriented to the rear of the home.

A special family area is located to the right of the dining room. The family room, nook, and kitchen can be completely closed off from the more formal part of the home or opened up for easy guest circulation when entertaining. A den off the living room provides privacy when needed for the older family members. The vaulted arch window gives this room a special touch of elegance.

The upstairs includes two secondary bedrooms, a bonus study or studio room and a luxurious master suite. Even the second bath has special features, such as double vanities and a specialty tub. Plentiful storage and large closets are available in all the bedrooms. The bonus area may be utilized as a fourth bedroom, additional storage or as a studio or hobby room.

PLAN SD-8815
(Specify basement or crawlspace when ordering.)

Upper floor:	1,198 sq. ft.
Main floor:	1,364 sq. ft.
Total living area:	2,562 sq. ft.

(Not counting basement, garage or bonus room)

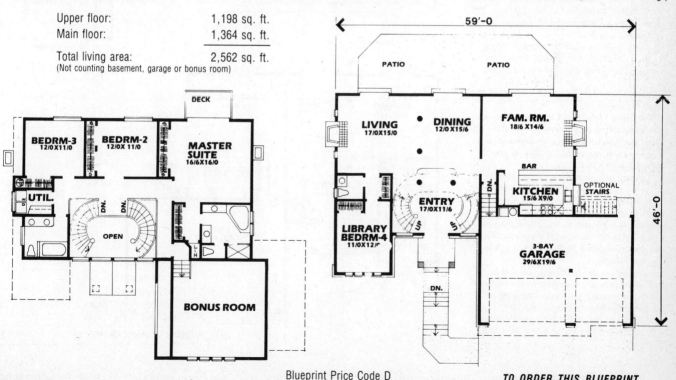

Blueprint Price Code D

Plan SD-8815

**TO ORDER THIS BLUEPRINT,
CALL TOLL-FREE 1-800-547-5570**
(Prices and details on pp. 12-15.)

Modern Luxury in Tudor Design

This modernized English Tudor home will bring a stately look to any neighborhood.

The entry is flanked by two bay windows, one in the library/den area, the other brightening up the bonus room over the garage. They work together to focus on the entry porch and court with a stone arch and brick background. Inviting bevel-glass entry doors open on a feast for the eyes — a granite floor, flowing to two circular stair cases. Both stairs going to the upper level are supported by colonial columns.

In the dining area there are two more colonial columns with arches separating the spacious living room from the dining area. The family room includes a grand fireplace, coved ceiling, and large sliding doors to the patio.

The living room has a traditional wood mantel and box beam ceiling, coved on all sides, that will instantly give you a feeling of welcoming warmth. The library could serve as a fifth bedroom.

Walking up the stairs, you are able to view the front yard through a two-story glass wall. At the top of the stairs there is no mistaking the master suite with its leaded-glass double doors. These lead to a grand bedroom suite with a coved ceiling. The luxurious bath includes a spa tub and separate shower.

Past the master bedroom you will be hidden in privacy, lounging in the bonus room — listening to music, reading, pursuing hobbies or exercising.

The top of the stairs to the left directs you to three other bedrooms with a hall bath.

Upper floor: 1,198 sq. ft.
Main floor: 1,364 sq. ft.

Total living area: 2,562 sq. ft.
(Not counting basement or garage)

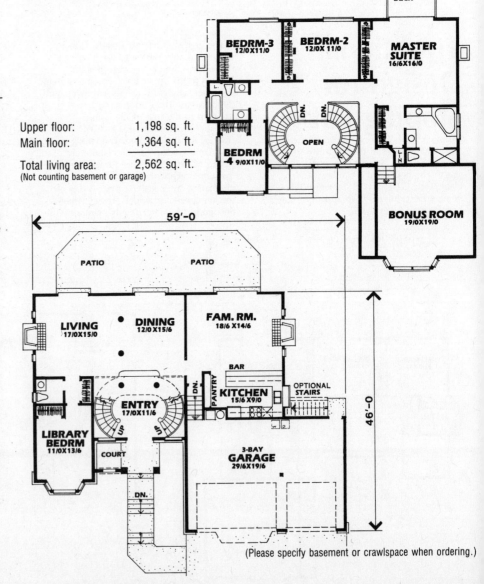

(Please specify basement or crawlspace when ordering.)

TO ORDER THIS BLUEPRINT, CALL TOLL-FREE 1-800-547-5570

(Prices and details on pp. 12-15.)

Blueprint Price Code D
Plan SD-8820

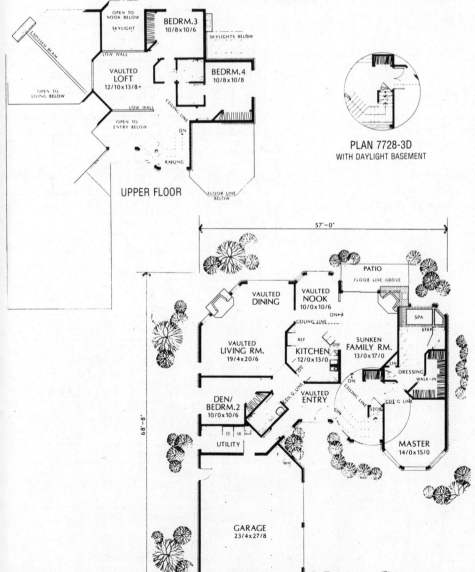

OPEN TO NOOK BELOW
SKYLIGHT
BEDRM. 3
10/8 x 10/6
SKYLIGHTS BELOW
LOW WALL
VAULTED LOFT
12/10 x 13/8+
BEDRM. 4
10/8 x 10/8
OPEN TO LIVING BELOW
LOW WALL
CEILING LINE
OPEN TO ENTRY BELOW
DN
RAILING

UPPER FLOOR

FLOOR LINE BELOW

PLAN 7728-3D
WITH DAYLIGHT BASEMENT

57'-0"

PATIO
FLOOR LINE ABOVE

VAULTED DINING
VAULTED NOOK
10/0 x 10/6
DN
CEILING LINE
SPA
STEP

VAULTED LIVING RM.
19/4 x 20/6
REF
KITCHEN
12/0 x 13/0
DW
SUNKEN FAMILY RM.
13/0 x 17/0
CEIL'G LINE
DRESSING
WALK-IN

68'-8"

DEN/ BEDRM. 2
10/0 x 10/6
VAULTED ENTRY
DN
CEILING LINE
CEIL'G LINE
STOR
MASTER
14/0 x 15/0

UTILITY
D W
F
WH

GARAGE
23/4 x 27/8

MAIN FLOOR

Executive Design

- All brick exterior with round-top windows.
- Master bedroom suite on main floor. All living areas to the rear.
- Den/bedroom on main floor with full bath.
- Two bedrooms and a loft on second floor. Each bedroom has own vanity.
- Right-angle attached garage. Good for corner lot. Could move garage doors to front.
- Great executive home. Good for both formal and informal entertaining.

Plans P-7728-3A & P-7728-3D

Bedrooms: 4	Baths: 3

Finished space:

Upper floor:	665 sq. ft.
Main floor:	1,988 sq. ft.

Total living area:	2,653 sq. ft.
Basement:	1,988 sq. ft.
Garage:	645 sq. ft.

Exterior Wall Framing:	2x6

Foundation options: (Specify)
Daylight basement: Plan P-7728-3D
Crawlspace: Plan P-7728-3A
(Foundation & framing conversion diagram available — see order form.)

Blueprint Price Code	D

Plans P-7728-3A & -3D

Dramatic, Soaring Lines

- This dramatic two-story offers a daylight basement option for hillside settings.
- Note the large island kitchen with adjoining nook and family room.
- Upstairs master suite includes splendid bath, walk-in closet and fireplace.
- Bonus space is available for office, exercise room, extra play space or additional bedroom.

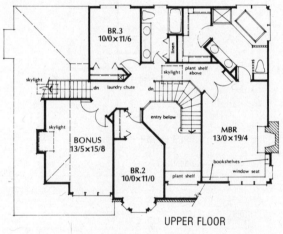

UPPER FLOOR

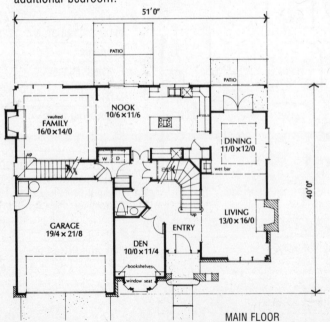

MAIN FLOOR

Plan CDG-2005

Bedrooms: 3-4	Baths: 2½

Space:	
Upper floor:	1,041 sq. ft.
Main floor:	1,386 sq. ft.
Bonus area:	231 sq. ft.
Total living area:	**2,658 sq. ft.**
Basement:	1,386 sq. ft.
Garage:	419 sq. ft.

Exterior Wall Framing:	2x4

Ceiling Heights:	
Upper floor:	8'
Main floor:	9'

Foundation options:
Daylight basement
Crawlspace.
(Foundation & framing conversion diagram available — see order form.)

Blueprint Price Code:	D

Plan CDG-2005

Simple Exterior, Luxurious Interior

- Modest and unassuming on the exterior, this design provides an elegant and spacious interior.
- Highlight of the home is undoubtedly the vast Great Room/ Dining area, with its vaulted ceiling, massive hearth and big bay windows.
- An exceptionally fine master suite is also included, with a large sleeping area, luxurious bath and big walk-in closet.
- A beautiful kitchen is joined by a bright bay-windowed breakfast nook; also note the large pantry.
- The lower level encompasses two more bedrooms and a generously sized game room and bar.

MAIN FLOOR

49'3"

50'8"

RAILING
DECK
HOT TUB
MASTER 19/0x14/0
VAULTED GREAT RM. 21/6x17/6
PLNTR.
SUNKEN TUB
DRESSING
WALK IN WARDROBE
BATH
VAULTED DINING 14/4x10/6
SKYLIGHT
PANTRY
VAULTED ENTRY
KITCHEN 13/6x10/6
GARAGE 21/4x21/8
REF.
DW
NOOK 10/0x10/0

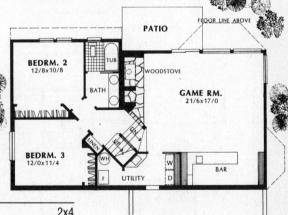

BASEMENT

PATIO
FLOOR LINE ABOVE
BEDRM. 2 12/8x10/8
TUB
WOODSTOVE
BATH
GAME RM. 21/6x17/0
BEDRM. 3 12/0x11/4
LINEN
WH
F
UTILITY
W D
BAR

Plan P-6595-3D

Bedrooms: 3	Baths: 2½

Space:	
Main floor:	1,530 sq. ft.
Lower level:	1,145 sq. ft.
Total living area:	2,675 sq. ft.
Garage:	462 sq. ft.

Exterior Wall Framing:	2x4

Foundation options:
Daylight basement only.
(Foundation & framing conversion diagram available — see order form.)

Blueprint Price Code:	D

Plan P-6595-3D

TO ORDER THIS BLUEPRINT,
CALL TOLL-FREE 1-800-547-5570
(Prices and details on pp. 12-15.)

Panoramic View for Scenic Site

- Large deck offers a panoramic view and plenty of space for outdoor living.
- Sunken living room features big windows and impressive fireplace.
- Living room is set off by railings, not walls, to create visual impact of big space.
- Master suite includes private bath, large closet, sitting area and access to deck.
- Lower level includes rec room with fireplace, two bedrooms, two baths and large utility area.

Plan NW-779

Bedrooms: 3	Baths: 3½
Space:	
Main floor:	1,450 sq. ft.
Lower floor:	1,242 sq. ft.
Total living area:	2,692 sq. ft.
Exterior Wall Framing:	2x6

Foundation options:
Daylight basement only.
(Foundation & framing conversion diagram available — see order form.)

Blueprint Price Code:	D

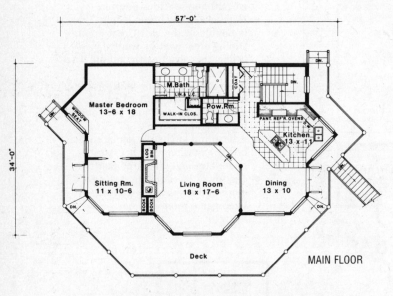

MAIN FLOOR

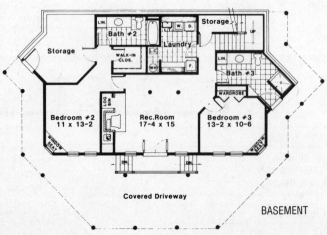

BASEMENT

TO ORDER THIS BLUEPRINT,
CALL TOLL-FREE 1-800-547-5570
(Prices and details on pp. 12-15.)

Plan NW-779

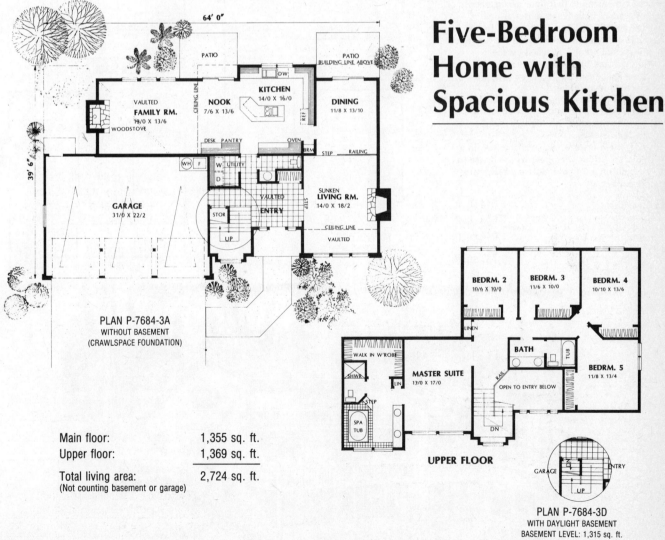

Five-Bedroom Home with Spacious Kitchen

PLAN P-7684-3A
WITHOUT BASEMENT
(CRAWLSPACE FOUNDATION)

UPPER FLOOR

PLAN P-7684-3D
WITH DAYLIGHT BASEMENT
BASEMENT LEVEL: 1,315 sq. ft.

Main floor:	1,355 sq. ft.
Upper floor:	1,369 sq. ft.
Total living area:	2,724 sq. ft.

(Not counting basement or garage)

Blueprint Price Code D

Plans P-7684-3A & -3D

TO ORDER THIS BLUEPRINT,
CALL TOLL-FREE 1-800-547-5570
(Prices and details on pp. 12-15.)

FRONT VIEW

Luxury on a Compact Foundation

Sky-lighted sloped ceilings, an intriguing stairway and overhead bridge and a carefully planned first floor arrangement combine to delight the senses as one explores this spacious 2737 sq. ft. home. A major element of the design is the luxurious master suite that is reached via the stairway and bridge. An abundance of closet space and an oversized bath are welcome features here.

Two bedrooms, generous bath facilities and a large family room provide lots of growing room for the younger members of the household.

All these features are available within a mere 36' width which allows the house to be built on a 50' wide lot — a real bonus these days.

Main floor:	1,044 sq. ft.
Upper level:	649 sq. ft.
Lower level:	1,044 sq. ft.
Total living area:	2,737 sq. ft.
(Not counting garage)	

(Exterior walls are 2x6 construction)

MAIN FLOOR
1044 SQUARE FEET

MASTER LOFT SUITE
649 SQUARE FEET

LOWER LEVEL
1044 SQUARE FEET

REAR VIEW

Blueprint Price Code D

Plan H-2110-1B

Take Full Advantage of Views

- This design is ideally suited to a front and side view lot which slopes up from the street.
- Visitors are welcomed into a vaulted entry which is overlooked by an open railing above.
- The entry, dining and living rooms are two steps down from the main floor, creating a separate zone for formal entertaining.
- Both the living and dining rooms are highlighted by 9' coffered ceilings.
- The den is light and airy, with French doors leading into the room and another pair of French doors leading out to a private deck. Direct access is provided to the adjoining full bath so that this room can easily be converted into a guest room.
- Skylights brighten the kitchen, which features a walk-in pantry, breakfast bay and an angled counter with eating bar that opens to the family room.
- Upstairs, the master bedroom is visually enlarged with a 10' coffered ceiling. An archway leads into a beautiful bath with dual vanities and spa tub. Optional skylights are available over the vanity area and large walk-in closet.
- The side-entering garage is tucked under the house and includes a spacious work area to the rear.

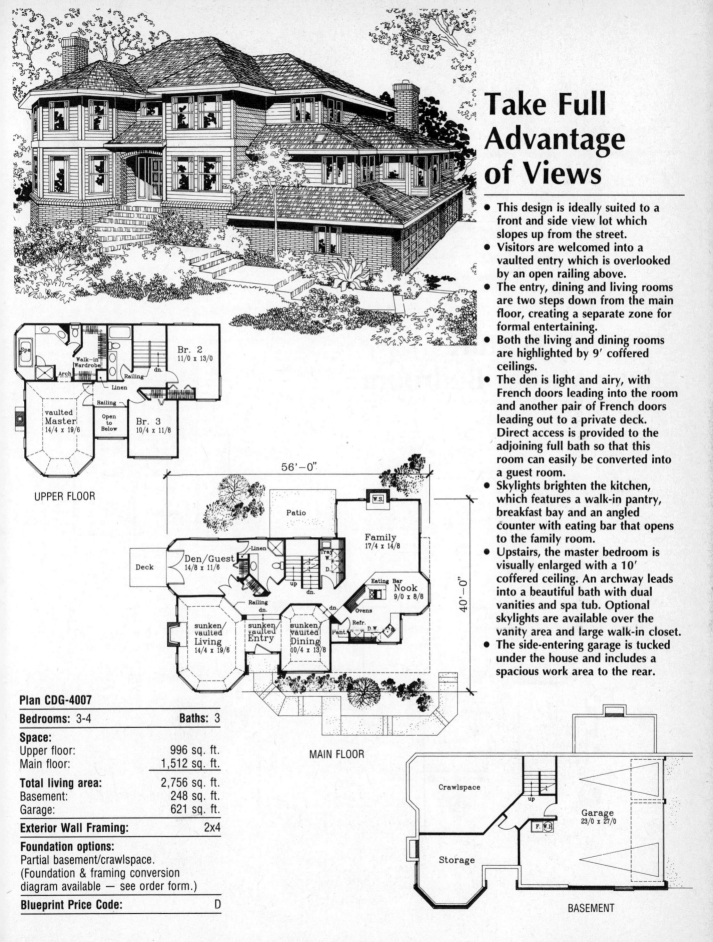

UPPER FLOOR

MAIN FLOOR

BASEMENT

Plan CDG-4007

Bedrooms: 3-4	Baths: 3

Space:	
Upper floor:	996 sq. ft.
Main floor:	1,512 sq. ft.

Total living area:	**2,756 sq. ft.**
Basement:	248 sq. ft.
Garage:	621 sq. ft.

Exterior Wall Framing:	**2x4**

Foundation options:
Partial basement/crawlspace.
(Foundation & framing conversion diagram available — see order form.)

Blueprint Price Code:	**D**

Plan CDG-4007

TO ORDER THIS BLUEPRINT, CALL TOLL-FREE 1-800-547-5570 (Prices and details on pp. 12-15.)

Two-Story Features
Deluxe Master Bedroom

First floor:	1,442 sq. ft.
Second floor:	823 sq. ft.
Total living area:	2,265 sq. ft.
Basement (Optional):	688 sq. ft.

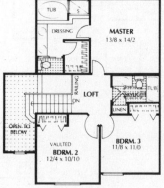

SECOND FLOOR

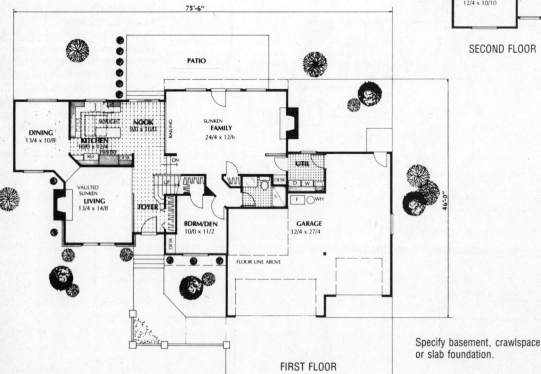

FIRST FLOOR

Specify basement, crawlspace
or slab foundation.

Blueprint Price Code C
Plan U-88-201

Nostalgic Exterior Appeal

- A lattice-trimmed front entry porch, repeated steep gables, and narrow lap siding all convey a nostalgic exterior appeal.
- The open-feeling plan offers plenty of excitement and livability for families in the 90's.
- The living room includes such dramatic features as a high-vaulted ceiling with loft overlook above, a two-story fireplace/stair tower with built-in wet bar, and high corner glass.
- The open kitchen overlooks a snack counter and skylit dining room.
- The main floor also includes a master bedroom with access to a dramatic bath and side deck as well as a den for TV watching or overnight guests.
- The two upstairs bedrooms plus loft will give the kids plenty of private space.

UDG-90009

Bedrooms: 3-4	Baths: 2

Space:

Upper floor:	554 sq. ft.
Main floor:	1,123 sq. ft.
Total living area:	1,677 sq. ft.
Basement:	1,123 sq. ft.
Garage:	544 sq. ft.

Exterior Wall Framing: 2x4

Foundation options:
Standard Basement.
(Foundation & framing conversion diagram available — see order form.)

Blueprint Price Code: B

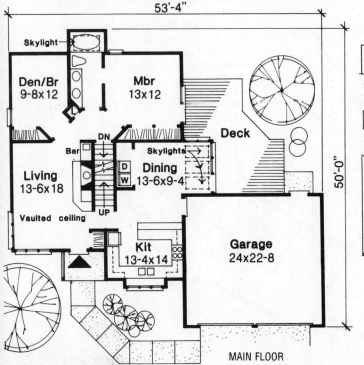

MAIN FLOOR

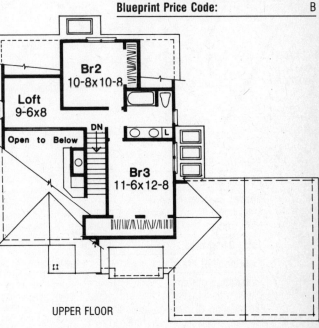

UPPER FLOOR

Plan UDG-90009

TO ORDER THIS BLUEPRINT,
CALL TOLL-FREE 1-800-547-5570
(Prices and details on pp. 12-15.)

Triple Play

- This playful design uses triple wings radiating from a central, spiral stairwell to create drama, both outside and in.
- The entry foyer opens to a view of the spiral stairs with a log support soaring up to the ridge.
- The eat-in kitchen and formal dining room surround the stairs, while just beyond is the large living room with fireplace and plenty of corner glass.
- The other two wings incorporate two bedrooms and a two-car garage.
- The walk-out lower level offers a large family room, a play room, an additional bedroom, a hobby and activity area and laundry facilites.

MAIN FLOOR

Plan CPS-994-SL

Bedrooms: 2	Baths: 1½
Space:	
Main floor:	1,430 sq. ft.
Lower floor:	1,430 sq. ft.
Total living area:	2,860 sq. ft.
Exterior Wall Framing:	2x6

Foundation options:
Daylight basement.
(Foundation & framing conversion
diagram available — see order form.)

Blueprint Price Code:	D

LOWER FLOOR

Plan CPS-994-SL

Contemporary Hillside Home

This three-level recreation home is designed to fit comfortably on a slope of approximately 20 degrees, with a fall of 15 to 17 feet for the depth of the building. Naturally the stability of the ground must be taken into consideration, and local professional advice should be sought. Otherwise, this home is designed to meet the requirements of the Uniform Building Code.

The pleasing contemporary nature of the exterior is calculated to blend into the surroundings as unobtrusively as possible, following the natural contours.

The modest roadside facade consisting of garage doors and a wooden entrance deck conceals the spacious luxury that lies beyond. Proceeding from the rustic deck into the skylighted entry hall, one is struck by the immensity of the living-dining room and the huge deck extending beyond. A massive masonry backdrop provides a setting for the pre-fab fireplace of your choice (this same structure incorporates the flue for a similar unit on the lower level).

Before descending from the entry hall, one must take notice of the balcony-type den, library, hobby or office room on this level — a private retreat from the activities below.

The efficient U-shaped kitchen has an adjoining attached breakfast bar for casual dining whenever the roomy dining room facilities are not required. A convenient laundry room is an important part of this housekeeping section.

The master bedroom suite occupies the remainder of the 1,256 sq. ft. contained on this level. The room itself, 12' x 16' in size, is served by a private full bathroom and two huge wardrobe closets. Direct access to the large deck provides opportunity for morning sit-ups or evening conversation under the stars. A final convenience on this level is the small lavatory for general use.

The focal point of the lower level is the spacious recreation room which is a duplicate size of the living room above. Flanking this room at either end are additional large bedrooms, one having a walk-in closet and the other a huge wall-spanning wardrobe. Another full bathroom serves this level. A small work shop or storage room completes this arrangement.

REAR VIEW

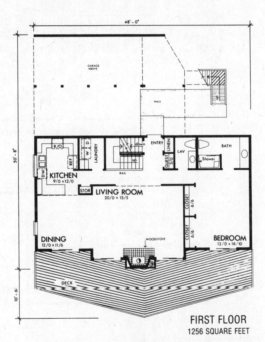

FIRST FLOOR
1256 SQUARE FEET

UPPER LEVEL
372 SQUARE FEET
528 SQUARE FEET - GARAGE

PLAN H-966-1B
WITH DAYLIGHT BASEMENT

(Exterior walls framed in 2x6 studs)

Upper level:	372 sq. ft.
Main floor:	1,256 sq. ft.
Basement:	1,256 sq. ft.
Total living area: (Not counting garage)	2,884 sq. ft.

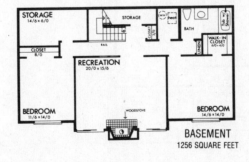

BASEMENT
1256 SQUARE FEET

Blueprint Price Code D

Plan H-966-1B

TO ORDER THIS BLUEPRINT, CALL TOLL-FREE 1-800-547-5570
(Prices and details on pp. 12-15.)

Dramatic Western Contemporary

- Dramatic and functional building features contribute to the comfort and desire of this family home.
- Master suite offers a spacious private bath and luxurious hydro spa.
- Open, efficient kitchen accommodates modern appliances, a large pantry, and a snack bar.
- Skylights shed light on the entryway, open staircase, and balcony.
- Upper level balcony area has private covered deck, and may be used as a guest room or den.

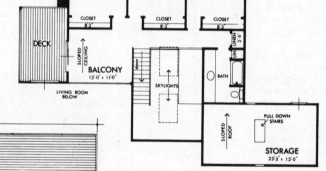

BEDROOM 11'-9" x 11'-9"
BEDROOM 11'-9" x 11'-9"
BEDROOM 11'-9" x 11'-9"
CLOSET 8'-3"
CLOSET 8'-3"
CLOSET 8'-3"
LIN LIN LINEN 3'-6"
DECK
SLOPED CEILING
BALCONY 13'-0" x 11'-0"
down
BATH
LIVING ROOM BELOW
SKYLIGHTS
SLOPED ROOF
PULL DOWN STAIRS
STORAGE 23'-3" x 12'-0"

UPPER FLOOR

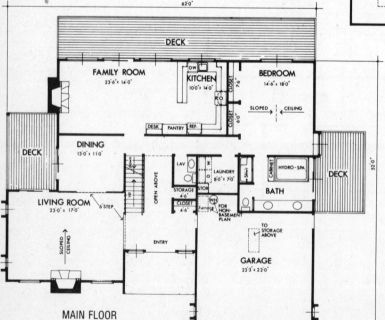

62'-0"
DECK
FAMILY ROOM 23'-6" x 14'-0"
KITCHEN 10'-0" x 14'-0"
DW
CLOSET 7'-6"
BEDROOM 14'-6" x 18'-0"
DESK PANTRY REF.
CLOSET 6'-0"
SLOPED CEILING
DINING 13'-0" x 11'-0"
DECK
LAV
LAUNDRY 8'-0" x 7'-0"
CARNET
HYDRO-SPA
DECK
52'-0"
OPEN ABOVE
STORAGE STOR
CLOSET 4'-6"
BATH
WH FURNACE FOR NON-BASEMENT PLAN
LIVING ROOM 23'-0" x 17'-0"
6" STEP
ENTRY
GARAGE 23'-3" x 22'-0"
TO STORAGE ABOVE

MAIN FLOOR

Plans H-3708-1 & -1A	
Bedrooms: 4	**Baths:** 2½
Space:	
Upper floor:	893 sq. ft.
Main floor:	2,006 sq. ft.
Total living area:	2,899 sq. ft.
Basement:	approx. 2,006 sq. ft.
Garage:	512 sq. ft.
Exterior Wall Framing:	2x6

Foundation options:
Daylight basement (Plan H-3708-1).
Crawlspace (Plan H-3708-1A).
(Foundation & framing conversion diagram available — see order form.)

Blueprint Price Code:	D

TO ORDER THIS BLUEPRINT, CALL TOLL-FREE 1-800-547-5570
(Prices and details on pp. 12-15.)

Plans H-3708-1 & -1A

Open Family/Nook/Kitchen Area

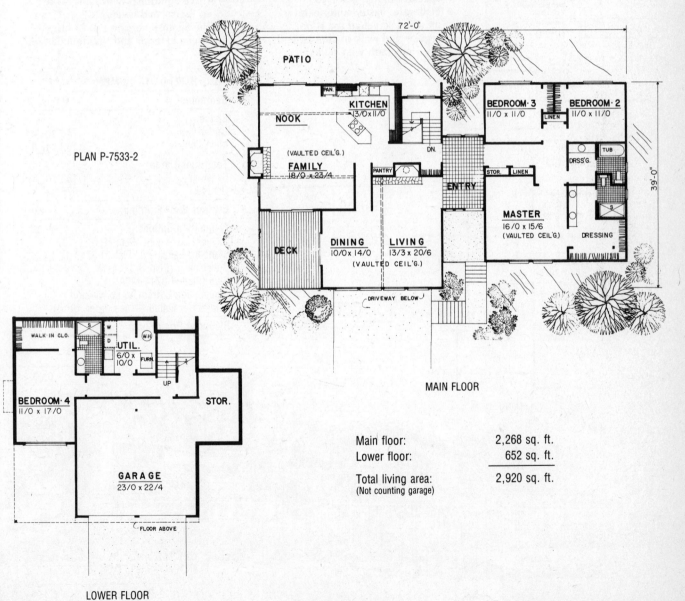

PLAN P-7533-2

72'-0"

PATIO

KITCHEN
13/0 x 11/0

NOOK

(VAULTED CEIL'G.)

FAMILY
18/0 x 23/4

PANTRY

DN.

ENTRY

DINING
10/0 x 14/0

LIVING
13/3 x 20/6

(VAULTED CEIL'G.)

DECK

DRIVEWAY BELOW

BEDROOM·3
11/0 x 11/0

LINEN

BEDROOM·2
11/0 x 11/0

TUB

DRSS'G.

STOR. LINEN

MASTER
16/0 x 15/6
(VAULTED CEIL'G.)

DRESSING

39'-0"

MAIN FLOOR

WALK-IN CLO.

UTIL.
6/0 x 10/0

FURN.

W·H

UP

BEDROOM·4
11/0 x 17/0

STOR.

GARAGE
23/0 x 22/4

FLOOR ABOVE

LOWER FLOOR

Main floor:	2,268 sq. ft.
Lower floor:	652 sq. ft.
Total living area:	2,920 sq. ft.
(Not counting garage)	

Blueprint Price Code D

Plan P-7533-2

TO ORDER THIS BLUEPRINT,
CALL TOLL-FREE 1-800-547-5570
(Prices and details on pp. 12-15.)

Pure Luxury in a Choice of Styles

- Southwestern colonial or Western contemporary exteriors are available when deciding if this spacious design is for you.
- Elaborate master suite features attached screened spa room, regular and walk-in closets, and luxurious bath with skylight.

- Study, large family and living room with sloped ceilings and rear patio are other points of interest.
- Three additional bedrooms make up the second level.
- The Spanish version (M2A) offers a stucco exterior and slab foundation.

Plans H-3714-1/1A/1B/M2A

Bedrooms: 4	Baths: 3
Space:	
Upper floor:	740 sq. ft.
Main floor:	2,190 sq. ft.
Total living area:	2,930 sq. ft.
Basement:	1,153 sq. ft.
Garage:	576 sq. ft.
Exterior Wall Framing:	2x6

Foundation options:
Daylight basement (Plan H-3714-1B).
Standard basement (Plan H-3714-1).
Crawlspace (Plan H-3714-1A).
Slab (Plan H-3714-M2A).
(Foundation & framing conversion diagram available — see order form.)

Blueprint Price Code: D

UPPER FLOOR

MAIN FLOOR

PLAN H-3714-M2A FRONT VIEW

TO ORDER THIS BLUEPRINT,
CALL TOLL-FREE 1-800-547-5570
(Prices and details on pp. 12-15.)

Plans H-3714-1/1A/1B/M2A

Master Suite Features Deluxe Bath

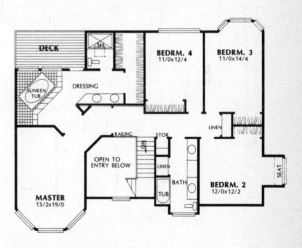

DECK

BEDRM. 4
11/0x12/4

BEDRM. 3
11/0x14/4

SH.

DRESSING

SUNKEN TUB

LINEN

OPEN TO ENTRY BELOW

RAILING

STOR.

UP

LINEN

BATH

TUB

SEAT

MASTER
13/2x19/0

BEDRM. 2
12/0x12/2

62'0"

DECK

DINING
12/0x14/8

KITCHEN
13/0x14/8

NOOK
9/0x16/8

CEILING LINE

DW

R

S

STOR.

PANTRY

DESK

SINK

W.

D.

BAR

FAMILY RM.
13/6x21/4

RAILING

RAILING

STEP

RAILING

STOR.

UTILITY
8/8x6/4

STEP

F

WH

ENTRY

BATH

UP

50'0"

SUNKEN
LIVING RM.
13/2x21/0

GARAGE
29/2x25/6

PLAN P-7662-3A
WITHOUT BASEMENT
(CRAWLSPACE FOUNDATION)

First floor: 1,538 sq. ft.
Second floor: 1,392 sq. ft.

Total living area: 2,930 sq. ft.
(Not counting basement or garage)

UP

ENTRY

BATH

PLAN P-7662-3D
WITH DAYLIGHT BASEMENT
BASEMENT LEVEL: 1,179 sq. ft.

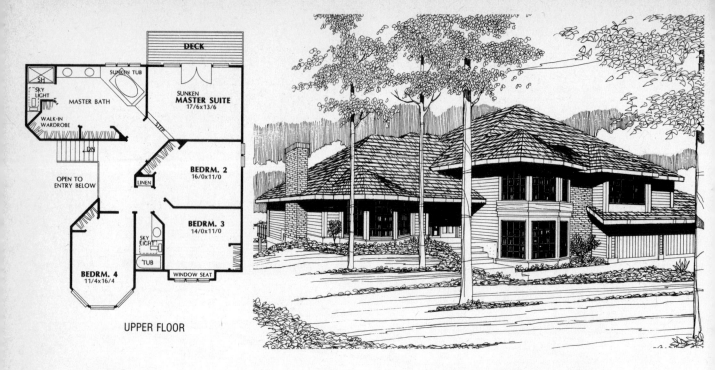

UPPER FLOOR

Labels within upper floor plan:
- SKY LIGHT
- SH
- MASTER BATH
- SUNKEN TUB
- DECK
- SUNKEN MASTER SUITE 17/6x13/6
- WALK-IN WARDROBE
- DN
- OPEN TO ENTRY BELOW
- STEP
- LINEN
- BEDRM. 2 16/0x11/0
- BEDRM. 3 14/0x11/0
- SKY LIGHT
- TUB
- BEDRM. 4 11/4x16/4
- WINDOW SEAT

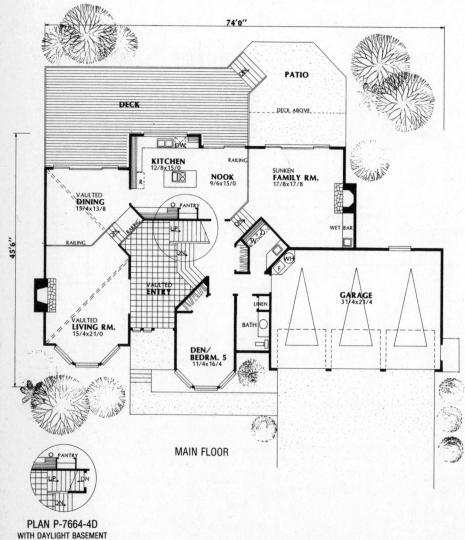

MAIN FLOOR

Labels within main floor plan:
- 74'0"
- 45'6"
- PATIO
- DECK
- DECK ABOVE
- KITCHEN 12/8x15/0
- DW
- RAILING
- NOOK 9/6x15/0
- SUNKEN FAMILY RM. 17/8x17/8
- R
- VAULTED DINING 15/4x13/8
- PANTRY
- UP
- RAILING
- DN
- WET BAR
- RAILING
- VAULTED ENTRY
- GARAGE 31/4x21/4
- VAULTED LIVING RM. 15/4x21/0
- WH
- F
- LINEN
- BATH
- DEN/ BEDRM. 5 11/4x16/4

PLAN P-7664-4D
WITH DAYLIGHT BASEMENT

- PANTRY
- UP
- DN

Creative Spaces

- Here's a home that is not only large, but extremely creative in its use of indoor space.
- A huge area is created by the combination of the vaulted living and dining rooms, which flow together visually but are separated by a railing.
- Another expansive space results from the kitchen/nook/family room arrangement, and their easy access to deck and patio.
- Upstairs, the master suite includes a lavish bath and generous closets.
- Three large secondary bedrooms share another full bath, and each has its own unique design feature.

Plans P-7664-4A & -4D

Bedrooms: 4-5	Baths: 2½

Space:

Upper floor:	1,254 sq. ft.
Main floor:	1,824 sq. ft.
Total living area:	**3,078 sq. ft.**
Basement:	1,486 sq. ft.
Garage:	668 sq. ft.

Exterior Wall Framing:	2x4

Foundation options:
Daylight basement (Plan P-7664-4D).
Crawlspace (Plan P-7664-4A).
(Foundation & framing conversion diagram available — see order form.)

Blueprint Price Code: E

Plans P-7664-4A & -4D

Impressive Home for Sloping Lot

PLAN Q-3080-1A
WITHOUT BASEMENT
(SLAB-ON-GRADE FOUNDATION)

First floor: 1,505 sq. ft.
Second floor: 1,575 sq. ft.

Total living area: 3,080 sq. ft.
(Not counting garage)

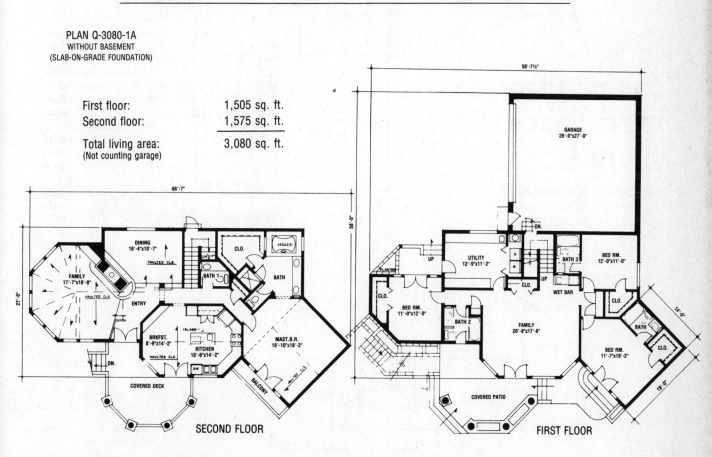

SECOND FLOOR

FIRST FLOOR

NOTE: This house was designed for a lot sloping down in the direction of the arrow.

Blueprint Price Code E

Plan Q-3080-1A

TO ORDER THIS BLUEPRINT,
CALL TOLL-FREE 1-800-547-5570
(Prices and details on pp. 12-15.)

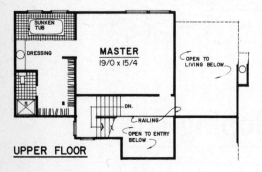

UPPER FLOOR

62'-0"

DECK

KITCHEN
11/4 x 15/4

FAMILY
17/0 x 13/4

NOOK
8/4 x 13/4

DINING
10/8 x 10/0

LIVING
13/0 x 17/0

DESK   PANTRY

DN.

ENTRY

UP   DN.

BEDROOM·2
10/0 x 10/6

LIN.

GARAGE
21/4 x 25/8

BEDROOM·3
10/0 x 11/2

44'-0"

Modest-Looking Plan Offers Space Galore

● Entire upper floor of almost 600 sq. ft. is devoted to master suite, including large closet and deluxe bath with sunken tub.

● Main floor includes spacious family room/nook/kitchen combination for casual family living.

● Living and dining areas flow together for more formal space for entertaining guests.

● Lower level, opening to the rear, includes 400 sq. ft. recreation area plus bath, utility area and fourth bedroom.

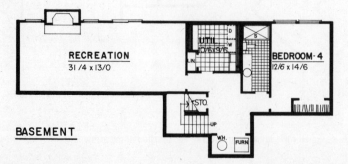

UTIL
10/6 x 9/6

D
W

S

RECREATION
31/4 x 13/0

BEDROOM·4
12/6 x 14/6

STO.

UP

WH.   FURN

BASEMENT

Plan P-7548-2D	
Bedrooms: 4	**Baths:** 3
Space:	
Upper floor:	584 sq. ft.
Main floor:	1,498 sq. ft.
Lower floor:	1,020 sq. ft.
Total living area:	3,102 sq. ft.
Garage:	547 sq. ft.
Exterior Wall Framing:	2x4

Foundation options:
Daylight basement only.
(Foundation & framing conversion diagram available — see order form.)

Blueprint Price Code: E

TO ORDER THIS BLUEPRINT,
CALL TOLL-FREE 1-800-547-5570

(Prices and details on pp. 12-15.)

Plan P-7548-2D

Executive Design Offers Daylight Basement Option

- Impressive exterior and exciting interior combine to create a great home for family living and entertaining as well.
- Sunken living room and dining room with raised ceiling flow together to make space for large gatherings.
- Family room, nook and island kitchen form great casual family area.
- Luxurious master suite includes deluxe bath and plenty of closet space.
- Large bonus area offers many possibilities for workroom, hobbies, exercise, play room and other uses.

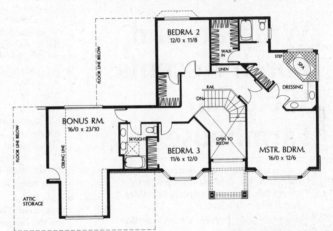

UPPER FLOOR

BEDRM. 2
12/0 x 11/8

BONUS RM.
16/0 x 23/10

BEDRM. 3
11/6 x 12/0

MSTR. BDRM.
16/0 x 12/6

ATTIC STORAGE

MAIN FLOOR

70' - 0"

48' - 6"

PATIO

FAMILY RM.
13/0 x 19/2

NOOK
10/0 x 12/8

KITCHEN
16/0 x 13/4

DINING
10/8 x 11/6

UTILITY

DEN
11/8 x 12/0

ENTRY

SUNKEN LIVING ROOM
16/0 x 16/0

GARAGE
31/4 x 20/4

Plans P-7718-3A & P-7718-3D

Bedrooms: 3	Baths: 2½

Space:

Upper floor:	1,188 sq. ft.
Main floor:	1,583 sq. ft.
Bonus area:	372 sq. ft.
Total living area:	**3,143 sq. ft.**
Daylight basement:	1,532 sq. ft.
Garage:	637 sq. ft.

Exterior Wall Framing:	2x6

Foundation options:
Daylight basement, Plan P-7718-3D
Crawlspace, Plan P-7718-3A
(Foundation & framing conversion diagram available — see order form.)

Blueprint Price Code: E

BASEMENT

Plans P-7718-3A & P-7718-3D

Wrap-around Porch Accents Victorian Farmhouse

- Fish-scale shingles and horizontal siding team with the detailed front porch to create this look of yesterday. The sides and rear are brick.
- The main level features a center section of informal family room and formal living and dining rooms. They can all be connected via French doors.
- A separate workshop is located on the main level and connected to the main house by a covered breezeway.
- The master bath ceiling is sloped and has built-in skylights. The kitchen and eating area have high sloped ceilings also. Typical ceiling heights are 8' on the basement and upper level and 10' on the main level.
- This home is energy efficient.
- This home is designed on a full daylight basement. The two-car garage is located on the basement level.

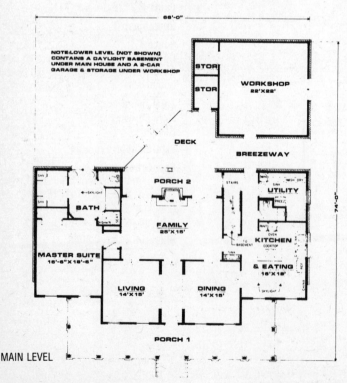

MAIN LEVEL

UPPER LEVEL

PLAN E-3103
WITH DAYLIGHT BASEMENT

Exterior walls are 2x6 construction.

Heated area:	3,153 sq. ft.
Unheated area	2,066 sq. ft.
Total area:	5,219 sq. ft.
(Not counting basement)	

TO ORDER THIS BLUEPRINT,
CALL TOLL-FREE 1-800-547-5570
76 (Prices and details on pp. 12-15.)

Blueprint Price Code E
Plan E-3103

Exceptional Design Maximizes the View to the Rear

PLAN P-6469-2D
WITH DAYLIGHT BASEMENT

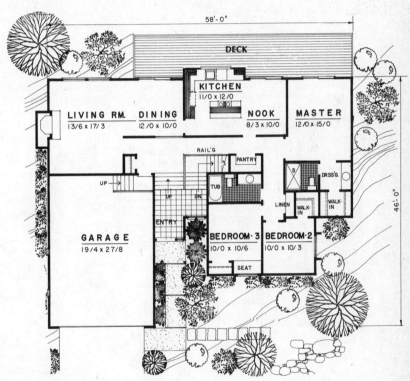

MAIN FLOOR

58'-0"

DECK

KITCHEN
11/0 x 12/0

LIVING RM.
13/6 x 17/3

DINING
12/0 x 10/0

NOOK
8/3 x 10/0

MASTER
12/0 x 15/0

RAIL'G.

PANTRY

UP

TUB

DRSS'G.

LINEN

WALK IN

WALK IN

UP DN

ENTRY

GARAGE
19/4 x 27/8

BEDROOM·3
10/0 x 10/6

BEDROOM·2
10/0 x 10/3

SEAT

46'-0"

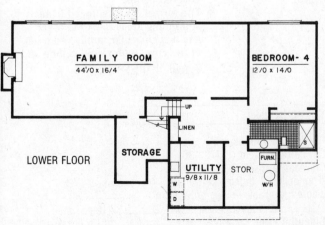

FAMILY ROOM
44'0 x 16/4

BEDROOM-4
12/0 x 14/0

UP

LINEN

STORAGE

UTILITY
9/8 x 11/8

STOR.

FURN.

W/H

W D

LOWER FLOOR

Main floor:	1,620 sq. ft.
Lower floor:	1,540 sq. ft.
Total living area: (Not counting garage)	3,160 sq. ft.

Blueprint Price Code E

Plan P-6469-2D

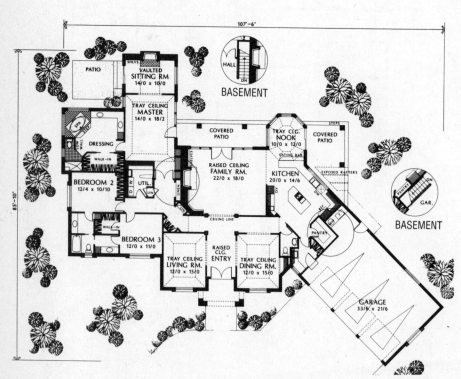

Texas-Style Estate

- This stately Texas-style single story is clad in brick and accented with staggered, sloping rooflines.
- Most alluring is the lavish master suite, featuring a vaulted sitting room with fireplace, a delightful private patio and a lavish bath with spacious dressing area, step-up spa and walk-in closet.
- The secondary bedrooms each provide a private entrance to the bathroom they share.
- The opposite end of the home offers an elongated kitchen with island work station, extended counter/eating bar and a nook with a bay window nestled between covered patios.
- The formal, tray-ceilinged living and dining areas flank the foyer, and a spectacular family room lies at the core, with raised ceiling and a huge fireplace.

Plans P-7722-3A & -3D

Bedrooms: 3	Baths: 2½

Space:

Total living area:

Main floor, basement version:	3,196 sq. ft.
Main floor, non-basement version:	3,140 sq. ft.
Basement:	3,196 sq. ft.
Garage:	720 sq. ft.

Exterior Wall Framing:	2x6

Ceiling Heights:	9'

Foundation options:
Daylight basement (P-7722-3D).
Crawlspace (P-7722-3A).
(Foundation & framing conversion diagram available — see order form.)

Blueprint Price Code:	E

Plans P-7722-3A & -3D

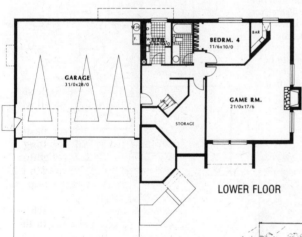

LOWER FLOOR

GARAGE
31/0x28/0

BEDRM. 4
11/6x10/0

BAR

GAME RM.
21/0x17/6

STORAGE

PLAN P-9059-3

Main floor: 2,239 sq. ft.
Upper floor: 958 sq. ft.

Total living area: 3,197 sq. ft.
(Not counting garage)

Exceptional Executive Designed for Uphill Slope

MAIN FLOOR

70'0"

DECK

NOOK
8/0x14/0

KITCHEN
12/10x16/6

BEDRM. 3
11/6x10/6

LIN

BEDRM. 2
11/0x10/6

VAULTED
FAMILY RM.
13/0x17/0

SUNKEN
TUB

DRESS'G

DINING
12/6x13/0

VAULTED
LIVING RM.
18/10x17/0

VAULTED
ENTRY

UP

MASTER
13/0x20/0

RAIL

PAN.

36'-6"

DRIVEWAY BELOW

RAIL

Blueprint Price Code E

Plan P-9059-3

Distinctive Executive Design

- Varying ceiling heights add visual interest — den is 9'; kitchen, 7' 2"; family room, 8' 7"; entry, 16' 6"; living room, 9' 6".
- Tri-level main floor includes living room, entry and den on one level, with steps down into the nook, kitchen and dining areas. Family room is another step down from the nook.
- Upper floor is two-level, with master

suite and two secondary bedrooms on one level and a loft and bonus area farther up.
- Gourmet island-type kitchen is loaded with counter space and cabinets, and a pantry is also included.
- Large, 415 sq. ft. bonus room can be finished off for exercise or play room, study or hobby workshop, home office or any number of other uses.

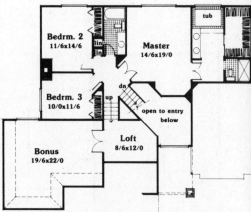

UPPER FLOOR

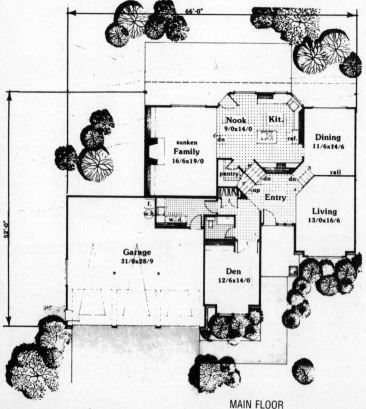

MAIN FLOOR

Plan R-4031

Bedrooms: 3	Baths: 2½

Finished Space:

Upper floor:	1,107 sq. ft.
Main floor:	1,699 sq. ft.
Bonus area:	415 sq. ft.

Total living area:	3,221 sq. ft.
Garage:	891 sq. ft.

Exterior Wall Framing:	2x4

Foundation options:
Crawlspace only.
(Foundation & framing conversion diagram available — see order form.)

Blueprint Price Code: E

Plan R-4031

Lower Level Opens to Rear in Spacious Hillside Design

- A huge living room with fireplace and dining room with railing overlook the stairway to the lower level of this walk-out, hillside design.
- The spacious country kitchen offers an island cooktop and unique skywall.
- Three to four bedrooms, an optional hobby room, and a family room with second fireplace, wet bar and attached deck occupy the lower level.

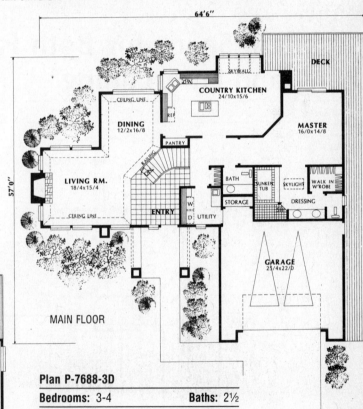

64'6"

57'0"

SKYWALL
DW
COUNTRY KITCHEN
24/10x15/6
CEILING LINE
DINING
12/2x16/8
REF
MASTER
16/0x14/8
PANTRY
RAILING
DN
LIVING RM.
18/4x15/4
BATH
SUNKEN TUB
SKYLIGHT
WALK IN W'ROBE
STORAGE
DRESSING
W
D
ENTRY
UTILITY
CEILING LINE

GARAGE
25/4x22/0

MAIN FLOOR

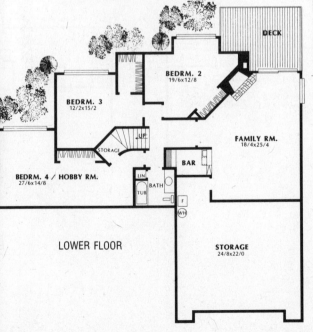

DECK

BEDRM. 2
19/6x12/8

BEDRM. 3
12/2x15/2

UP

STORAGE

FAMILY RM.
18/4x25/4

BEDRM. 4 / HOBBY RM.
27/6x14/8

BAR

LIN
TUB BATH
F
WH

LOWER FLOOR

STORAGE
24/8x22/0

Plan P-7688-3D	
Bedrooms: 3-4	**Baths:** 2½
Space:	
Main floor:	1,624 sq. ft.
Lower floor:	1,624 sq. ft.
Total living area:	3,248 sq. ft.
Garage:	557 sq. ft.
Storage:	620 sq. ft.
Exterior Wall Framing:	2x4
Foundation options: Daylight basement. (Foundation & framing conversion diagram available — see order form.)	
Blueprint Price Code:	E

Plan P-7688-3D

Abundant Space for Both Family Living and Entertaining

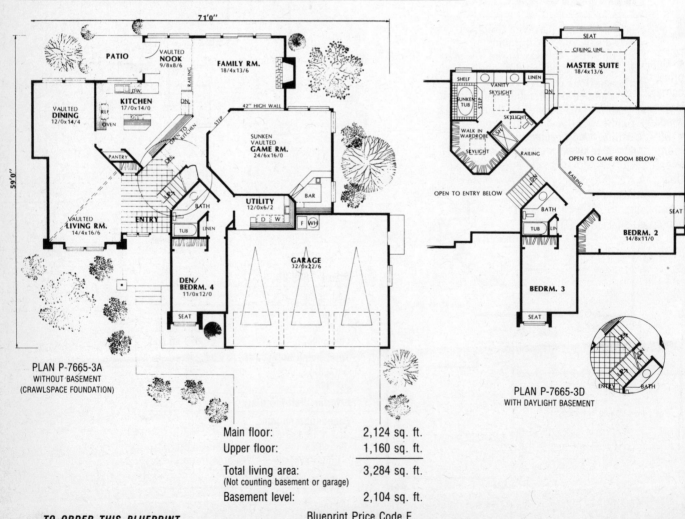

71'0"

PATIO

VAULTED NOOK
9/8x8/6

FAMILY RM.
18/4x13/6

VAULTED DINING
12/0x14/4

KITCHEN
17/0x14/0

OPEN TO KITCHEN

SUNKEN VAULTED GAME RM.
24/6x16/0

42" HIGH WALL

59'0"

PANTRY

BATH

UTILITY
12/0x6/2

BAR

VAULTED LIVING RM.
14/4x16/6

ENTRY

LINEN

TUB

D W

F WH

DEN/ BEDRM. 4
11/0x12/0

GARAGE
32/0x22/6

SEAT

PLAN P-7665-3A
WITHOUT BASEMENT
(CRAWLSPACE FOUNDATION)

SEAT

CEILING LINE

MASTER SUITE
18/4x13/6

SHELF

LINEN

SUNKEN TUB

STEP

VANITY SKYLIGHT

SKYLIGHT

WALK IN WARDROBE

SKYLIGHT

RAILING

OPEN TO GAME ROOM BELOW

OPEN TO ENTRY BELOW

RAILING

BATH

TUB

LIN

SEAT

BEDRM. 2
14/8x11/0

BEDRM. 3

SEAT

PLAN P-7665-3D
WITH DAYLIGHT BASEMENT

ENTRY

BATH

Main floor:	2,124 sq. ft.
Upper floor:	1,160 sq. ft.
Total living area: (Not counting basement or garage)	3,284 sq. ft.
Basement level:	2,104 sq. ft.

Blueprint Price Code E

Plans P-7665-3A & P-7665-3D

Traditional Design with Three Living Levels

- Upper level provides spectacular private master retreat with deluxe bath, private deck, raised bed area, large walk-in closet and large windows to the rear.
- Main floor includes spacious living room, library and formal dining room.
- Large kitchen adjoins sunny nook. Utility area also on main floor.
- Lower level features large family room, game room, wine cellar, two bedroms and bath.

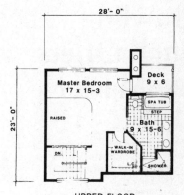

UPPER FLOOR

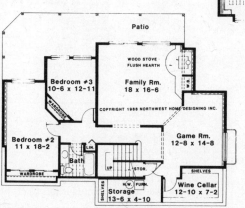

LOWER FLOOR

MAIN FLOOR

Plan NW-855

Bedrooms: 3	Baths: 2½

Space:

Upper floor:	549 sq. ft.
Main floor:	1,388 sq. ft.
Lower floor:	1,371 sq. ft.
Total living area:	3,308 sq. ft.
Garage:	573 sq. ft.

Exterior Wall Framing:	2x6

Foundation options:
Daylight basement only.
(Foundation & framing conversion diagram available — see order form.)

Blueprint Price Code:	E

Sprawling Ranch Offers Two Master Suites

- This sprawling one-story offers a myriad of excitement and a Southwestern flair.
- At the center of attention is the versatile family room with raised ceiling, three-sided entry, great fireplace and a spectacular window wall overlooking the rear, covered patio.
- The raised-ceilinged entry is flanked by formal dining and living rooms, each with large front-facing windows.
- The highly functional kitchen has an island cooktop, plenty of counter space and an eating bar dividing it from the vaulted nook; a convenient pantry and utility room are just around the corner.
- Two lavish master suites lie on opposite ends of the rear patio, each with its own step-up spa, sitting room, three-way fireplace, and attached private patio!

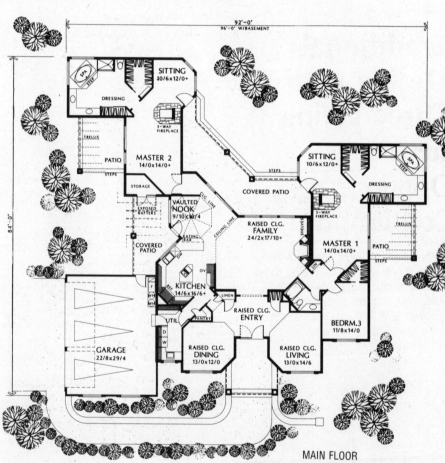

MAIN FLOOR

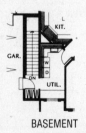

BASEMENT

Plans P-7727-3A & -3D

Bedrooms: 3	Baths: 3	Ceiling Heights: 9'

Space:

Total living area:

Main floor, basement version:	3,374 sq. ft.	
Main floor, non-basement version:	3,288 sq. ft.	
Basement:	3,374 sq. ft.	
Garage:	665 sq. ft.	

Foundation options:
Daylight basement (P-7727-3D).
Crawlspace (P-7727-3A).
(Foundation & framing conversion diagram available — see order form.)

Exterior Wall Framing:	2x6	Blueprint Price Code:	E

TO ORDER THIS BLUEPRINT, CALL TOLL-FREE 1-800-547-5570 (Prices and details on pp. 12-15.)

Plans P-7727-3A & -3D

Luxurious, Open Contemporary

This contemporary "open concept" plan is great for the established family and couples who enjoy entertaining. The vaulted "Great Room" features an overhead balcony. Breakfast, kitchen and dining areas feature standard ceilings, which emphasize the height of the vaulted Great Room.

A centrally located stone fireplace is the home's focal point, offering visual privacy to first floor areas. Major areas of the home are oriented to a view toward the rear.

This home is 81'6" wide by 52' deep, excluding your custom deck configuration. Total square footage of home is 3,425 sq. ft., not including the oversized garage.

First floor:	2,016 sq. ft.
Second floor:	1,409 sq. ft.
Total living area:	3,425 sq. ft.

(Not counting garage or basement)

PLAN S-52382-HS
CRAWLSPACE

PLAN S-52382-HS-B
WITH DAYLIGHT BASEMENT

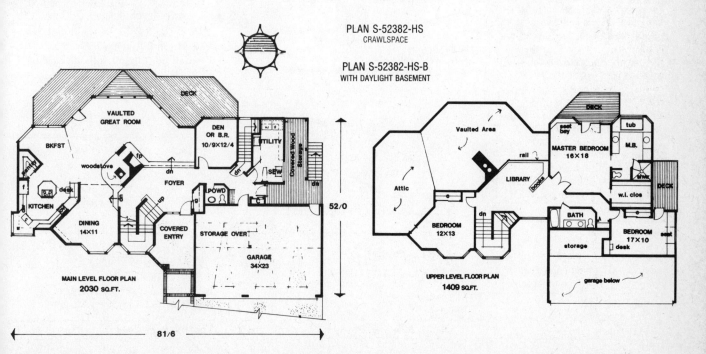

Blueprint Price Code E

Plans S-52382-HS & -HS-B

TO ORDER THIS BLUEPRINT,
CALL TOLL-FREE 1-800-547-5570
(Prices and details on pp. 12-15.)

85

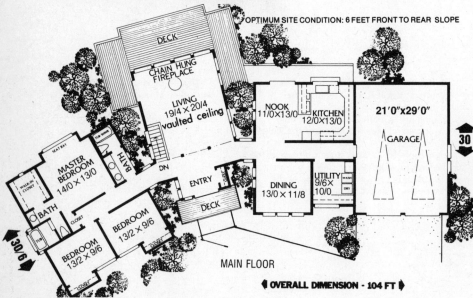

OPTIMUM SITE CONDITION: 6 FEET FRONT TO REAR SLOPE

DECK

CHAIN HUNG FIREPLACE

LIVING 19/4 × 20/4 vaulted ceiling

NOOK 11/0×13/0

KITCHEN 12/0×13/0

21'0"x29'0"

GARAGE

30

DN

MASTER BEDROOM 14/0 × 13/0

BATH

WALK-IN CLOSET

SEAT BAY

ENTRY

DINING 13/0 × 11/8

UTILITY 9/6× 10/0

WASH DRY

BATH

CLOSET

BEDROOM 13/2 × 9/6

BEDROOM 13/2 × 9/6

DECK

30/6

MAIN FLOOR

◀ OVERALL DIMENSION - 104 FT ▶

Angled Ranch Provides Panoramic View

- Designed for lots that slope down from the street.
- Sleeping wing is isolated for quiet, privacy.
- Vaulted living room opens onto large deck.
- Lower level includes 700 sq. ft. game room with half-bath and 470 sq. ft. all-purpose room.
- Can be ordered without basement for flat lot situations.

Plan SD-2026

Bedrooms: 3	Baths: 2½

Space:

Main floor:	2,273 sq. ft.
Lower floor:	1,370 sq. ft.
Total living area:	**3,643 sq. ft.**
Garage:	609 sq. ft.

Exterior Wall Framing:	2x4

Foundation options:
  Daylight basement.
  Crawlspace.
(Foundation & framing conversion diagram available — see order form.)

Blueprint Price Code:

Without basement:	C
With basement:	F

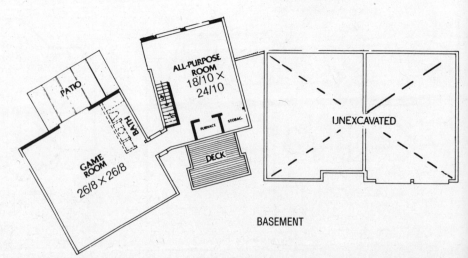

ALL-PURPOSE ROOM 18/10 × 24/10

PATIO

BATH

UNEXCAVATED

GAME ROOM 26/8 × 26/8

FURNACE

STORAG.

DECK

BASEMENT

Plan SD-2026

Family Living Centers on Unique Kitchen Design

- Large five-sided kitchen includes work/cooktop island and loads of cabinet and counter space.
- Multi-level design adds interest for sloping lot.
- Dining room, vaulted nook and vaulted family room radiate off the kitchen, which also adjoins the foyer area.
- Opulent master suite includes luxurious bath, sitting area and abundant closet space.
- Living room soars to height of unusual diagonal exposed beam.
- Den (including fireplace) is available for home office, library or guest room.

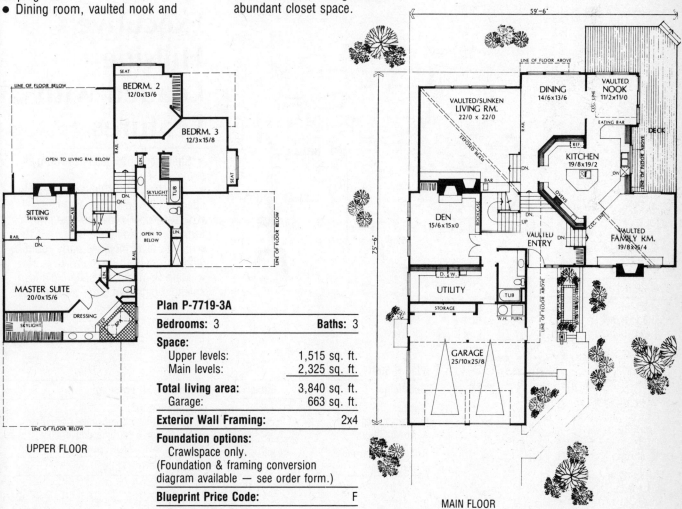

UPPER FLOOR

MAIN FLOOR

Plan P-7719-3A

Bedrooms: 3	Baths: 3

Space:

Upper levels:	1,515 sq. ft.
Main levels:	2,325 sq. ft.
Total living area:	**3,840 sq. ft.**
Garage:	663 sq. ft.

Exterior Wall Framing:	2x4

Foundation options:
Crawlspace only.
(Foundation & framing conversion diagram available — see order form.)

Blueprint Price Code:	F

Plan P-7719-3A

***TO ORDER THIS BLUEPRINT,
CALL TOLL-FREE 1-800-547-5570***
(Prices and details on pp. 12-15.)

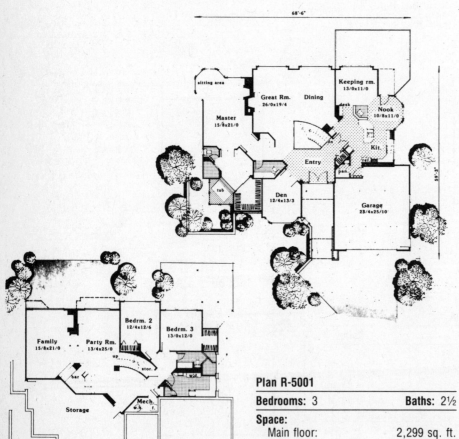

68'-6"

59'-3"

sitting area

Great Rm.
26/0x19/4

Master
15/8x21/0

Dining

Keeping rm.
13/0x11/0

Nook
10/8x11/0

Kit.

Entry

tub

Den
12/4x13/3

Garage
23/4x25/10

Family
15/8x21/0

Party Rm.
13/4x25/0

Bedrm. 2
12/4x12/6

Bedrm. 3
13/0x12/0

bar

up

stor.

w.i.

Storage

Mech.

Lower Floor

Executive Hillside Loaded with Features

- Sheltered entry leads to roomy foyer.
- "Keeping room" and nook adjoin spacious island kitchen.
- Great Room provides space for formal entertaining.
- Lower level includes party room with bar and family room.
- Main floor master suite includes splendid bath and large walk-in closet.

Plan R-5001

Bedrooms: 3	Baths: 2½

Space:

Main floor:	2,299 sq. ft.
Lower floor:	1,581 sq. ft.

Total living area: 3,880 sq. ft.
Garage: 603 sq. ft.

Exterior Wall Framing: 2x4

Foundation options:
Daylight basement only.
(Foundation & framing conversion diagram available — see order form.)

Blueprint Price Code: F

Plan R-5001

Elegance and Luxury

PLAN P-9061-4

Upper floor:	2,714 sq. ft.
Lower floor:	1,517 sq. ft.
Total living area: (Not counting garage)	4,231 sq. ft.

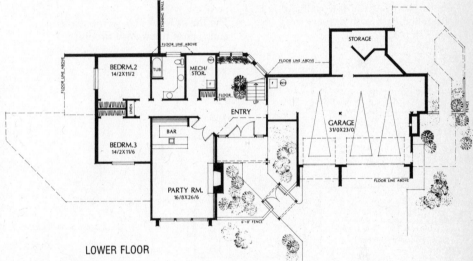

LOWER FLOOR

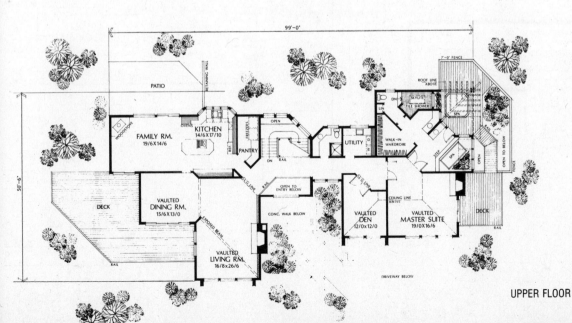

UPPER FLOOR

Blueprint Price Code G

Plan P-9061-4

Spectacular Spaces

- Spectacular multi-level living is yours in this sun-drenched contemporary.
- Dramatic vaulted ceilings that soar to the upper loft are found in the kitchen, dining and living rooms; the sunken living room has a fireplace and a low wall that continues into the adjoining dining room; double doors open to a side deck. The vaulted kitchen on the other side features an island cooktop bar and breakfast nook.
- The secluded, sunken master suite on the other end of the home has a beautiful front window wall and attached bath with dressing area and step-up spa tub.

- The upper level accommodates three additional bedrooms, a full bath, a library and a work or play area.
- The lower level houses the garage and a pool room with fireplace.

Plan P-7720-2D

Bedrooms: 4	Baths: 2½

Space:

Upper floor:	1,348 sq. ft.
Main floor:	2,468 sq. ft.
Lower floor:	678 sq. ft.
Total living area:	4,494 sq. ft.
Garage:	1,072 sq. ft.

Exterior Wall Framing:	2x4

Foundation options:
Daylight basement.
(Foundation & framing conversion diagram available — see order form.)

Blueprint Price Code:	G

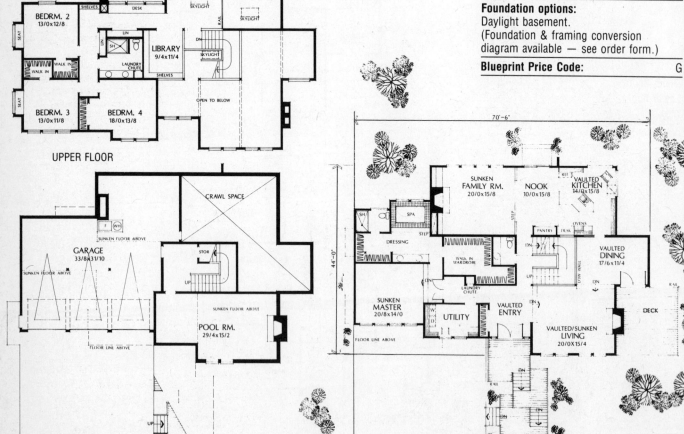

UPPER FLOOR

BASEMENT

MAIN FLOOR

Plan P-7720-2D

UPPER FLOOR

Bdrm. 3
13/0x14/6

Bdrm. 2
20/6x12/0

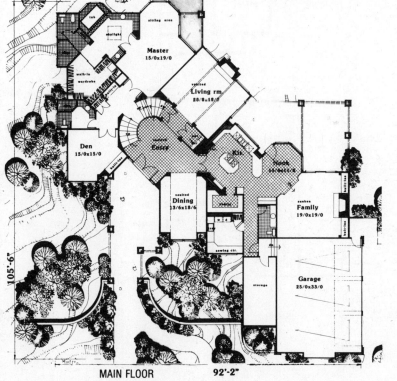

Master
15/0x19/0

vaulted Living rm.
20/0x18/0

Den
15/0x15/0

Entry

Kit.

Nook

vaulted Dining
13/6x18/6

sunken Family
19/0x19/0

sewing ctr.

storage

Garage
25/0x33/0

105'-6"

MAIN FLOOR   92'-2"

Grandeur and Elegance at Every Turn

- For a family that's looking for a home that is truly outstanding in both beauty and space, here's a design that's hard to beat.
- Grandeur abounds, beginning right at the entry and extending up circular stairways to a master suite and quiet den.

- A few more steps up brings you to two additional bedrooms, each with private baths.
- On the main floor, the living room is 350 sq. ft. and boasts a vaulted ceiling.
- A huge kitchen provides plenty of space for food preparation for daily meals and parties alike.
- A sunny nook connects with a spacious family room with fireplace.
- Designed to fit on an upward slope, this plan also includes a partial basement with a wine cellar and storage area under the den.

Plan R-4029	
Bedrooms: 3	**Baths:** 4½
Space:	
Upper floor:	972 sq. ft.
Main floor:	3,346 sq. ft.
Total living area:	4,318 sq. ft.
Basement:	233 sq. ft.
Garage:	825 sq. ft.
Exterior Wall Framing:	2x4
Ceiling Heights:	9'

Foundation options:
Crawlspace and partial basement only.
(Foundation & framing conversion diagram available — see order form.)

Blueprint Price Code:	G

Plan R-4029

TO ORDER THIS BLUEPRINT,
CALL TOLL-FREE 1-800-547-5570
(Prices and details on pp. 12-15.)

Sprawling Design
Offers Grand Spaces

PLAN Q-5000-1
WITH BASEMENT

Main level:	3,495 sq. ft.
Lower level:	1,505 sq. ft.
Total living area: (Not counting garage)	5,000 sq. ft.

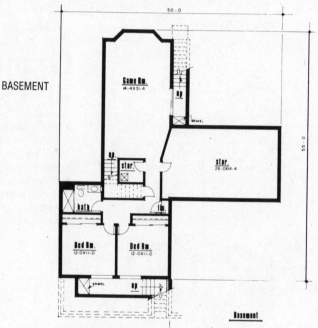

BASEMENT

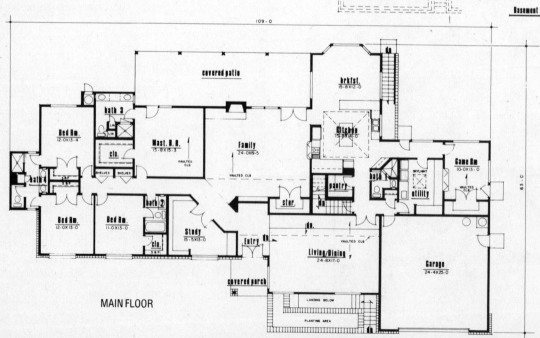

MAIN FLOOR

Blueprint Price Code G
Plan Q-5000-1

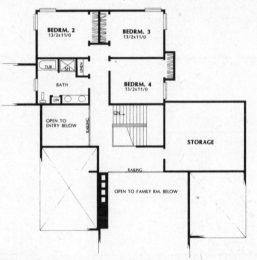

Space, Space and More Space in Three-Level Home

Main floor:	2,670 sq. ft.
Upper floor:	917 sq. ft.
Lower floor:	1,918 sq. ft.
Total living area: (Not counting garage)	5,505 sq. ft.

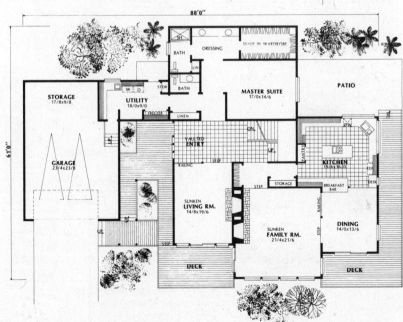

BEDRM. 2
13/2x11/0

BEDRM. 3
13/2x11/0

TUB SH

LINEN

BATH

BEDRM. 4
13/2x11/0

LIN

OPEN TO
ENTRY BELOW

RAILING

STORAGE

RAILING

OPEN TO FAMILY RM. BELOW

88'0"

STORAGE
17/8x9/8

UTILITY
18/0x9/0

W D

STOR

BATH

LINEN

SH

BATH DRESSING

WALK IN WARDROBE

LIN

MASTER SUITE
17/0x14/6

PATIO

61'0"

GARAGE
23/4x23/8

UP

VAULTED
ENTRY

DN

RAILING

STEP

KITCHEN
19/6x16/0

UP

DN

REF

DESK

SUNKEN
LIVING RM.
14/8x19/6

STEP

STORAGE

STEP

BREAKFAST
BAR

DECK

SUNKEN
FAMILY RM.
21/4x21/6

STEP

RAILING

DINING
14/0x13/6

DECK

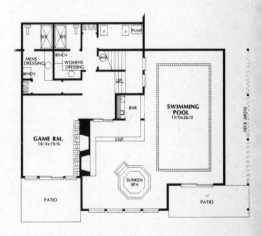

SH SH F F PUMP

MENS
DRESSING

BENCH

BENCH

WOMENS
DRESSING

WH

BAR

UP

GAME RM.
14/4x19/6

STEP

SWIMMING
POOL
13/0x26/0

DECK ABOVE

PATIO

SUNKEN
SPA

PATIO

Blueprint Price Code G

Plan P-7679-4D

TO ORDER THIS BLUEPRINT, CALL TOLL-FREE 1-800-547-5570
(Prices and details on pp. 12-15.)

93

Handsome Chalet Design Features View

- Roomy floor plan will make this chalet something you'll yearn for all year long.
- Massive fireplace in living room is a pleasant welcome after a day in the cold outdoors.
- Open kitchen has two entrances for smoother traffic.
- Generous laundry facilities and large bath are unexpected frills you'll appreciate.
- Upper floor bedrooms feature sloped ceilings and plenty of storage space.
- Optional basement plan affords more storage and general use space.

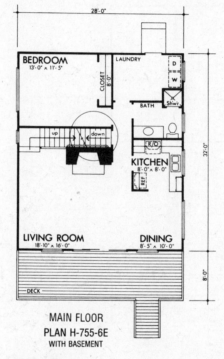

MAIN FLOOR
PLAN H-755-6E
WITH BASEMENT

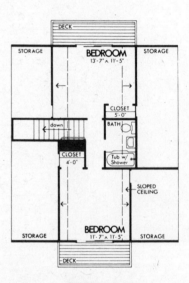

UPPER FLOOR

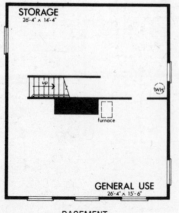

BASEMENT

PLAN H-755-5E
WITHOUT BASEMENT

WATER HEATER & FURNACE
LOCATED IN LAUNDRY RM.

Plans H-755-5E & -6E

Bedrooms: 3	Baths: 2

Space:

Upper floor:	454 sq. ft.
Main floor:	896 sq. ft.
Total without basement:	1,350 sq. ft.
Basement:	896 sq. ft.
Total with basement:	2,246 sq. ft.
Exterior Wall Framing:	2x4

Foundation options:
Daylight basement (Plan H-755-6E).
Crawlspace (Plan H-755-5E).
(Foundation & framing conversion diagram available — see order form.)

Blueprint Price Code:

Without basement:	A
With basement:	C

TO ORDER THIS BLUEPRINT,
CALL TOLL-FREE 1-800-547-5570
(Prices and details on pp. 12-15.)

Plans H-755-5E & -6E

MASTER BEDROOM
14'-0" x 14'-0"

STORAGE

STORAGE

Shwr

BATH

OPEN TO BELOW

WALK-IN CLOSET

ACCESS DOORS

down

UPPER FLOOR

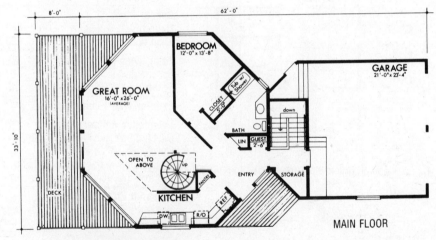

8'-0"   62'-0"

33'-10"

BEDROOM
12'-0" x 13'-8"

GARAGE
21'-0" x 23'-4"

GREAT ROOM
16'-0" x 26'-0"
(average)

CLOSET
5'-0"

Tub w/ Shower

BATH

LIN

GUEST
2'-6"

down

OPEN TO ABOVE

up

PANTRY

ENTRY

STORAGE

DECK

KITCHEN

REF

DW

R/O

MAIN FLOOR

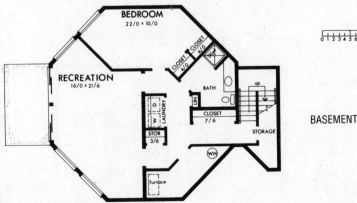

BEDROOM
22/0 x 10/0

CLOSET 4/0   CLOSET 7/0

up

RECREATION
16/0 x 21/6

BATH

LIN

W D LAUNDRY

STOR 3/6

CLOSET 7/6

STORAGE

furnace

WH

BASEMENT

0 1 2 3 4 5 6 7 8 9 10   15   20
SCALE

Octagonal Vacation Retreat

- Octagonal shape offers a view on all sides.
- Living, dining, and meal preparation are combined in a single Great Room, interrupted only by a provocative spiral staircase.
- Winding staircase allows continuous observance of activities below.
- Extraordinary master suite is bordered by glass, a private bath, and dressing room.
- Attached garage has room for boat, camper, or extra automobile.

Plans H-964-1A & -1B

Bedrooms: 2-3	Baths: 2-3

Space:

Upper floor:	346 sq. ft.
Main floor:	1,067 sq. ft.

Total living area:	1,413 sq. ft.
Basement:	approx. 1,045 sq. ft.
Garage:	512 sq. ft.
Storage (2nd floor)	134 sq. ft.

Exterior Wall Framing:	2x6

Foundation options:
Daylight basement (Plan H-964-1B).
Crawlspace (Plan H-964-1A).
Foundation & framing conversion diagram available — see order form.)

Blueprint Price Code:

Without basement:	A
With basement:	C

Unique, Dramatic Floor Plan

- An expansive and impressive Great Room, warmed by a wood stove, features an island kitchen that's completely open in design.
- A passive solar sun room is designed to collect and store heat from the sun, while also providing a good view of the surroundings.
- Upstairs, you'll see a glamorous master suite with a private bath and huge walk-in closet.
- The daylight basement adds a sunny sitting room, third bedroom and large recreation room.

PLAN P-536-2A
WITHOUT BASEMENT

Plans P-536-2A & -2D

Bedrooms: 2-3	Baths: 2-3
Space:	
Upper floor:	642 sq. ft.
Main floor:	863 sq. ft.
Total living area:	1,505 sq. ft.
Basement:	863 sq. ft.
Garage:	445 sq. ft.
Exterior Wall Framing:	2x4

Foundation options:
Daylight basement (Plan P-536-2D).
Crawlspace (Plan P-536-2A).
(Foundation & framing conversion diagram available — see order form.)

Blueprint Price Code:
Without basement:	B
With basement:	C

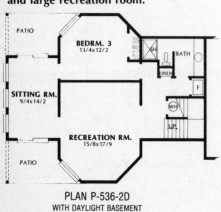

PLAN P-536-2D
WITH DAYLIGHT BASEMENT

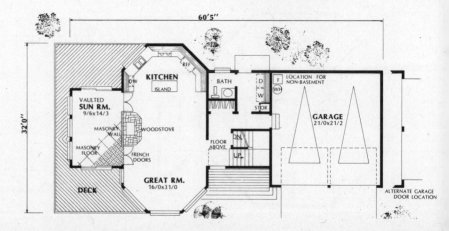

Plans P-536-2A & -2D

FRONT VIEW

Economical Design

REAR VIEW

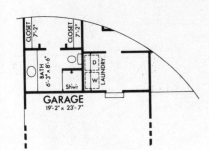

MAIN FLOOR
PLAN H-868-1A
WITHOUT BASEMENT

- Uninterrupted glass and a full, rear deck afford a sweeping view of the outdoors.
- Rear orientation provides a seclusion from street and neighbors.

- Open, flexible family living areas allow for efficient traffic flow.
- Optional daylight basement plan offers recreation room, additional bedroom and third bath.

Plans H-868-1 & -1A	
Bedrooms: 3-4	Baths: 2-3

Space:	
Main floor:	1,525 sq. ft.

Total living area:	1,525 sq. ft.
Basement:	1,420 sq. ft.
Garage:	426 sq. ft.

Exterior Wall Framing:	2x4

Foundation options:
Daylight basement (Plan H-868-1).
Crawlspace (Plan H-868-1A).
(Foundation & framing conversion diagram available — see order form.)

Blueprint Price Code:

Without basement	B
With basement	D

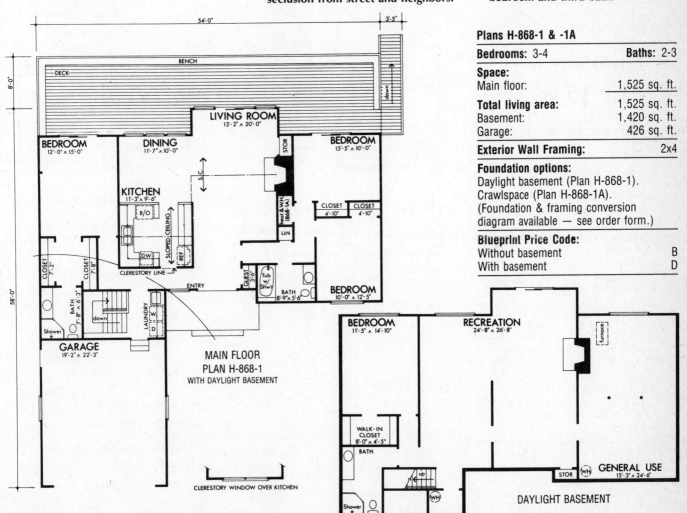

MAIN FLOOR
PLAN H-868-1
WITH DAYLIGHT BASEMENT

CLERESTORY WINDOW OVER KITCHEN

DAYLIGHT BASEMENT

Plans H-868-1 & -1A

UPPER FLOOR

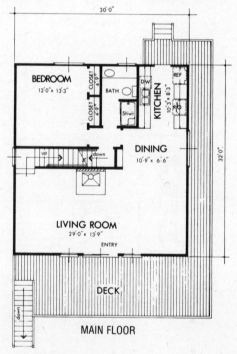

MAIN FLOOR

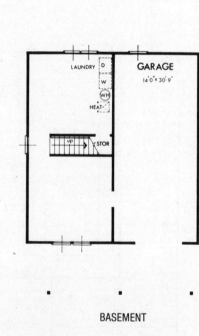

BASEMENT

Chalet for All Seasons

- Rustic exterior makes this design suitable for a lakefront, beach, or wooded setting.
- Patterned railing and wood deck edge the front and side main level, while a smaller deck assumes a balcony role.
- Designed for relaxed, leisure living, the main level features a large L-shaped Great Room warmed by a central free-standing fireplace.
- Upper level offers a second bath and added sleeping accommodations.

Plans H-858-2

Bedrooms: 3	Baths: 2

Space:	
Upper floor:	576 sq. ft.
Main floor:	960 sq. ft.
Total without basement:	1,536 sq. ft.
Basement:	530 sq. ft.
Total with basement:	2,066 sq. ft.
Garage: 430 sq. ft. (included in basement)	

Exterior Wall Framing:	2x6

Foundation options:
Daylight basement.
(Foundation & framing conversion diagram available — see order form.)

Blueprint Price Code:

Without basement:	B
With basement	C

Plan H-858-2

Raised Living for Heightened Views

- Picture your new home nestled into an upsloping lot with an entire living room window wall looking back to your panoramic view.
- The raised main level gives a better view of the surroundings, without being blocked by a road, cars, or low trees. The resulting larger windows and walk-out on the lower level avoid a basement feeling in the rec room.
- The sunken living room, at the top of a half-flight of stairs, has a dramatic cathedral ceiling highlighted by angled transom windows.
- A see-through fireplace separates the living room from the formal dining room, also with a cathedral ceiling.
- The kitchen incorporates a spacious breakfast bay overlooking the rear deck.
- The main floor also houses three bedrooms and two full baths.

Plan AX-8486-A

Bedrooms: 3	**Baths:** 2

Space:

Main floor:	1,630 sq. ft.
Basement & rec room:	978 sq. ft.
Total living area:	2,608 sq. ft.
Garage:	400 sq. ft.
Storage area:	110 sq. ft.

Exterior Wall Framing:	2x4

Foundation options:
Daylight basement.
(Foundation & framing conversion diagram available — see order form.)

Blueprint Price Code:	D

Plan AX-8486-A

TO ORDER THIS BLUEPRINT, *CALL TOLL-FREE 1-800-547-5570* (Prices and details on pp. 12-15.)

Contrasting Rustic and Contemporary

- In this design, contemporary styling is combined with the rustic atmosphere of a country lodge, for a home that will serve equally well for year-round or recreational living.
- A studio-type master bedroom is isolated upstairs, and includes a private bath, a balcony overlooking the living room below and a private outdoor deck.
- Interior touches include diagonal paneling, an open-beamed, cathedral ceiling and a massive stone fireplace with raised hearth.
- The main floor offers easy access to three large decks.
- Three foundation options include a daylight basement with recreation room, standard basement or crawlspace.

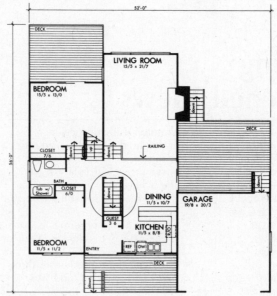

MAIN FLOOR

UPPER FLOOR

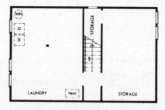

WITHOUT BASEMENT
(CRAWLSPACE FOUNDATION)

STANDARD BASEMENT

DAYLIGHT BASEMENT

Plans H-834-5, -5A & -5B

Bedrooms: 3	Baths: 2

Space:

Upper floor:	399 sq. ft.
Main floor:	1,249 sq. ft.
Total without basement:	1,648 sq. ft.
Daylight basement:	1,249 sq. ft.
Total with basement:	2,897 sq. ft.
Standard basement:	640 sq. ft.
Garage:	398 sq. ft.

Exterior Wall Framing:	2x4

Foundation options:
Daylight basement (H-834-5B).
Standard basement (H-834-5).
Crawlspace (H-834-5A).
(Foundation & framing conversion diagram available — see order form.)

Blueprint Price Code:

Without basement:	B
With standard basement:	C
With daylight basement:	D

Plans H-834-5, -5A & -5B

REAR VIEW

Sunny Family Living

- Pleasant-looking and unassuming from the front, this plan breaks into striking, sun-catching angles at the rear.
- The living room sun roof gathers passive solar heat, which is stored in the tile floor and the two-story high masonry backdrop to the wood stove.
- A 516-square-foot master suite with private bath and balcony makes up the second floor.
- The main floor offers two more bedrooms and a full bath.

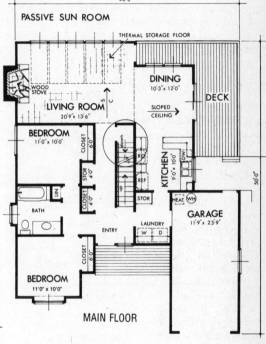

MAIN FLOOR

PASSIVE SUN ROOM BELOW

SLOPED CEILING

BALCONY RAILING

BEDROOM
17'3" x 13'3"

WALK-IN CLOSET
10'9" x 6'6"

BATH

UPPER FLOOR

STOR

WITHOUT BASEMENT
(CRAWLSPACE FOUNDATION)

RECREATION
20'6" x 13'6"

GAME AREA
10'9" x 20'9"

GENERAL USE
13'0" x 14'6"

HEAT

BATH

Shwr

BASEMENT

FRONT VIEW

Plans H-947-1A & -1B

Bedrooms: 3	Baths: 2-3
Space:	
Upper floor:	516 sq. ft.
Main floor:	1,162 sq. ft.
Total without basement:	1,678 sq. ft.
Daylight basement:	966 sq. ft.
Total with basement:	2,644 sq. ft.
Garage:	279 sq. ft.
Exterior Wall Framing:	2x6

Foundation options:
Daylight basement (H-947-1B).
Crawlspace (H-957-1A).
(Foundation & framing conversion diagram available — see order form.)

Blueprint Price Code:
Without basement: B
With basement: D

Plans H-947-1A & -1B

TO ORDER THIS BLUEPRINT,
CALL TOLL-FREE 1-800-547-5570
(Prices and details on pp. 12-15.)

Surrounded by Decks

- Wrap-around deck offers a panoramic view of the surroundings as well as space for outdoor living and relaxation.
- Angular arrangement of garage, breezeway, and home provides front-yard privacy and a visual barrier to front bedrooms from street traffic.
- Exciting L-shaped dining room, attached sunken living room, and deck create a perfect atmosphere for entertaining.
- Basement is available with either a concrete floor (Plan H-2083), a framed floor for steep sloping sites (Plan H-2083-B), or on a crawlspace (Plan H-2083-A).

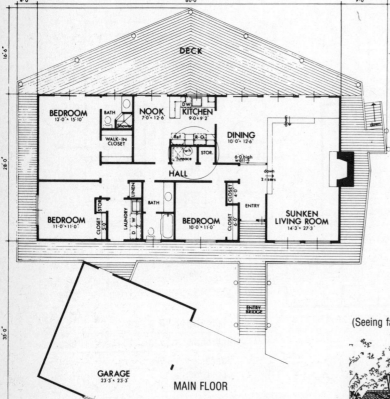

MAIN FLOOR

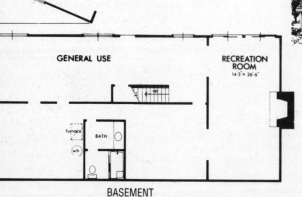

BASEMENT

Plans H-2083, -A & -B	
Bedrooms: 3	Baths: 2-3
Space:	
Main floor:	1,660 sq. ft.
Basement:	1,660 sq. ft.
Total living area	
with basement:	3,320 sq. ft.
Garage:	541 sq. ft.
Exterior Wall Framing:	2x4

Foundation options:
Daylight basement (Plans H-2083 & H-2083-B).
Crawlspace (Plan H-2083-A).
(Foundation & framing conversion diagram available — see order form.)

Blueprint Price Code:	
Without basement:	B
With basement:	E

(Seeing facing page for alternate floor plan).

PLAN H-2083
(CONCRETE)
WITH DAYLIGHT BASEMENT

PLAN H-2083-B
CRAWLSPACE
WITH WOOD-FRAMED
LOWER LEVEL

Plans H-2083, -A & -B

FRONT VIEW

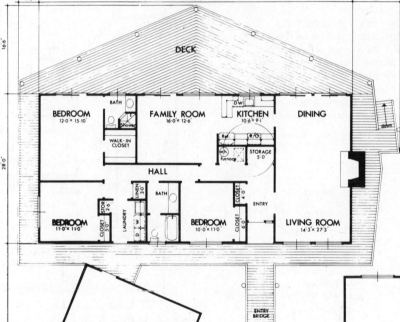

MAIN FLOOR

BASEMENT

Gracious Indoor/ Outdoor Living

- A clean design makes this plan adaptable to almost any climate or setting.
- Perfect for a scenic, hillside lot, the structure and wrap-around deck offers a spanning view.
- Kitchen is flanked by family and dining rooms, allowing easy entrance from both.
- Foundation options include a daylight basement on concrete slab (H-2083-1), a wood-framed lower level (H-2083-1B), and a crawlspace (H-2083-1A).

PLAN H-2083-1
WITH DAYLIGHT BASEMENT
(ON CONCRETE SLAB)

PLAN H-2083-1B
(WITH WOOD-FRAMED LOWER LEVEL)

(See facing page for both rear view and alternate floor plan.)

Plans H-2083-1, -1A & -1B

Bedrooms: 3	Baths: 2-3

Space:

Main floor:	1,660 sq. ft.
Basement:	1,660 sq. ft.

Total living area:

with basement:	3,320 sq. ft.
Garage:	541 sq. ft.

Exterior Wall Framing: 2x4

Foundation options:
Daylight basement (Plan H-2083-1 or -1B).
Crawlspace (Plan H-2083-1A).
(Foundation & framing conversion diagram available — see order form.)

Blueprint Price Code:

Without basement:	B
With basement:	E

TO ORDER THIS BLUEPRINT,
CALL TOLL-FREE 1-800-547-5570
(Prices and details on pp. 12-15.) **103**

Plans H-2083-1, -1A & -1B

Ideal Home for a Narrow Lot

- This design features a room arrangement that is wide-open, yet confined to an economical width of only 28'.
- The entryway greets you with a balconied staircase and lovely bay window.
- The Great Room, dining area, and kitchen are arranged so no one is excluded from conversation or on-going activities.
- Other highlights include a woodstove/stone hearth in the Great Room, a large outdoor deck off the dining area, and a spacious U-shaped kitchen with breakfast bar.
- Second level features a master suite with walk-through closet and private bath.

UPPER FLOOR

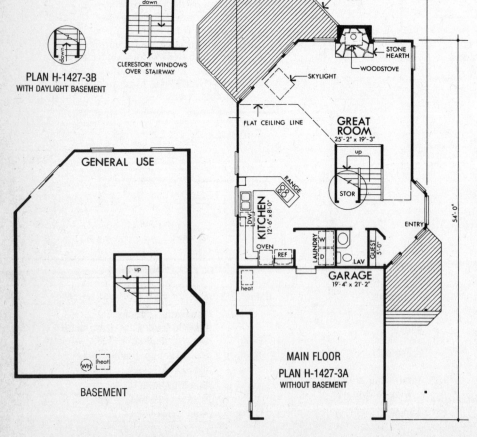

PLAN H-1427-3B
WITH DAYLIGHT BASEMENT

GENERAL USE

BASEMENT

MAIN FLOOR
PLAN H-1427-3A
WITHOUT BASEMENT

Plans H-1427-3A & -3B	
Bedrooms: 3	Baths: 2½
Space:	
Upper floor:	880 sq. ft.
Main floor:	810 sq. ft.
Total without basement:	**1,690 sq. ft.**
Basement:	810 sq. ft.
Total with basement:	**2,500 sq. ft.**
Garage:	443 sq. ft.
Exterior Wall Framing:	**2x4**

Foundation options:
Daylight basement.
Crawlspace.
Foundation & framing conversion diagram available — see order form.)

Blueprint Price Code:	
Without basement:	B
With basement:	D

Plans H-1427-3A & -3B

Panoramic View Embraces Outdoors

- This geometric design takes full advantage of scenic sites.
- Living area faces a glass-filled wall and wrap-around deck.
- Open dining/living room arrangement is complemented by vaulted ceilings, an overhead balcony, and a 5-ft-wide fireplace.
- 12' deep main deck offers generous space for outdoor dining and entertaining.

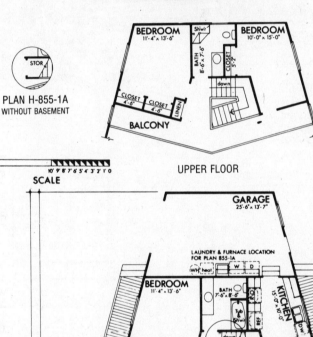

STOR

PLAN H-855-1A
WITHOUT BASEMENT

SCALE

UPPER FLOOR

BEDROOM
11'-4" x 13'-6"

BEDROOM
10'-0" x 15'-0"

BATH
8'-6" x 7'-6"

CLOSET
5'-2"

CLOSET
4'-6"

CLOSET
4'-6"

LINEN

BALCONY

MAIN FLOOR

GARAGE
25'-6" x 13'-7"

LAUNDRY & FURNACE LOCATION
FOR PLAN 855-1A

BEDROOM
11'-4" x 13'-6"

BATH
7'-6" x 8'-6"

KITCHEN
15'-0" x 10'-0"

REF

CLOSET
4'-3"

CLOSET
5'-0"

CLOSET

ENTRY

BALCONY LINE

LIVING/DINING ROOM
41'-0" x 15'-9"

DECK

42'-0"
56'-0"
50'-0"
61'-0"

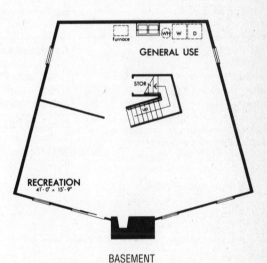

GENERAL USE

furnace

WH W D

STOR

RECREATION
41'-0" x 15'-9"

BASEMENT

Plans H-855-1 & -1A

Bedrooms: 3	Baths: 2
Space:	
Upper floor:	625 sq. ft.
Main floor:	1,108 sq. ft.
Total living area:	1,733 sq. ft.
Basement:	approx. 1,108 sq. ft.
Garage:	346 sq. ft.
Exterior Wall Framing:	2x6

Foundation options:
Daylight basement (Plan H-855-1).
Crawlspace (Plan H-855-1A).
(Foundation & framing conversion diagram available — see order form.)

Blueprint Price Code:
Without basement	B
With basement	D

Plans H-855-1 & -1A

Solar Flair

- Full window walls and a sun room with glass roof act as passive energy collectors in this popular floor plan.
- Expansive living room features wood stove and vaulted ceilings.
- Dining room shares a breakfast counter with the merging kitchen.
- Convenient laundry room is positioned near kitchen and garage entrance.
- Second level is devoted entirely to the private master suite, featuring vaulted ceiling and a balcony view to the living room below.

Plans H-877-5A & -5B

Bedrooms: 3-4	Baths: 2-3

Space:

Upper floor:	332 sq. ft.
Main floor:	1,200 sq. ft.
Sun room:	162 sq. ft.
Total living area:	**1,744 sq. ft.**
Basement:	approx. 1,200 sq. ft.
Garage:	457 sq. ft.

Exterior Wall Framing:	2x6

Foundation options:
Daylight basement (Plan H-877-5B).
Crawlspace (Plan H-877-5A).
(Foundation & framing conversion diagram available — see order form.)

Blueprint Price Code:

Without finished basement:	B
With finished basement:	D

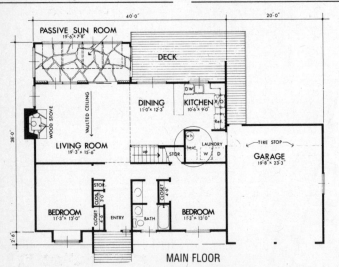

MAIN FLOOR

PLAN H-877-5B
WITH BASEMENT

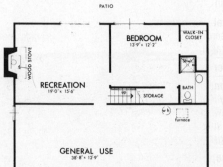

UPPER FLOOR

BASEMENT

FRONT VIEW

Plans H-877-5A & -5B

Indoor-Outdoor Living

- Attention-getting pentagonal-shaped home is ideal for full-time or vacation living.
- Huge, two-story high living/dining area takes up half of the main floor, ideal for family gatherings.
- Compact, but functional kitchen features breakfast bar and adjacent laundry room that can also serve as a pantry and/or mudroom.
- Open stairway leads to second-floor balcony hallway overlooking the main level living area.
- Upper level has room for two additional bedrooms and a second bath.

Plans H-855-2 & -2A

Bedrooms: 3	Baths: 2

Space:

Upper floor:	660 sq. ft.
Main floor:	1,174 sq. ft.

Total living area:	1,834 sq. ft.
Basement:	approx. 1,174 sq. ft.
Garage:	277 sq. ft.

Exterior Wall Framing:	2x4

Foundation options:
Daylight basement (Plan H-855-2).
Crawlspace (Plan H-855-2A).
(Foundation & framing conversion diagram available — see order form.)

Blueprint Price Code:

Without basement	B
With basement	E

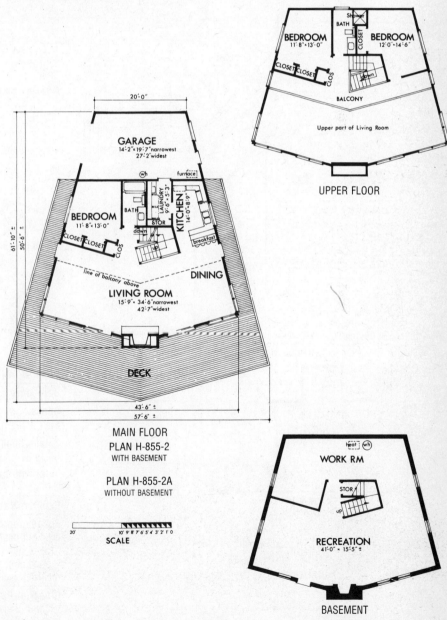

MAIN FLOOR
PLAN H-855-2
WITH BASEMENT

PLAN H-855-2A
WITHOUT BASEMENT

SCALE

UPPER FLOOR

BASEMENT

Plans H-855-2 & -2A

Spacious Octagon

- Highly functional main floor plan makes traffic easy and minimizes wasted hall space.
- Double-sized entry opens to spacious octagonal living room with central fireplace and access to all rooms.
- U-shaped kitchen and attached dining area allow for both informal and formal occasions.
- Contiguous bedrooms each have independent deck entrances.
- Exciting deck borders entire home.

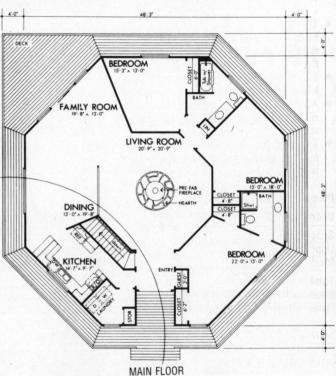

MAIN FLOOR

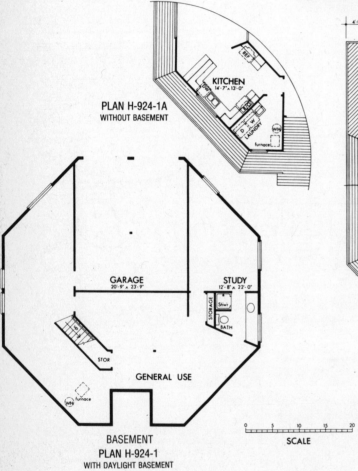

PLAN H-924-1A
WITHOUT BASEMENT

BASEMENT
PLAN H-924-1
WITH DAYLIGHT BASEMENT

SCALE

Plans H-924-1 & -1A		
Bedrooms: 3-4		**Baths:** 2-3
Space:		
Main floor:		1,888 sq. ft.
Total without basement:		1,888 sq. ft.
Basement:		1,395 sq. ft.
Total with basement:		3,283 sq. ft.
Garage:		493 sq. ft.
Exterior Wall Framing:		2x4

Foundation options:
Daylight basement (Plan H-924-1).
Crawlspace (Plan H-924-1A).
(Foundation & framing conversion diagram available — see order form.)

Blueprint Price Code:
Without basement: B
With basement: E

Plans H-924-1 & -1A

An Octagonal Home with a Lofty View

- There's no better way to avoid the ordinary than by building an octagonal home and escaping from square corners and rigid rooms.
- The roomy main floor offers plenty of space for full-time family living or for a comfortable second home retreat.
- The vaulted entry hall leads to the bedrooms on the right or down the hall to the Great Room.
- Warmed by a wood stove, the Great Room offers a panoramic view of the surrounding scenery.
- The center core of the main floor houses two baths, one of which contains a spa tub and is private to the master bedroom.
- This plan also includes a roomy kitchen and handy utility area.
- A large loft is planned as a recreation room, also with a wood stove.
- The daylight basement version adds another bedroom, bath, garage and large storage area.

Plans P-532-3A & -3D

Bedrooms: 3-4	Baths: 2-3

Space:

Upper floor:	355 sq. ft.
Main floor:	1,567 sq. ft.

Total living area:	**1,922 sq. ft.**
Basement living area:	430 sq. ft.
Garage (included in basement):	
	approx. 735 sq. ft.
Storage:	approx. 482 sq. ft.

Exterior Wall Framing: 2x4

Foundation options:
Daylight basement (Plan P-532-3D).
Crawlspace (Plan P-532-3A).
(Foundation & framing conversion diagram available — see order form.)

Blueprint Price Code:

Without basement:	B
With basement:	C

FRONT VIEW

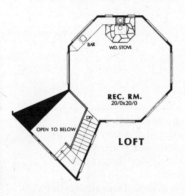

BAR WD. STOVE

REC. RM.
20/0x20/0

OPEN TO BELOW DN

LOFT

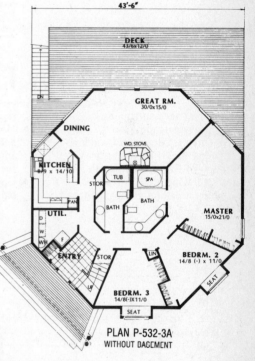

43'-6"

DECK
43/6x12/0

DN

GREAT RM.
30/0x15/0

DINING

WD. STOVE

KITCHEN
8/9 x 14/10

STOR TUB SPA

BATH BATH

MASTER
15/0x21/0

PAN

UTIL.

D W WH

F

ENTRY STOR

LIN

BEDRM. 2
14/8 (-) x 11/0

SEAT

BEDRM. 3
14/8(-)X11/0

SEAT

PLAN P-532-3A
WITHOUT BASEMENT

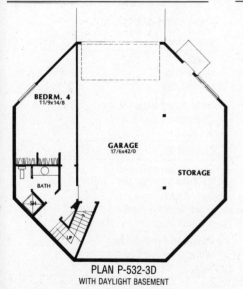

BEDRM. 4
11/9x14/8

GARAGE
17/6x42/0

STORAGE

BATH

SH

LP

PLAN P-532-3D
WITH DAYLIGHT BASEMENT

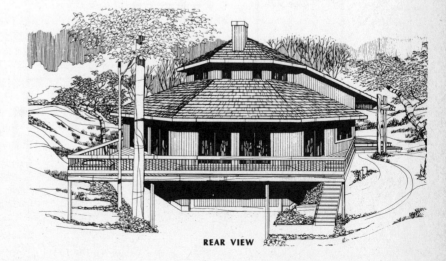

REAR VIEW

Plans P-532-3A & -3D

Decked-Out for Fun

- Spacious deck surrounds this comfortable cabin/chalet.
- Sliding glass doors and windows blanket the living-dining area, indulged with raised hearth and a breathtaking view.
- Dining area and compact kitchen separated by breakfast bar.
- Master bedroom, laundry room and bath complete first floor; two additional bedrooms located on second floor.
- Upper level also features impressive balcony room with exposed beams

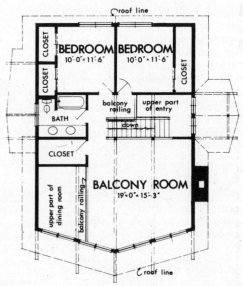

UPPER FLOOR

Plans H-919-1 & -1A

Bedrooms: 3	Baths: 2

Space:	
Upper floor:	869 sq. ft.
Main floor:	1,064 sq. ft.

Total living area:	**1,933 sq. ft.**
Basement:	475 sq. ft.
Garage:	501 sq. ft.

Exterior Wall Framing:	2x6

Foundation options:
Daylight basement (Plan H-919-1).
Crawlspace (Plan H-919-1A).
(Foundation & framing conversion diagram available — see order form.)

Blueprint Price Code:
Without finished basement:	B
With finished basement:	C

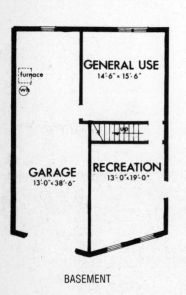

BASEMENT

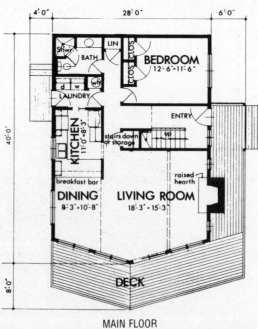

MAIN FLOOR

Plans H-919-1 & -1A

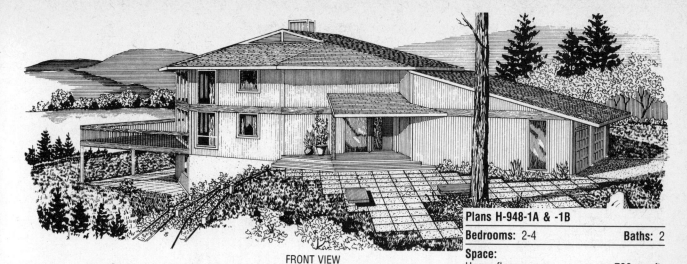

FRONT VIEW

Octagonal Sunshine Special

- Octagon homes offer the ultimate for taking advantage of a view, and are fascinating designs even for more ordinary settings.
- This plan offers a huge, house-spanning living/dining area with loads of glass and a masonry collector wall to store solar heat.
- The 700-square-foot upper level is devoted entirely to an enormous master suite, with a balcony overlooking the living room below, a roomy private bath and a large closet/dressing area.
- Scissor-trusses allow vaulted ceilings over the two-story-high living room and the master suite.
- A second roomy bedroom and full bath are offered downstairs, along with an efficient kitchen, a laundry area and inviting foyer.
- A daylight basement option offers the potential for more bedrooms, hobbies, work rooms or recreational space.

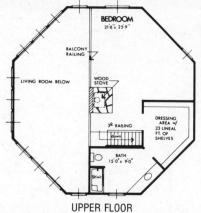

UPPER FLOOR

Plans H-948-1A & -1B	
Bedrooms: 2-4	Baths: 2
Space:	
Upper floor:	700 sq. ft.
Main floor:	1,236 sq. ft.
Total without basement:	1,936 sq. ft.
Daylight basement:	1,236 sq. ft.
Total with basement:	3,172 sq. ft.
Garage:	550 sq. ft.
Exterior Wall Framing:	2x6

Foundation options:
Daylight basement (H-948-1B).
Crawlspace (H-948-1A).
(Foundation & framing conversion diagram available — see order form.)

Blueprint Price Code:	
Without basement:	B
With basement:	E

MAIN FLOOR

WITHOUT BASEMENT (CRAWLSPACE FOUNDATION)

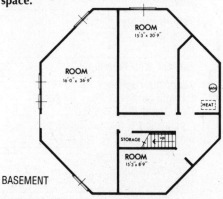

BASEMENT

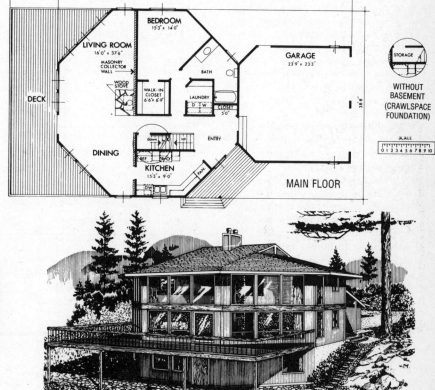

REAR VIEW

Plans H-948-1A & -1B

Excellent Family Design

- Long sloping rooflines and bold design features make this home attractive for any neighborhood.
- Inside, a vaulted entry takes visitors into an impressive vaulted Great Room with a wood stove and window-wall facing the house-spanning rear deck.
- Clerestory windows flanking the stove area and large windows front and rear flood the Great Room with natural light.
- The magnificent kitchen includes a stylish island and opens to the informal dining area which in turn flows into the Great Room.
- Two bedrooms on the main floor share a full bath, and bedroom #2 boasts easy access to the rear deck which spans the width of the house.
- The upstairs comprises an "adult retreat," with a roomy master suite, luxurious bath with double sinks, and a large walk-in closet.
- A daylight basement version adds another 1,410 sq. ft. of space for entertaining and recreation, plus a fourth bedroom and a large shop/storage area.

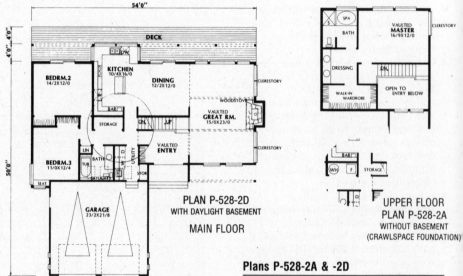

PLAN P-528-2D
WITH DAYLIGHT BASEMENT
MAIN FLOOR

UPPER FLOOR
PLAN P-528-2A
WITHOUT BASEMENT
(CRAWLSPACE FOUNDATION)

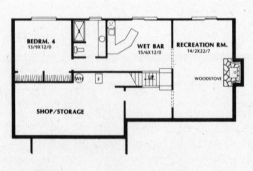

Plans P-528-2A & -2D	
Bedrooms: 3-4	**Baths:** 2-3

Space:	
Upper floor:	498 sq. ft.
Main floor:	1,456 sq. ft.
Total living area:	**1,954 sq. ft.**
Basement:	1,410 sq. ft.
Garage:	502 sq. ft.
Exterior Wall Framing:	2x4

Foundation options:
Daylight basement (Plan P-528-2D).
Crawlspace (Plan P-528-2A).
(Foundation & framing conversion diagram available — see order form.)

Blueprint Price Code:

Without basement:	B
With basement:	E

Plans P-528-2A & -2D

Traditional Split Level

- A traditional exterior and a compact interior characterize this split level.
- An extensive deck along the rear of the home can be entered through the dining room and master bedroom; another deck sits off the living room, which also offers a fireplace and large front windows.
- The kitchen provides a handy breakfast bar, also convenient to the dining room; both are situated above the living room.
- The master suite and two additional bedrooms complete the upper level.
- Below are laundry and utility facilities and a generous family room.

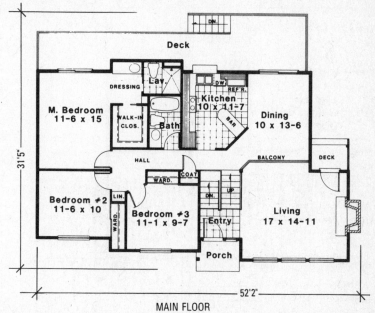

MAIN FLOOR

LOWER FLOOR

Plan NW-413

Bedrooms: 3	Baths: 2½

Space:

Main/upper floor:	1,315 sq. ft.
Lower floor:	345 sq. ft.
Total living area:	1,660 sq. ft.
Garage:	633 sq. ft.

Exterior Wall Framing:	2x6

Foundation options:
Daylight basement.
(Foundation & framing conversion diagram available — see order form.)

Blueprint Price Code:	B

Plan NW-413

Split Entry with Country Kitchen

- The split entry of this updated traditional opens up to a large vaulted living room with fireplace and a lovely country kitchen with sliders to a deck.
- Down the hall you'll find the vaulted master suite with large walk-in closet and private bath.
- Two additional bedrooms and a second bath are also included.
- The lower level is unfinished and left up to the owner to choose its function; room for a third bath and laundry facilities is provided.

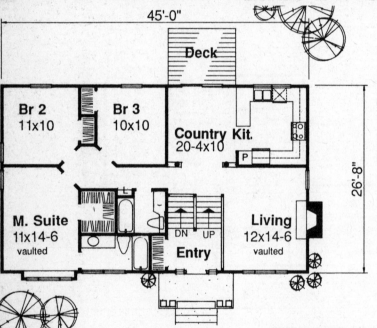

45'-0"

Deck

Br 2 11x10

Br 3 10x10

Country Kit. 20-4x10

P

26'-8"

M. Suite 11x14-6 vaulted

DN UP

Entry

Living 12x14-6 vaulted

MAIN FLOOR

Plan B-90012

Bedrooms: 3	Baths: 2-3

Space:

Main/upper level:	1,203 sq. ft.
Basement:	460 sq. ft.
Total living area:	**1,663 sq. ft.**
Garage:	509 sq. ft.

Exterior Wall Framing:	2x4

Foundation options:
Daylight basement.
(Foundation & framing conversion diagram available — see order form.)

Blueprint Price Code:	B

Garage 23-6x21-8

D W Mechanical

FURN WH FD

UP

Bonus Space 12x14-6

BASEMENT

TO ORDER THIS BLUEPRINT,
CALL TOLL-FREE 1-800-547-5570

Plan B-90012

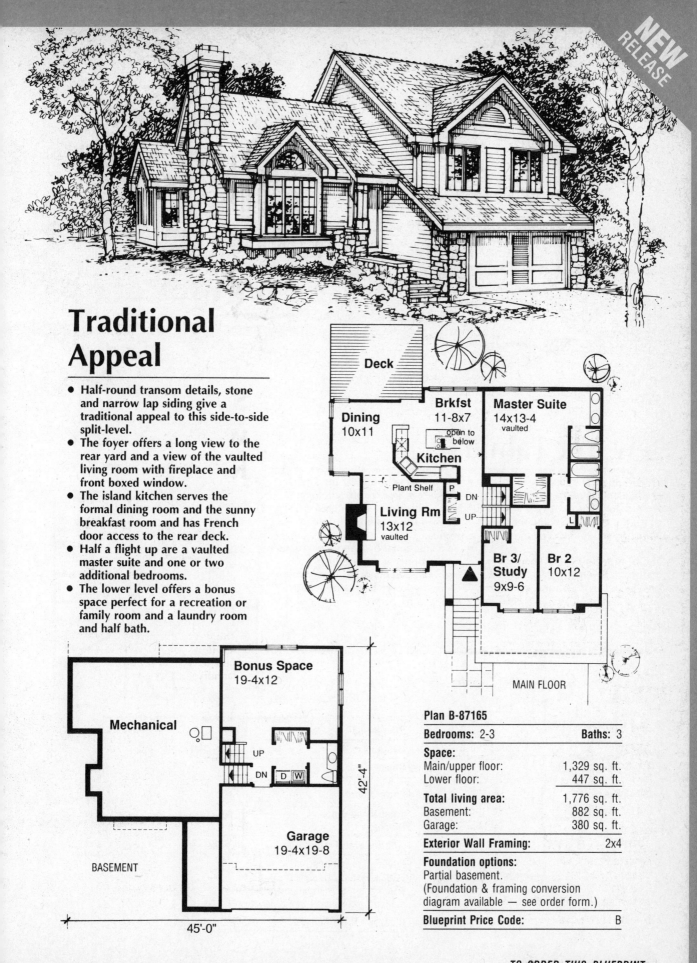

Traditional Appeal

- Half-round transom details, stone and narrow lap siding give a traditional appeal to this side-to-side split-level.
- The foyer offers a long view to the rear yard and a view of the vaulted living room with fireplace and front boxed window.
- The island kitchen serves the formal dining room and the sunny breakfast room and has French door access to the rear deck.
- Half a flight up are a vaulted master suite and one or two additional bedrooms.
- The lower level offers a bonus space perfect for a recreation or family room and a laundry room and half bath.

Deck

Dining
10x11

Brkfst
11-8x7

Master Suite
14x13-4
vaulted

open to below

Kitchen

Plant Shelf

P

DN

UP

Living Rm
13x12
vaulted

Br 3/
Study
9x9-6

Br 2
10x12

L

MAIN FLOOR

Bonus Space
19-4x12

Mechanical

UP

DN   D W

Garage
19-4x19-8

BASEMENT

42'-4"

45'-0"

Plan B-87165

Bedrooms: 2-3	Baths: 3

Space:

Main/upper floor:	1,329 sq. ft.
Lower floor:	447 sq. ft.

Total living area:	1,776 sq. ft.
Basement:	882 sq. ft.
Garage:	380 sq. ft.

Exterior Wall Framing:	2x4

Foundation options:
Partial basement.
(Foundation & framing conversion diagram available — see order form.)

Blueprint Price Code:	B

Plan B-87165

NEW RELEASE

New Yet Familiar

- You'll find style and value in this newly planned split entry home.
- Ground-hugging front roof lines cover the vaulted Great Room, dining room, kitchen and master bedroom.
- The front-facing Great Room features a lovely fireplace flanked by windows and entrance to a deck; it is overlooked by a balcony dining room above.

- The breakfast room off the kitchen also offers an exciting adjoining deck, which may be entered through the master bedroom as well.
- Two additional bedrooms are found on the upper level; a fourth bedroom and generous family room share the lower level with a bath and laundry room.

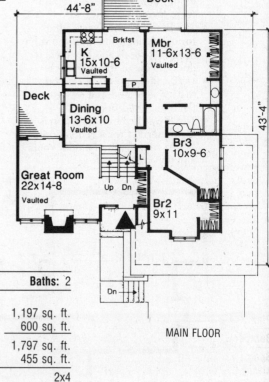

MAIN FLOOR

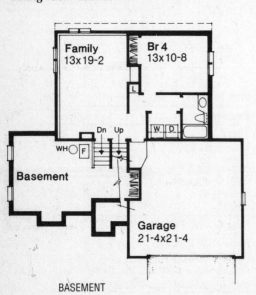

BASEMENT

Plan B-903

Bedrooms: 4	Baths: 2
Space:	
Main/upper floor:	1,197 sq. ft.
Lower floor:	600 sq. ft.
Total living area:	1,797 sq. ft.
Garage:	455 sq. ft.
Exterior Wall Framing:	2x4
Foundation options: Partial basement. (Foundation & framing conversion diagram available — see order form.)	
Blueprint Price Code:	B

Plan B-903

Spirited Split

- A lovely front porch, expressed timber and ascending exterior stairs create an anticipation that is well rewarded inside this three-bedroom split-level.
- The vaulted living room off the foyer has a handsome fireplace and front window; it joins the formal dining room with wet bar.
- Also vaulted are the kitchen and breakfast room, with pantry and entrance to the wrapping rear deck.
- Up several steps is the elegant vaulted master bedroom and private skylit bath with plant shelf above the tub and walk-in closet; two additional bedrooms and a second bath are also included.
- The lower level offers a half bath, laundry room and a bonus area with bar.

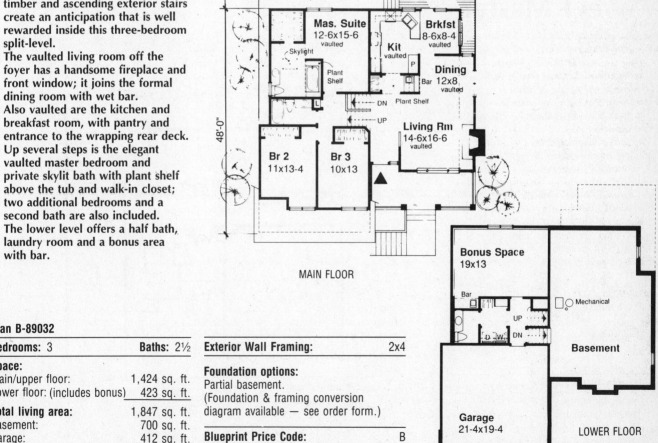

MAIN FLOOR

LOWER FLOOR

Plan B-89032

Bedrooms: 3	Baths: 2½

Space:

Main/upper floor:	1,424 sq. ft.
Lower floor: (includes bonus)	423 sq. ft.
Total living area:	**1,847 sq. ft.**
Basement:	700 sq. ft.
Garage:	412 sq. ft.

Exterior Wall Framing:	2x4

Foundation options:
Partial basement.
(Foundation & framing conversion diagram available — see order form.)

Blueprint Price Code:	B

Plan B-89032

Sweet Master Suite

- Traditional stone veneer & New England shingle exterior.
- Arch top window at bedroom/study.
- Bedroom/study can also be used as an office.
- Great Room features vaulted ceiling, fireplace & French doors to outdoor living deck.
- Kitchen includes all amenities plus breakfast eating bar.
- Main floor laundry/mudroom.
- Master suite features coffered ceiling and Master bath with walk-in closets.
- Full basement.

Plan CPS-1155-C

Bedrooms: 3	Baths: 2

Space:	
Total living area:	1,848 sq. ft.
Basement:	1,848 sq. ft.
Garage:	513 sq. ft.

Exterior Wall Framing:	2x6

Foundation options:
Daylight basement.
(Foundation & framing conversion diagram available — see order form.)

Blueprint Price Code:	B

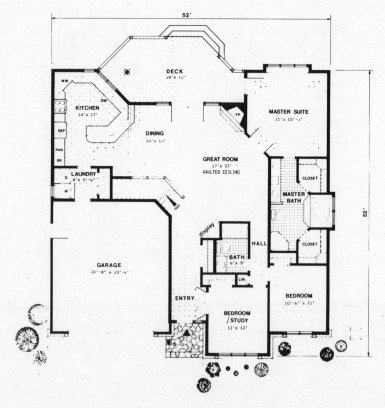

MAIN FLOOR

Plan CPS-1155-C

A Blend of Extras

- A sophisticated blend of country and contemporary design flows through this exceptional home.
- Specially designed for a side sloping lot, the home has a tuck-under garage and an open, economical interior.
- Attractive features include vaulted ceilings, a front wrapping deck, a rear deck off the family room, skylights, interior plant shelves in the kitchen and master bath, and an optional fourth bedroom, guest room or study.
- The vaulted family room is uniquely set below the main level, separated from the nook by a handrail.
- Three bedrooms and two full baths are found on the upper floor.

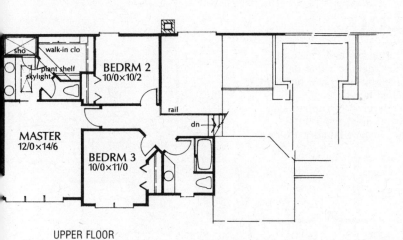

UPPER FLOOR

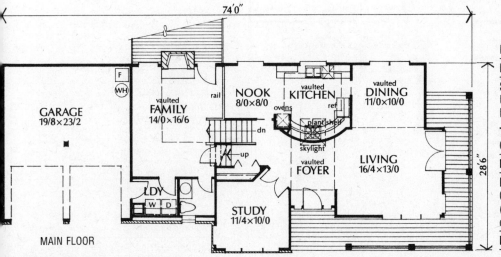

MAIN FLOOR

Plan CDG-4005	
Bedrooms: 3-4	Baths: 2½

Space:	
Upper floor:	732 sq. ft.
Main floor:	1,178 sq. ft.
Total living area:	**1,910 sq. ft.**
Garage:	456 sq. ft.

Exterior Wall Framing:	2x4

Foundation options:
Crawlspace.
(Foundation & framing conversion diagram available — see order form.)

Blueprint Price Code:	B

Plan CDG-4005

Indoor/Outdoor
Living on A Sloping Lot

- The wood siding, the front deck, and the multi-paned exterior of this Northwest contemporary will beckon you up to the entry stairs and inside.
- The two-story entry opens up to a vaulted living room with tall windows, exposed beam ceiling and adjoining dining area which accesses the hand-railed deck.
- An updated kitchen offers a walk-in

pantry, eating bar and breakfast nook with sliders to a rear deck.
- A fireplace and rear patio highlight the attached family room.
- A washer/dryer in the upper level bath is convenient to all three bedrooms, making laundry a breeze.

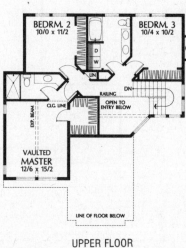

UPPER FLOOR

BASEMENT

MAIN FLOOR

Plan P-7737-4D

Bedrooms: 3	Baths: 2½
Space:	
Upper floor:	802 sq. ft.
Main floor:	1,158 sq. ft.
Total living area:	1,960 sq. ft.
Garage/basement:	736 sq. ft.
Exterior Wall Framing:	2x6

Foundation options:
Daylight basement.
(Foundation & framing conversion diagram available — see order form.)

Blueprint Price Code:	B

Plan P-7737-4D

Stately Multi-Level

- Off the split entry of this exciting multi-level home is a vaulted, sunken living room with fireplace and front boxed window.
- An open half wall makes the kitchen and bayed dining area loft-like above.

- The modern vaulted master suite has beautiful boxed window and bath with windowed jacuzzi tub.
- The lower level family room offers views and access to adjoining patio; an extra bedroom, bath and office or bonus space are also included.

Plan B-89007	
Bedrooms: 4	**Baths: 3**
Space:	
Main floor:	1,536 sq. ft.
Lower level:	602 sq. ft.
Total living area:	**2,138 sq. ft.**
Basement:	360 sq. ft.
Garage:	420 sq. ft.
Exterior Wall Framing:	2x4

Foundation options:
Partial basement.
(Foundation & framing conversion diagram available — see order form.)

Blueprint Price Code: C

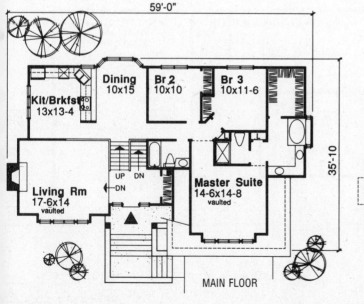

MAIN FLOOR

59'-0"
35'-10"

Dining 10x15
Br 2 10x10
Br 3 10x11-6
Kit/Brkfst 13x13-4
UP DN
DN
Living Rm 17-6x14 vaulted
Master Suite 14-6x14-8 vaulted

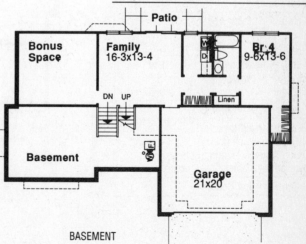

BASEMENT

Patio
Bonus Space
Family 16-3x13-4
Br. 4 9-6x13-6
DN UP
Linen
Basement
Garage 21x20

Plan B-89007

Today's Tradition

- The traditional two-story design is brought up to today's standards with this exciting new design.
- The front half of the main floor is devoted to formal entertaining. The living and dining rooms offer symmetrical bay windows overlooking the wrap-around front porch.
- The informal living zone faces the rear deck and yard. It includes a family room with fireplace and beamed ceiling as well as a modern kitchen with cooktop island and snack bar.
- There are four large bedrooms and two full baths on the upper sleeping level.

Plan AGH-2143

Bedrooms: 4	Baths: 2½

Space:	
Upper floor:	1,047 sq. ft.
Main floor:	1,096 sq. ft.
Total living area:	**2,143 sq. ft.**
Daylight basement:	1,096 sq. ft.
Garage:	852 sq. ft.

Exterior Wall Framing:	2x4

Foundation options:
Daylight basement.
(Foundation & framing conversion diagram available — see order form.)

Blueprint Price Code:	C

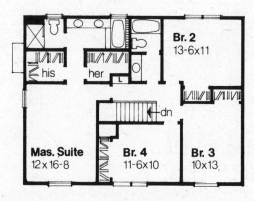

Br. 2
13-6x11

his   her

Mas. Suite
12 x 16-8

Br. 4
11-6x10

Br. 3
10x13

dn

UPPER FLOOR

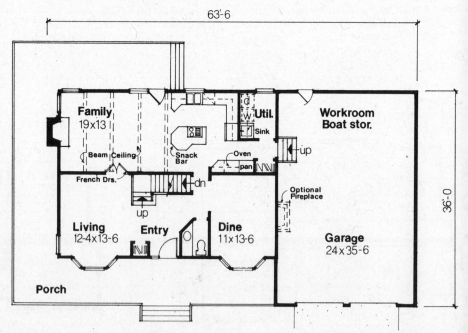

63'-6

36'-0

Family
19x13

Util.

Workroom
Boat stor.

Beam Ceiling

Snack Bar

Sink

Oven

pan

up

Optional Fireplace

French Drs.

dn

up

Living
12-4x13-6

Entry

Dine
11x13-6

Garage
24 x 35-6

Porch

MAIN FLOOR

Plan AGH-2143

Three Bedroom Split Entry

- This lovely split entry combines contemporary and traditional styling in an affordable floor arrangement.
- The main/upper level houses the sleeping rooms, two baths, convenient laundry facilities, and the main living areas.
- A formal dining room is divided from the foyer by an open handrail; the room can also overlook the front yard through a large, boxed window wall.
- The adjacent living room boasts a handsome fireplace and sliders to the rear patio.
- A large versatile bonus space and garage are found on the lower level.

MAIN FLOOR

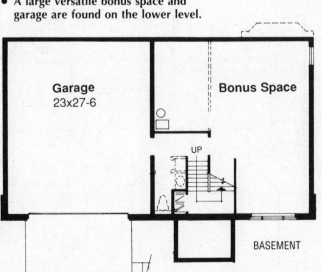

BASEMENT

Plan B-90014

Bedrooms: 3	Baths: 2-3

Space:

Main/upper floor:	1,549 sq. ft.
Basement:	750 sq. ft.
Total living area:	2,299 sq. ft.
Garage:	633 sq. ft.

Exterior Wall Framing:	2x4

Foundation options:
Daylight basement.
(Foundation & framing conversion diagram available — see order form.)

Blueprint Price Code:	C

Plan B-90014

Difficult Site, No Problem

- Designed to accommodate an irregular site, this traditionally styled exterior has an interior with modern conveniences.
- The kitchen is well-planned to serve both the dining room and a spacious octagonal breakfast nook.
- A large living room with window seat and fireplace and a generous-sized family room provide ample space for entertaining and family activities.
- The master bedroom suite features a large bath with step-up jacuzzi tub, walk-in closet, and a private study entered through double doors.
- Room for three additional bedrooms and a full bath are located on the upper floor.

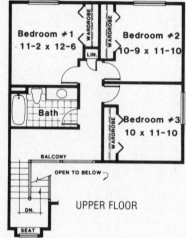

UPPER FLOOR

Bedroom #1
11-2 x 12-6

WARDROBE

Bedroom #2
10-9 x 11-10

LIN.

Bath

WARDROBE

Bedroom #3
10 x 11-10

BALCONY

OPEN TO BELOW

DN.

SEAT

Plan NW-660

Bedrooms: 4	Baths: 2½

Space:	
Upper floor:	700 sq. ft.
Main floor:	1,720 sq. ft.
Lower/basement:	106 sq. ft.

Total living area:	2,526 sq. ft.
Garage:	659 sq. ft.

Exterior Wall Framing:	2x6

Foundation options:
Daylight basement.
(Foundation & framing conversion diagram available — see order form.)

Blueprint Price Code:	D

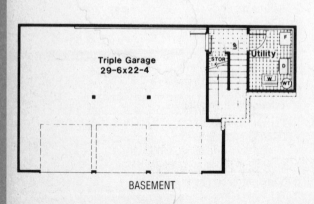

Triple Garage
29-6x22-4

STOR.

Utility

F

S

W

D

WT

BASEMENT

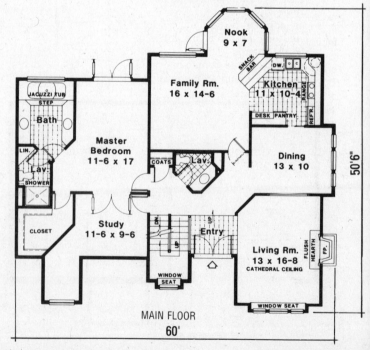

Nook
9 x 7

SNACK BAR

Family Rm.
16 x 14-6

DW.

Kitchen
11 x 10-4

FRIDGE

DESK   PANTRY

REFR.

JACUZZI TUB
STEP

Bath

LIN.

Lav.

SHOWER

Master
Bedroom
11-6 x 17

COATS

Lav.

Dining
13 x 10

CLOSET

Study
11-6 x 9-6

Entry

Living Rm.
13 x 16-8
CATHEDRAL CEILING

FLUSH HEARTH

FP.

WINDOW SEAT

WINDOW SEAT

MAIN FLOOR
60'

50'6"

Plan NW-660

Great Room With Deck

- Brick details and a small covered front porch accent the exterior of this open sloping lot design.
- The entry opens to an exciting living/dining room combination with large attached deck, fireplace and easy access to the modern island kitchen.
- An office, guest room or fourth bedroom and second bedroom share a bath on the other side of the living room.
- A beautiful master suite is tucked away on the opposite end of the home for privacy; amenities here include a walk-in closet, stunning corner windows and a convenient bath built for two.
- The lower level houses an extra bedroom, bath, storage space and a large rec room with patio.

Plan NW-104

Bedrooms: 3-4	Baths: 3

Space:

Main floor:	1,760 sq. ft.
Lower/basement:	843 sq. ft.
Total living area:	**2,603 sq. ft.**
Garage:	468 sq. ft.

Exterior Wall Framing:	2x6

Foundation options:
Daylight basement.
(Foundation & framing conversion diagram available — see order form.)

Blueprint Price Code:	D

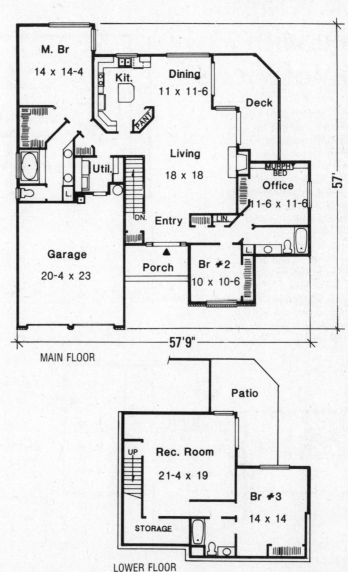

MAIN FLOOR

LOWER FLOOR

Plan NW-104

Deck Wraps Home with Plenty of Views

- A full deck and an abundance of windows surround this exciting two-level contemporary.
- Skywalls are found in the kitchen and dining room; the kitchen also features an island kitchen.
- The brilliant living room boasts a huge fireplace and cathedral ceiling, besides the stunning window wall.
- The master bedroom offers private access to the deck and an attached bath with dual vanities, large tub and a walk-in closet.
- A generous-sized family room and two extra bedrooms share the lower level with a two-car garage and storage area.

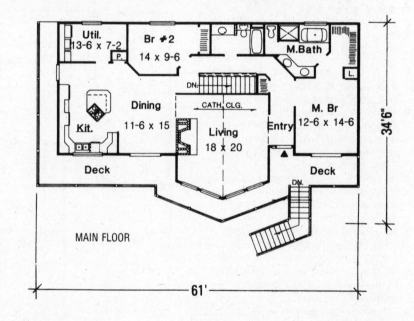

MAIN FLOOR

61'

34'6"

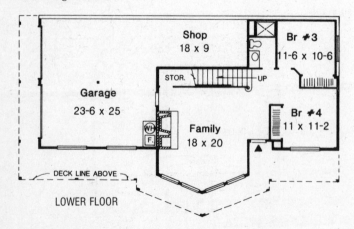

LOWER FLOOR

Plan NW-579

Bedrooms: 2-4	Baths: 2-3

Space:

Main/upper floor:	1,707 sq. ft.
Lower floor:	901 sq. ft.
Total living area:	**2,608 sq. ft.**
Shop:	162 sq. ft.
Garage:	588 sq. ft.
Exterior Wall Framing:	**2x6**

Foundation options:
Daylight basement.
(Foundation & framing conversion diagram available — see order form.)

Blueprint Price Code:	D

Plan NW-579

Well-Planned Walkout

- A dramatic double-back stair atrium descending from the Great Room to the bonus family room below ties the main floor design to the walkout lower level.
- A traditional exterior leads into a dramatic, open-feeling interior.
- The vaulted Great Room and dining room are separated by stylish columns.
- A see-thru fireplace is shared by the Great Room and the exciting kitchen with octagonal breakfast bay.
- A double-doored den/guest room opens off the Great Room.
- The spacious main floor master suite includes a huge walk-in closet and lavish master bath.

Plan AG-9105

Bedrooms: 3-4	Baths: 2½

Space:

Main floor:	1,838 sq. ft.
Daylight basement:	800 sq. ft.
Total living area:	**2,638 sq. ft.**
Unfinished basement area:	1,038 sq. ft.
Garage:	462 sq. ft.
Exterior Wall Framing:	**2x6**

Foundation options:
Daylight basement.
(Foundation & framing conversion diagram available — see order form.)

Blueprint Price Code:	D

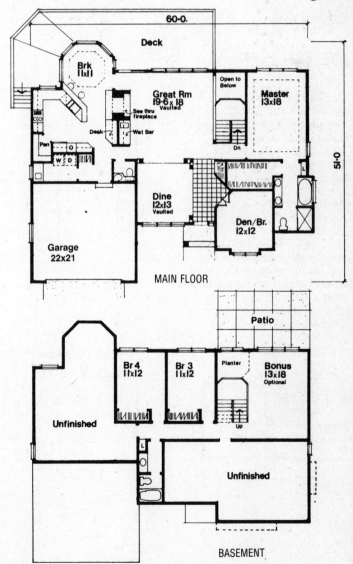

MAIN FLOOR

BASEMENT

Plan AG-9105

127

Farmhouse for Sloping Lot

- A covered porch wraps around the front of this lovely farmhouse styled two-story.
- Inside, the vaulted foyer opens to the living room and upstairs landing.
- The open staircase overlooks both the living room and adjoining dining room.
- A family room with fireplace and a breakfast nook join the kitchen on the other side of a counter bar.
- Upstairs, an arched opening adorns the entrance to the master bedroom's private bath; three secondary bedrooms share a second full bath.

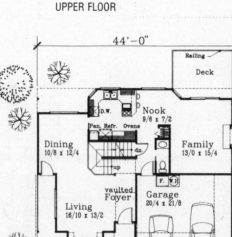

UPPER FLOOR

Br. 2 10 8 x 12 0
Walk-in Wardrobe
Master 11 8 x 11 6
Railing
Arch
Walk in
Walk in
dn.
Railing
Spa
Br. 4 12 1 x 11 8
Open to Below
Br. 3 10 8 x 11 8
Plants
Walk in

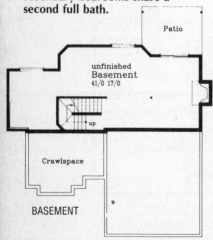

Patio

unfinished Basement 41/0 17/0

up

Crawlspace

BASEMENT

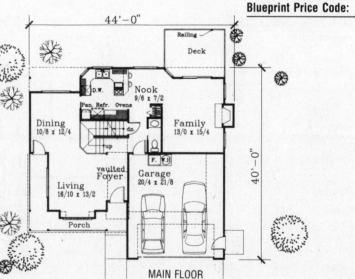

44'-0"

Railing

Deck

40'-0"

D.W.
Nook 9/6 x 7/2
Pan. Refr. Ovens
Dining 10/8 x 12/4
dn.
up
Family 13/0 x 15/4
F.
W.H.
vaulted Foyer
Garage 20/4 x 21/8
Living 16/10 x 13/2
Porch

MAIN FLOOR

Plan CDG-4013	
Bedrooms: 4	**Baths:** 2½

Space:	
Upper floor:	1,077 sq. ft.
Main floor:	888 sq. ft.
Lower floor:	682 sq. ft.
Total living area:	2,647 sq. ft.
Garage:	441 sq. ft.

Exterior Wall Framing:	2x4

Foundation options:
Daylight basement.
(Foundation & framing conversion diagram available — see order form.)

Blueprint Price Code:	D

Plan CDG-4013

Compact Fun

- This cozy cottage is perfect for a scenic, sloping site.
- Entrance to the main level is through a wrapping deck off the front stairway; the succeeding combination living/dining area is divided only by a central two-way fireplace.
- An island kitchen, a bedroom with dual closets and a full bath complete the main level.
- Upstairs you'll find two additional bedrooms, a bath and a library loft area that overlooks the living area below.
- Room for a family and game room with fireplace and soda bar and a television area, bath and laundry room are found on the lower level, also with an attached patio.

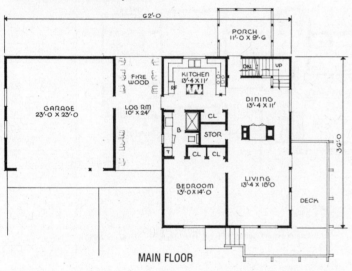

MAIN FLOOR

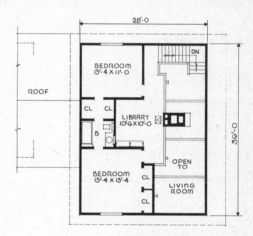

UPPER FLOOR

LOWER FLOOR

Plan CPS-987	
Bedrooms: 3	**Baths:** 3

Space:	
Upper floor:	511 sq. ft.
Main floor:	1,008 sq. ft.
Lower floor:	1,248 sq. ft.
Total living area:	2,767 sq. ft.
Garage:	529 sq. ft.
Exterior Wall Framing:	2x6

Foundation options:
Daylight basement.
(Foundation & framing conversion diagram available — see order form.)

Blueprint Price Code:	D

Plan CPS-987

REAR VIEW

Exciting Interior Bridge

- A spectacular second floor sky bridge overlooks the sun-drenched living room, brightened by a fireplace and brilliant windows that reach up two stories.
- Porches off the dining room and family room, a deck off the den, and bay windows in the nook and sitting room upstairs provide access and views to the outdoors.
- The combination family room, nook and kitchen make family dining and entertaining an open, but intimate experience.
- Room for three to four bedrooms is included.

Plan NW-915

Bedrooms: 3-4	Baths: 3

Space:	
Upper floor:	1,522 sq. ft.
Lower floor:	1,267 sq. ft.
Total living area:	**2,789 sq. ft.**
Garage:	731 sq. ft.

Exterior Wall Framing:	2x6

Foundation options:
Daylight basement.
(Foundation & framing conversion diagram available — see order form.)

Blueprint Price Code:	D

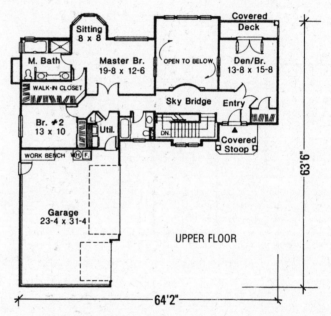

UPPER FLOOR

63'6"

64'2"

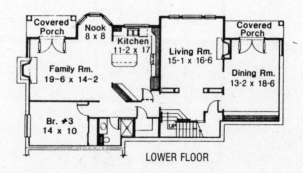

LOWER FLOOR

Plan NW-915

Angled Spaciousness

- This slope-to-the-front home looks impressive with the hip roof and generous windows.
- Upon entry, you may step up into the formal living room with fireplace, high ceiling and large window seats at each end, or into the dining room.
- The adjoining nook and kitchen have front sun deck and rear patio; the attached family room offers a corner wood stove and front bay window.
- A private bath and deck, walk-in closet and beautiful corner windows accentuate the master suite.
- An exciting game room and two additional bedrooms are found on the lower level.

Plan NW-507

Bedrooms: 3	Baths: 2½

Space:

Main floor:	1,963 sq. ft.
Lower floor:	917 sq. ft.
Total living area:	**2,880 sq. ft.**
Garage:	679 sq. ft.
Shop:	140 sq. ft.
Storage:	181 sq. ft.
Exterior Wall Framing:	2x6

Foundation options:
Daylight basement.
(Foundation & framing conversion diagram available — see order form.)

Blueprint Price Code:	D

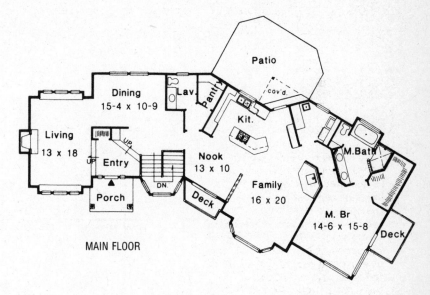

MAIN FLOOR

83' × 48'2"

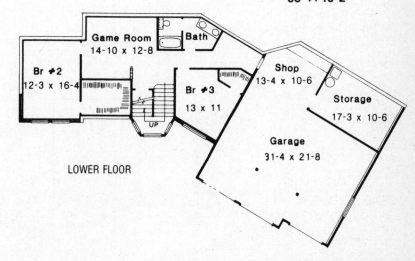

LOWER FLOOR

Plan NW-507

TO ORDER THIS BLUEPRINT, CALL TOLL-FREE 1-800-547-5570
(Prices and details on pp. 12-15.) **131**

Luxurious Tudor

- Rarely will you find a Tudor home designed to complement a side sloping lot like this one.
- Inside the towering brick entryway, an 11' vaulted foyer opens to a spacious living and dining room with French doors that reveal a piano room beautifully accented by a semi-circular wall of windows.
- The family room to the rear of the home adjoins the kitchen for an open entertaining area which can be completely closed off, or extended to a rear deck.
- A private, semi-circular deck off the master bedroom upstairs, vaulted ceilings, a window seat and a large attached bath with romantic corner spa tub highlight the upper level.
- Two additional bedrooms, bonus space, another full bath and laundry facilities are also included.

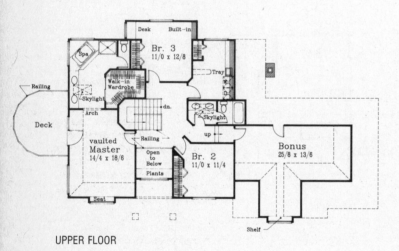

UPPER FLOOR

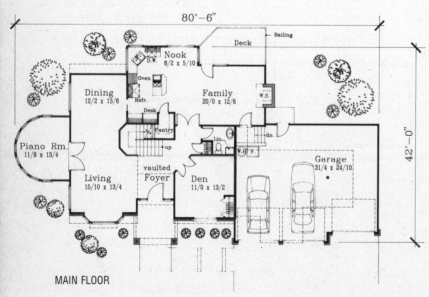

MAIN FLOOR

Plan CDG-4010

Bedrooms: 3-5	Baths: 2½
Space:	
Upper floor:	1,204 sq. ft.
Main floor:	1,462 sq. ft.
Bonus room:	388 sq. ft.
Total living area:	3,054 sq. ft.
Garage:	778 sq. ft.
Exterior Wall Framing:	2x4

Foundation options:
Crawlspace.
(Foundation & framing conversion diagram available — see order form.)

Blueprint Price Code:	E

Plan CDG-4010

Multi-Level Living

- Brick trim, a hip roof and bay windows add finishing touches to the facade of this great Northwestern traditional designed for a side slope.
- Inside, the bedrooms and bayed living room with fireplace occupy the main level; up several stairs you'll find the formal dining room, kitchen, nook and family room.
- A generous island cooktop/eating bar, pantry, and nook with access to a rear deck are only steps away from the relaxing family room.
- The lower level has a fourth bedroom, utility facilities and a large rec room with woodstove, along with the three-car garage.

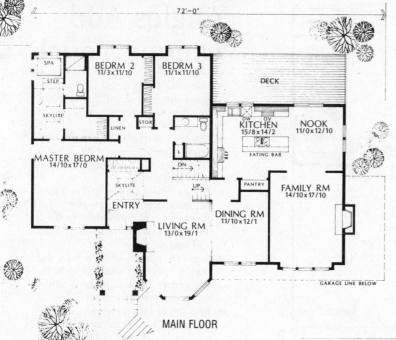

MAIN FLOOR

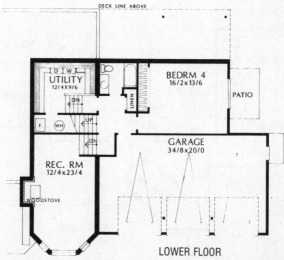

LOWER FLOOR

Plan P-7746-3D

Bedrooms: 4	Baths: 3

Space:

Main floor:	2,324 sq. ft.
Lower floor:	921 sq. ft.
Total living area:	3,245 sq. ft.
Garage:	693 sq. ft.
Exterior Wall Framing:	2x6

Foundation options:
Daylight basement.
(Foundation & framing conversion diagram available — see order form.)

Blueprint Price Code:	E

Plan P-7746-3D

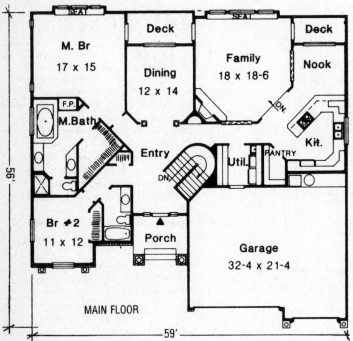

SEAT

M. Br
17 x 15

Deck

Dining
12 x 14

Family
18 x 18-6

Deck

Nook

F.P.

M.Bath

Entry

Kit.

DN.

DN.

Util.

PANTRY

Br #2
11 x 12

Porch

Garage
32-4 x 21-4

56'

MAIN FLOOR

59'

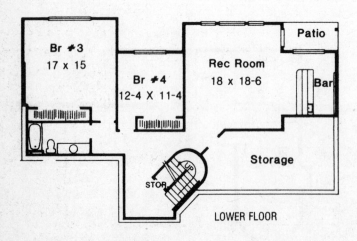

Br #3
17 x 15

Br #4
12-4 X 11-4

Rec Room
18 x 18-6

Patio

Bar

STOR.

Storage

LOWER FLOOR

Angles Add Unique Touch

- Columns, brick detail and archways grace the exterior of this spacious four-bedroom home with daylight basement.
- The main living areas are all oriented to the rear, with outdoor views possible from decks, window seats and patio.
- The beautiful sunken family room has an angled entrance and fireplace; it is convenient to the modern kitchen with pantry, nook and worktop bar.
- A gas fireplace visible to both the master bedroom and master bath and luxury tub will make it hard to leave this private retreat.
- Two secondary bedrooms, a bath and a spacious rec room with wet bar and patio are located on the lower level.

Plan NW-885

Bedrooms: 4	Baths: 3
Space:	
Main floor:	2,003 sq. ft.
Lower floor:	1,383 sq. ft.
Total living area:	3,386 sq. ft.
Garage:	690 sq. ft.
Exterior Wall Framing:	2x6

Foundation options:
Daylight basement.
(Foundation & framing conversion diagram available — see order form.)

Blueprint Price Code: E

Plan NW-885

Handsome Hill-Hugging Haven

- Multiple octagonal rooms allow this dramatic home to take full advantage of surrounding views.
- A dazzling two-story entry greets guests from the three-car garage motor courtyard.
- Once inside the front door, a soaring dome ceiling catches the eye past the octagonal stairway.
- A sunken living and dining room

with cathedral and domed ceiling face out to the rear deck and views.
- The octagonal island kitchen and breakfast nook are sure to please.
- The main floor den features a second fireplace and front-facing window seat.
- The entire second floor houses the master bedroom suite with a sensational master bath.

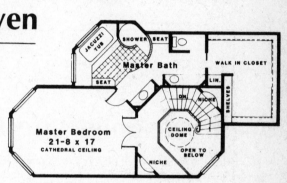

UPPER FLOOR

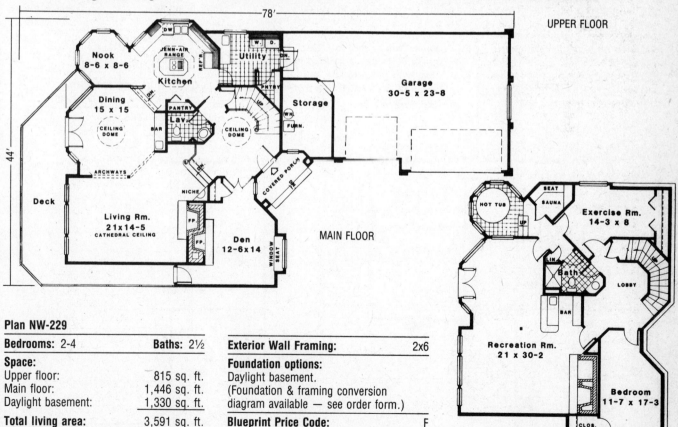

MAIN FLOOR

BASEMENT

Plan NW-229

Bedrooms: 2-4	Baths: 2½

Space:

Upper floor:	815 sq. ft.
Main floor:	1,446 sq. ft.
Daylight basement:	1,330 sq. ft.
Total living area:	**3,591 sq. ft.**

Exterior Wall Framing: 2x6

Foundation options:
Daylight basement.
(Foundation & framing conversion diagram available — see order form.)

Blueprint Price Code: F

Plan NW-229

Well Seasoned Lifestyle

- This delightful multi-leveled plan is perfect for hillside living.
- Off the spacious entry and down several stairs is the vaulted living room and bayed library; a deck is bordered on two sides with each room.
- The formal dining room is vaulted and set beyond a columned arcade of plants; adjoining is a step-up family room with fireplace, wet bar and deck.
- The kitchen offers an island worktop and bayed breakfast nook.
- A U-shaped stairway climbs to the upper floor with a loft space or fourth bedroom, a vaulted master suite with bay window and luxury bath, and two additional bedrooms with dual baths.

Plan B-89030-L	
Bedrooms: 3-4	**Baths:** 3½
Space:	
Upper floor:	1,402 sq. ft.
Main floor:	2,002 sq. ft.
Total living area:	3,404 sq. ft.
Garage total:	780 sq. ft.
Exterior Wall Framing:	2x4
Foundation options:	
Daylight basement.	
(Foundation & framing conversion diagram available — see order form.)	
Blueprint Price Code:	E

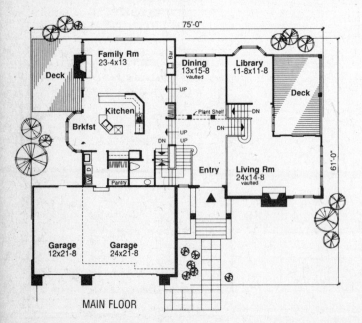

MAIN FLOOR

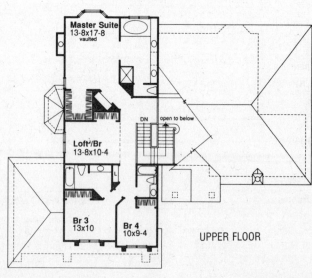

UPPER FLOOR

Plan B-89030-L

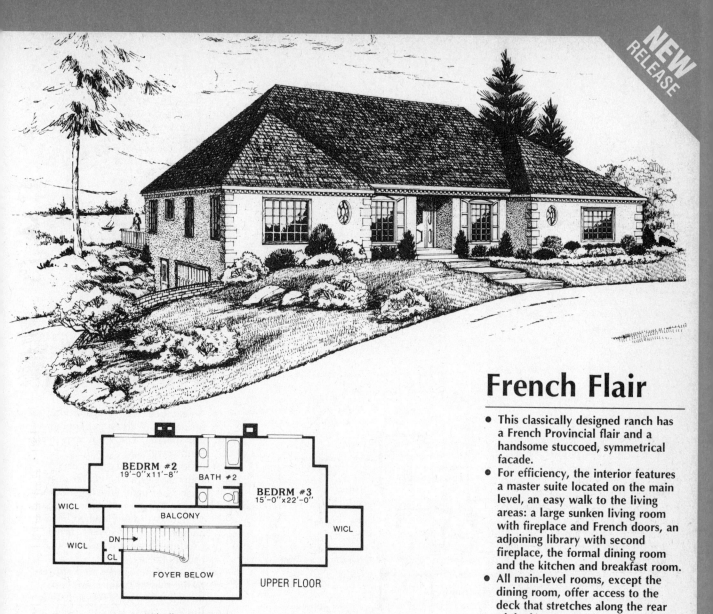

BEDRM #2
19'-0" x 11'-8"

BATH #2

BEDRM #3
15'-0" x 22'-0"

WICL

WICL

WICL

BALCONY

DN

CL

FOYER BELOW

UPPER FLOOR

70'-0" OVERALL

WOOD DECK

DN

DN

FRENCH DRS.

FRENCH DRS.

FRENCH DRS.

BKFST
11'-5" x 9'-0"

FIREPLACE

FIREPLACE

PANT

REF

LIVING RM
26'-8" x 16'-2"

LIBRARY
15'-0" x 23'-0"

MASTER
BEDRM
13'-3" x 20'-0"

S
S
KITCHEN
11'-5" x 12'-0"

DW

DN

DN

UP

FOYER

40'-0" OVERALL

ANTE FOYER

GALLERY

WICL

DINING RM
14'-0" x 18'-0"

WET BAR

CL

PORCH

CL

CL

LAV

LC

LAUN RM

D W

DN

MSTR BATH

MAIN FLOOR

Plan AX-8619

French Flair

- This classically designed ranch has a French Provincial flair and a handsome stuccoed, symmetrical facade.
- For efficiency, the interior features a master suite located on the main level, an easy walk to the living areas: a large sunken living room with fireplace and French doors, an adjoining library with second fireplace, the formal dining room and the kitchen and breakfast room.
- All main-level rooms, except the dining room, offer access to the deck that stretches along the rear of the home.
- A reception area off the foyer has room for coats and an attractive wet bar.
- The upper level provides for two generous children's or guest rooms.
- A full basement houses a side-entry, two-car garage (not shown).

Plan AX-8619

Bedrooms: 3	Baths: 2½

Space:

Upper floor:	1,068 sq. ft.
Main floor:	2,592 sq. ft.
Total living area:	**3,660 sq. ft.**
Basement (includes garage):	2,592 sq. ft.

Exterior Wall Framing:	2x4

Foundation options:
Daylight basement.
(Foundation & framing conversion diagram available — see order form.)

Blueprint Price Code:	F

Private Master Bedroom Loft

- An exciting deck wraps around the formal living areas and kitchen of this spacious contemporary, perfect for a scenic site.
- Inside, an eye-catching curved staircase lies at the center of the open floor plan, which includes a sunken living room with fireplace, an updated island kitchen with pantry, nook and lovely corner window above the sink, and a private library.
- The upper loft is devoted entirely to the master suite; attractions include a private deck and study, fireplace, huge walk-in closet, and a bath with separate shower and luxury tub.
- The lower level provides space for two additional bedrooms, a rec room, full bar with wine storage and attached patio.

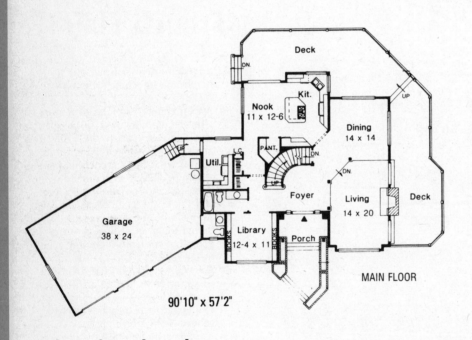

90'10" x 57'2"

MAIN FLOOR

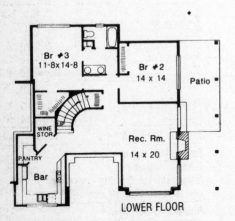

LOWER FLOOR

UPPER FLOOR

Plan NW-917

Bedrooms: 3-4	Baths: 3½
Space:	
Upper floor:	905 sq. ft.
Main floor:	1,587 sq. ft.
Lower floor:	1,289 sq. ft.
Total living area:	3,781 sq. ft.
Garage:	912 sq. ft.
Exterior Wall Framing:	2x6

Foundation options:
Daylight basement.
(Foundation & framing conversion diagram available — see order form.)

Blueprint Price Code:	F

Plan NW-917

Luxurious Multi-Level Offers Options

- Classic, symmetrical lines set the tone for this impressive, open layout and design.
- Sunken formal living areas, coved ceilings, arched openings and a fireplace and wood stove highlight the main floor.

- A wraparound deck encloses the family room and kitchen/nook.
- Four bedrooms, laundry room and a large bonus area over the garage complete the upper floor.
- Room for an extra bedroom, recreational room with walk-out

patio and a bath is found in the lower level.

UPPER FLOOR

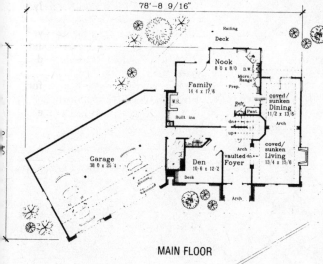

MAIN FLOOR

LOWER FLOOR

Plan CDG-4011

Bedrooms: 5-7	Baths: 3-4

Space:

Upper floor:	1,161 sq. ft.
Bonus room:	734 sq. ft.
Main floor:	1,298 sq. ft.
Lower floor:	752 sq. ft.

Total living area:	3,945 sq. ft.
Garage:	963 sq. ft.

Exterior Wall Framing:	2x4

Foundation options:
Daylight basement.
(Foundation & framing conversion diagram available — see order form.)

Blueprint Price Code:	F

***TO ORDER THIS BLUEPRINT,
CALL TOLL-FREE 1-800-547-5570***
(Prices and details on pp. 12-15.)

Plan CDG-4011

An Array Of Luxuries

- This luxury home would ideally be built into a hill to allow full use of the home's basement.
- A panoramic view is captured from every primary room, including a deck that stretches along the rear of the home.
- Luxurious amenities inside include an island kitchen with separate walk-in pantry, window-enclosed nook, a huge family room with wood stove and rear window wall, a formal dining room with window seat, and a formal sunken living room.
- Other extras are the master bedroom with step-down onto the deck, roomy walk-in closet and a private bath with bayed step-up spa tub, separate shower and work area.
- Downstairs you'll find an exciting recreation room with wood stove and eye-catching bar, plus room for two additional bedrooms, a full bath and storage space.

Plan NW-744

Bedrooms: 4	Baths: 3½

Space:	
Main floor:	2,539 sq. ft.
Lower/basement:	1,703 sq. ft.
Total living area:	**4,242 sq. ft.**
Garage:	904 sq. ft.

Exterior Wall Framing:	2x6

Foundation options:
Daylight basement.
(Foundation & framing conversion diagram available — see order form.)

Blueprint Price Code:	G

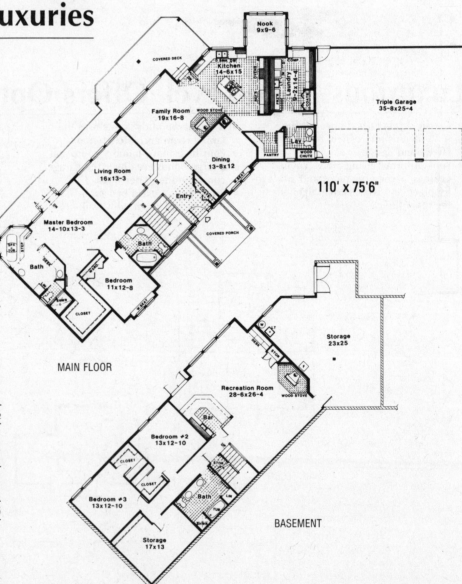

110' x 75'6"

MAIN FLOOR

BASEMENT

TO ORDER THIS BLUEPRINT,
CALL TOLL-FREE 1-800-547-5570

140 (Prices and details on pp. 12-15.)

Plan NW-744

For The Large, Active Family

- This spacious, multi-level home is ideal for the large, active family.
- Elegance is certainly not forgotten, however; note the coved ceiling in the foyer and dining room, the luxurious sunken living room with fireplace, the modern island kitchen and adjoining bayed nook,

wet bar and grand family room with added fireplace and entertainment deck.
- A brilliant master suite on the upper floor boasts a private bath with bayed window and spa tub,

separate shower and walk-in closet; three additional bedrooms are also offered.
- The lower level is devoted to extra-curricular activities, movie watching and entertaining.

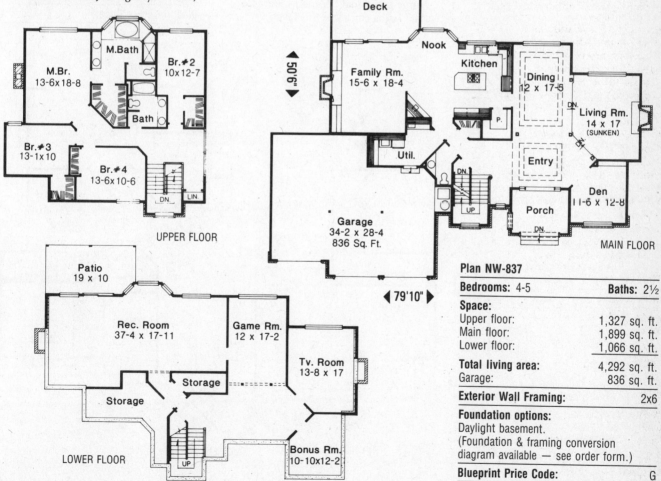

UPPER FLOOR

MAIN FLOOR

LOWER FLOOR

Plan NW-837

Bedrooms: 4-5	Baths: 2½

Space:

Upper floor:	1,327 sq. ft.
Main floor:	1,899 sq. ft.
Lower floor:	1,066 sq. ft.
Total living area:	4,292 sq. ft.
Garage:	836 sq. ft.

Exterior Wall Framing:	2x6

Foundation options:
Daylight basement.
(Foundation & framing conversion diagram available — see order form.)

Blueprint Price Code:	G

Plan NW-837

NEW RELEASE

Exciting Game Room Fun

- A spectacular game room with a large wet bar, sink and refrigerator shares the lower main level with a den or fifth bedroom, and a huge family room with bay window, massive fireplace and double-door entrance to a rear deck.
- The spacious kitchen features an angled cooktop and eating bar, handy pantry and attached vaulted nook.
- Opposite the vaulted foyer is an exciting vaulted living and dining room combination with multi bay windows, large fireplace, and third entrance to the rear deck.
- The upper level houses a stunning master bedroom with tray ceiling, rear bay window and elevated dressing area with skylight; three large additional bedrooms and two full baths complete this level.

Plans P-7714-3A & -3D

Bedrooms: 4-5	Baths: 4

Space:

Upper floor:	1,889 sq. ft.
Main floor:	2,509 sq. ft.
Total living area:	**4,398 sq. ft.**
Basement:	2,509 sq. ft.
Garage:	711 sq. ft.

Exterior Wall Framing:	**2x6**

Foundation options:
Daylight basement (P-7714-3D).
Crawlspace (P-7714-3A).
(Foundation & framing conversion diagram available — see order form.)

Blueprint Price Code:	**G**

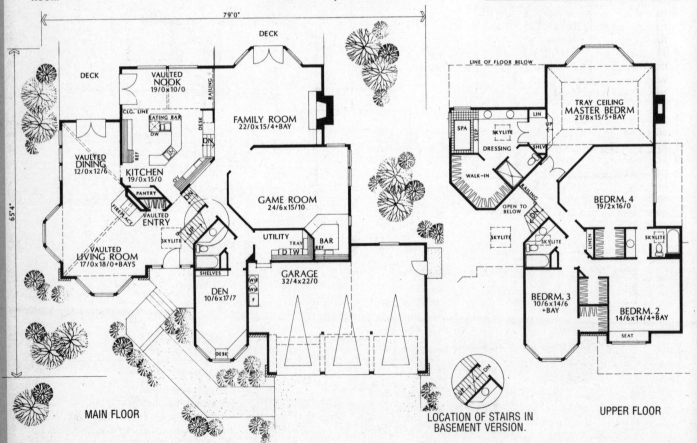

MAIN FLOOR

LOCATION OF STAIRS IN BASEMENT VERSION.

UPPER FLOOR

Plans P-7714-3A & -3D

A Home With Recreation In Mind

- A step-down three-car garage is hidden by the graceful arched window treatment of this luxurious two-story with finished lower level.
- Off the covered front porch and two-story foyer is a bayed living room with fireplace and formal dining room with deck.
- The combination island kitchen and nook adjoin the large family room with wood stove; the study to the rear of the home could be used as an extra bedroom.
- An elegant master suite and three additional bedrooms are found on the upper level.
- The lower level is perfect for parties and family activities; included are a pool room, rec room with wet bar and hot tub, a guest room, shop area and attached outdoor patios.

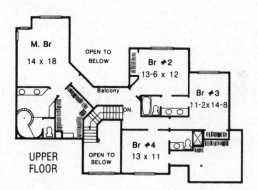

UPPER FLOOR

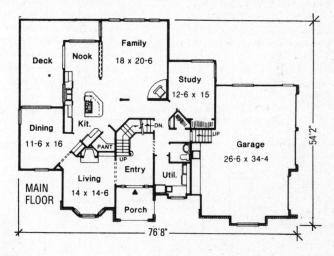

MAIN FLOOR

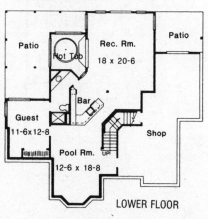

LOWER FLOOR

Plan NW-785

Bedrooms: 4-6		Baths: 4½

Space:

Upper floor:	1,613 sq. ft.
Main floor:	1,888 sq. ft.
Lower floor:	1,365 sq. ft.
Total living area:	4,866 sq. ft.
Garage:	910 sq. ft.

Exterior Wall Framing: 2x6

Foundation options:
Daylight basement.
(Foundation & framing conversion diagram available — see order form.)

Blueprint Price Code: G

Plan NW-785

TO ORDER THIS BLUEPRINT, **CALL TOLL-FREE 1-800-547-5570** (Prices and details on pp. 12-15.)

Ultra Modern, Ultra Luxury

- An intriguing exterior befits the equally striking interior of this contemporary, stuccoed two-story home.
- Up curved steps, through double front doors and into a beautiful open foyer affords you a view of an exciting sunken activities room with fireplace and step-down window seat.
- A pair of bedrooms and a full bath are a few steps away.
- Two flights above the foyer is the main level that includes a formal living room with ceiling mirror, a private deck shared with the master bedroom and an attached semi-circular front deck; also featured on this level is a step-up family room with see-through fireplace to the dining room, both with open beamed ceilings.
- The spectacular master bedroom offers a huge walk-in closet and private luxury bath with spa tub and sauna!

Plan SD-9015	
Bedrooms: 3-4	**Baths:** 2 full, 2 half
Space:	
Main/upper floor:	4,107 sq. ft.
Lower floor:	2,277 sq. ft.
Total living area:	6,384 sq. ft.
Garage:	834 sq. ft.
Exterior Wall Framing:	2x4
Foundation options: Daylight basement. (Foundation & framing conversion diagram available — see order form.)	
Blueprint Price Code:	G

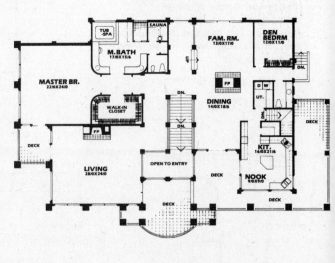

LOWER LEVEL

MAIN FLOOR

Plan SD-9015

Week-End Retreat

For those whose goal is a small, affordable retreat at the shore or in the mountains, this plan may be the answer. Although it measures less than 400 sq. ft. of living space on the main floor, it lacks nothing in comfort and convenience. A sizeable living room boasts a masonry hearth on which to mount your choice of wood stove or pre-fab fireplace. There is plenty of room for furniture, including a dining table.

The galley type kitchen is a small marvel of compact convenience and utility, even boasting a dishwasher and space for a stackable washer and dryer. The wide open nature of the first floor guarantees that even the person working in the kitchen area will still be included in the party. On the floor plan, a dashed line across the living room indicates the limits of the balcony bedroom above. In front of this line, the A-frame shape of the living room soars from floor boards to the ridge beam high above. Clerestory windows lend a further note of spaciousness and unity with nature's outdoors. A huge planked deck adds to the indoor-outdoor relationship.

A modest sized bedroom on the second floor is approached by a standard stairway, not an awkward ladder or heavy pull-down stairway as is often the case in small A-frames. The view over the balcony rail to the living room below adds a note of distinction. The unique framing pattern allows a window at either end of the bedroom, improving both outlook and ventilation.

A compact bathroom serves both levels and enjoys natural daylight through a skylight window.

First floor:	391 sq. ft.
Upper level:	144 sq. ft.
Total living area:	535 sq. ft.

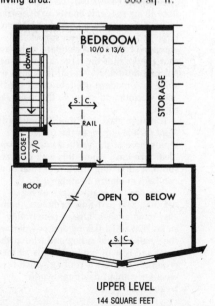

UPPER LEVEL
144 SQUARE FEET

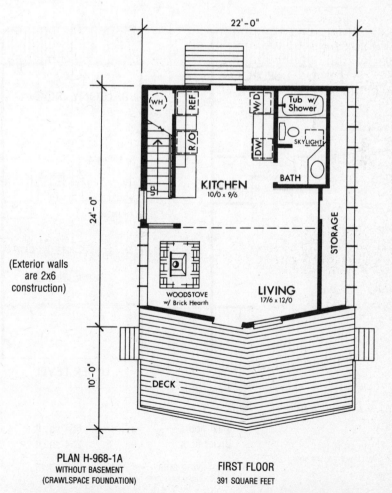

(Exterior walls are 2x6 construction)

PLAN H-968-1A
WITHOUT BASEMENT
(CRAWLSPACE FOUNDATION)

FIRST FLOOR
391 SQUARE FEET

Carefree Vacation Home

Scoffers and non-believers had a field day when the A-Frame first began to appear. Impractical, some said; uncomfortable, declared others; too expensive, ugly and more. And yet people built them and enjoyed them — and like the Volkswagen Bug, found them to be economical and practical, and yes, even beautiful to many beholders. Through the years, there has been a steady demand for these ubiquitous structures, and Plan H-15-1 is one of our more popular models. With this design, you will not be experimenting or pioneering because it has been built sucessfully many times.

Though it covers only 654 sq. ft. of main floor living space, it boasts an oversized living/dining room, a U-shaped kitchen, large bedroom and closet spaces, fully equipped bath plus a standard stairway (not a ladder) to the large second floor balcony dormitory. An old fashioned wood stove or a modern pre-fabricated fireplace adds warmth and cheer to the main living room.

The huge glass wall that dominates the front facade enhances the romantic atmosphere of the vaulted interior. And in ideal locations, where this wall can face south, a surprising amount of solar energy can help minimize heating costs.

One particular advantage of the A-Frame as a part-time or holiday home is easy maintenance. Use of penetrating stains that resist flaking and powdering on the small areas of siding and trim at the front and rear of the building is all that is required. The rest is roofing which resists weather without painting or other treatment.

MAIN FLOOR

26'-0"

DECK

STORAGE

BATH

Shwr

REF

KITCHEN
9'-2" x 8'-8"

DW

R/O

LIN

STOR

up

BEDROOM
11'-8" x 10'-0"

CLOSET
5'-0"

STORAGE

WOODSTOVE

LIVING ROOM
23'-8" x 11'-6"

DECK

4'-0"

28'-0"

10'-0"

PLAN H-15-1
CRAWLSPACE FOUNDATION

UPPER LEVEL

DECK

S. C.

BALCONY ROOM
15'-6" x 12'-4"

RAILINGS

down

OPEN TO
LIVING RM.

SLOPED CEILING

Main floor:	654 sq. ft.
Upper floor:	254 sq. ft.
Total living area:	908 sq. ft.

(Not counting basement or garage)

Blueprint Price Code A
Plan H-15-1

Compact, Easy to Build

This compact vacation or retirement home is economical and easy to construct. Only 24' x 46' for the daylight basement version, it nonetheless contains all the necessities and some of the luxuries one desires in a three-bedroom home. The non-basement version measures 24' x 44'.

Overall width for both versions including deck and carport is 50'.

One luxury is the separate, private bath adjoining the master bedroom; another is the double "His & Hers" wardrobe closets for the same room. The other two bedrooms are equipped with good-sized closets and share a second bathroom. Even if you choose the basement version, the convenience of first floor laundry facilities is yours.

The open stairway to the basement adds 3' to the visual size of the living room. A

pre-fab fireplace is located to allow enjoyment of a cozy hearth and a beautiful view from the same chair.

The plans are so completely detailed that a handyman amateur might frame this building (with the help of a few friends). Why not try it? (Be sure to order a materials list, too!)

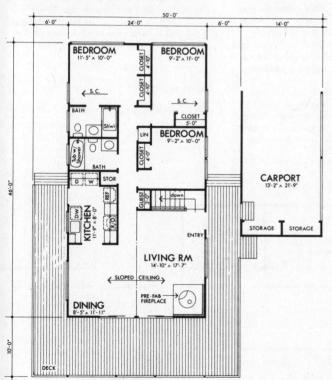

PLAN H-18
WITH DAYLIGHT BASEMENT
1104 SQUARE FEET

PLAN H-18-A
WITHOUT BASEMENT
1056 SQUARE FEET

Total living area: 1,104 sq. ft.
(Not counting basement or carport)

Blueprint Price Code A

Plans H-18 & H-18-A

TO ORDER THIS BLUEPRINT,
CALL TOLL-FREE 1-800-547-5570
(Prices and details on pp. 12-15.) **147**

Neatly Packaged Leisure Home

This pitched-roof two-story contemporary leisure home is accented with solid wood siding, placed vertically and diagonally, and it neatly packages three bedrooms and a generous amount of living space into a 1,271 sq. ft. plan that covers a minimum of ground space.

Half the main floor is devoted to the vaulted Great Room, which is warmed by a woodstove and opens out through sliding glass doors to a wide deck. The U-shaped kitchen adjacent to the Great Room has a

window looking onto the deck and a circular window in the front wall. The master bedroom, a full bath and the utility room complete the 823 sq. ft. first floor.

Stairs next to the entry door lead down to the daylight basement, double garage and workroom, or up to the second floor. An open railing overlooking the Great Room and clerestory windows add natural light and enhance the open feeling of the home. The two bedrooms share another full bathroom.

Main floor:	823 sq. ft.
Upper floor:	448 sq. ft.
Total living area:	1,271 sq. ft.

(Not counting basement or garage)

BASEMENT
PLAN P-520-D
WITH DAYLIGHT BASEMENT

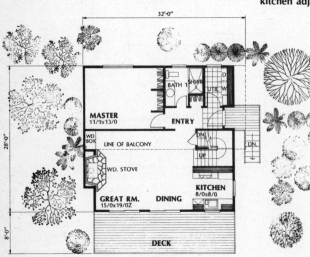

MAIN FLOOR

UPPER FLOOR

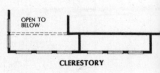

CLERESTORY

TO ORDER THIS BLUEPRINT,
CALL TOLL-FREE 1-800-547-5570
(Prices and details on pp. 12-15.)

Blueprint Price Code A
Plan P-520-D

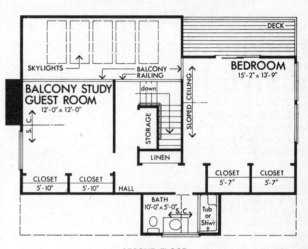

REAR VIEW

Solar Heat in Rustic Design

The first level, with only 623 sq. ft., is basically one huge room divided into areas for lounging, dining and cooking. A spacious deck, spanning the rear of the home, provides for outdoor living. Bathroom, laundry, closet space and stairwell complete the first floor.

Upstairs, two large rooms serve as bedrooms or for a variety of other purposes. Balcony railings unite the upper levels with the Great Room below. Linen and storage closets are opposite the fully equipped bathroom. Five huge skylight windows across the rear slope of the roof flood the entire home with solar light and heat, achieving a dramatic effect throughout. Exterior walls are of 2x6 framing.

FIRST FLOOR
623 SQUARE FEET

DECK

KITCHEN
9'-5" x 8'-1"

DW

REF

BOAT OR SKI-MOBILE
5'-0" x 14'-0"

BALCONY LINE

WOODSTOVE

GUEST
4'-0"

down

up

down

SKIS

GARAGE
10'-0" x 23'-0"

GREAT ROOM
12'-0" x 23'-0"

ENTRY

BATH
5'-0" x 5'-0"

SKI ROOM LAUNDRY
5'-0" x 8'-9"

W D

PORCH

6'-0" HIGH SCREEN WALL

38'-0"
22'-6"   15'-6"
8'-0"
24'-0"
5'-6"

PLAN H-953-1B
WITH DAYLIGHT BASEMENT

WH

STOR

heat

PLAN H-953-1A
WITHOUT BASEMENT
(CRAWL SPACE FOUNDATION)

SECOND FLOOR
689 SQUARE FEET

SKYLIGHTS

BALCONY RAILING

DECK

BEDROOM
15'-2" x 13'-9"

BALCONY STUDY GUEST ROOM
12'-0" x 12'-0"

down

STORAGE

SLOPED CEILING

S.C.

LINEN

CLOSET
5'-10"

CLOSET
5'-10"

HALL

CLOSET
5'-7"

CLOSET
5'-7"

BATH
10'-0" x 5'-0"

S.C.

Tub or Shw'r

First floor:	623 sq. ft.
Second floor:	689 sq. ft.
Total living area:	1,312 sq. ft.

(Not counting basement or garage)

Blueprint Price Code A
Plans H-953-1A & H-953-1B

TO ORDER THIS BLUEPRINT, CALL TOLL-FREE 1-800-547-5570 (Prices and details on pp. 12-15.) **149**

Economical and Stylish

A distinctive roof and window treatment on the kitchen extension lend a traditional look to this otherwise contemporary three-bedroom home of 1,362 sq. ft., which is only 40' wide to conserve lot space.

The brick and wood fence, with built-in planters, sets off the front courtyard and the walkway to the angled front door and entry hall. The vaulted, open-beam ceiling of the dining area and great room sweeps from the foyer to the large fireplace, flanked by windows, on the back wall.

The vaulted, U-shaped kitchen is washed with sunlight through the multi-paned arched window overlooking the front courtyard. A door from the dining area leads out to an optional courtyard and back to the large deck or patio set into the back corner of the house.

The large master bedroom suite has a sitting room, with a door leading to the patio, plus a dressing room, private bath and a spacious walk-in closet. The other two bedrooms share the hall bathroom.

In the daylight basement version of the plan, stairs replace the utility room just off the entry hall.

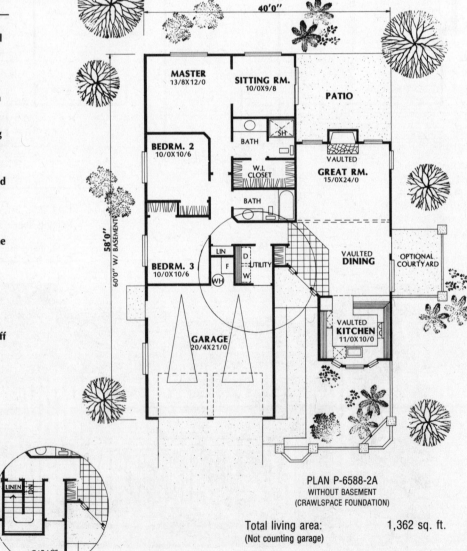

PLAN P-6588-2D
WITH DAYLIGHT BASEMENT

Main floor: 1,403 sq. ft.
Basement level: 1,303 sq. ft.

PLAN P-6588-2A
WITHOUT BASEMENT
(CRAWLSPACE FOUNDATION)

Total living area: 1,362 sq. ft.
(Not counting garage)

Blueprint Price Code A
Plans P-6588-2A & 2D

Narrow Lot Design with Daylight Basement Option

- This thoroughly modern plan exhibits beautiful traditional touches in its exterior design.
- A gracious courtyard-like area leads visitors to a side door with a vaulted entry area.
- A delightful kitchen/nook area is just to the right of the entry, and includes abundant window space and a convenient utility room.
- The vaulted living and dining areas join together to create an impressive space for entertaining and family living.
- The master suite boasts a large closet and private bath.
- Daylight basement option adds almost 1,500 square feet of space to the home.

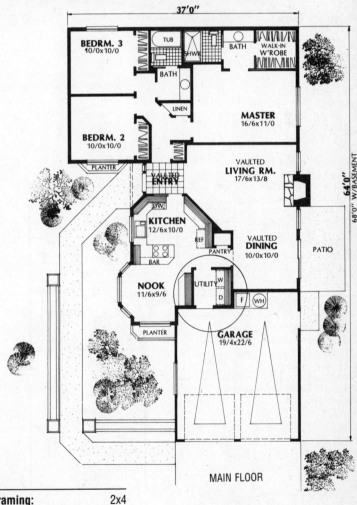

MAIN FLOOR

BASEMENT STAIR DETAIL

Plans P-6598-2A & -2D

Bedrooms: 3	Baths: 2

Space:

Main floor, non-basement plan:	1,375 sq. ft.
Main floor, basement version:	1,470 sq. ft.
Basement:	1,470 sq. ft.
Garage:	435 sq. ft.

Exterior Wall Framing:	2x4

Foundation options:
Daylight basement, Plan P-6598-2D.
Crawlspace, Plan P-6598-2A.
(Foundation & framing conversion diagram available — see order form.)

Blueprint Price Code:	A

Plans P-6598-2A & -2D

(Alternate, included in blueprints)

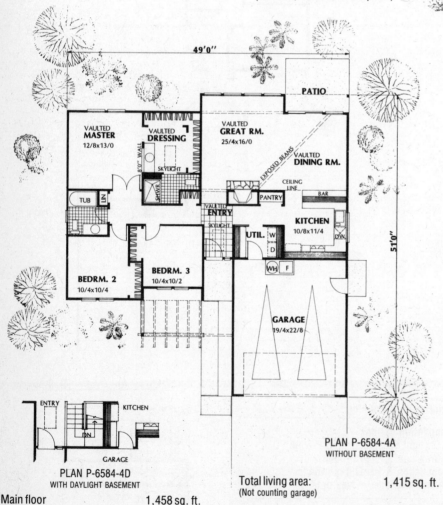

49'0''

PATIO

VAULTED
MASTER
12/8x13/0

VAULTED
DRESSING

VAULTED
GREAT RM.
25/4x16/0

EXPOSED BEAMS

VAULTED
DINING RM.

8'/0'' WALL

SKYLIGHT

CEILING
LINE

BAR

TUB

LIN

SHWR

PANTRY

VAULTED
ENTRY

KITCHEN
10/8x11/4

SKYLIGHT

UTIL.

W
D

DW.

BEDRM. 2
10/4x10/4

BEDRM. 3
10/4x10/2

WH

F

GARAGE
19/4x22/8

51'0''

ENTRY

KITCHEN

DN

GARAGE

PLAN P-6584-4D
WITH DAYLIGHT BASEMENT

PLAN P-6584-4A
WITHOUT BASEMENT

Main floor   1,458 sq. ft.
Lower floor   1,413 sq. ft.

Total living area: 1,415 sq. ft.
(Not counting garage)

Distinctive Contemporary Offers Two Exterior Designs

An open-arbor entry porch, boxed chimney, horizontal board siding and semihipped rooflines lend a custom look to the exterior of this contemporary ranch home. And the home's 1,415 sq. ft. interior is equally distinctive.

The front entry hall, which separates the spacious, open living area from the comfortably sized bedroom wing, has a vaulted ceiling with skylight for a dramatic first impression. The great room also has a vaulted ceiling, plus a long window wall (with sliding-glass door off the dining area opening onto a partly covered patio) and large fireplace.

There's an efficient U-shaped kitchen with pantry storage and an adjacent utility room. (In the daylight basement version, the utility room is replaced by stairs, and the entry to the garage is relocated.) A large master bedroom suite also has a vaulted ceiling with a skylight in the wardrobe/dressing area.

Blueprint Price Code A
Plans P-6584-4A & 4D

FRONT VIEW

All-Season Chalet

A guided tour from the front entry of this home takes you into the central hallway that serves as the hub of traffic to the main floor level. From here, convenience extends in every direction and each room is connected in a step-saving manner. Besides the master bedroom with twin closets, a full bathroom with stall shower is placed adjacent to a common wall that also serves the laundry equipment.

The living room and dining area are connected to allow for the expandable use of the dining table should the need arise for additional seating. The kitchen is open ended onto the dining area and has all the modern conveniences and built-in details.

A raised deck flanks the gable end of the living zone and extends outward for a distance of 8'.

A full basement is reached via a stairway connecting with the central hallway. The basement provides ample storage plus room for the central heating system. Another interesting feature is the garage placed under the home where the owner may not only store his automobile but such things as a boat and trailer and other sporting equipment.

First floor: 1,008 sq. ft.
Second floor: 462 sq. ft.
Total living area: 1,470 sq. ft.
(Not counting basement or garage)

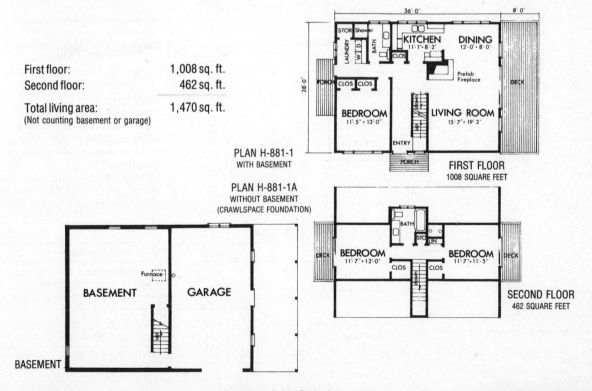

PLAN H-881-1
WITH BASEMENT

PLAN H-881-1A
WITHOUT BASEMENT
(CRAWLSPACE FOUNDATION)

FIRST FLOOR
1008 SQUARE FEET

SECOND FLOOR
462 SQUARE FEET

Blueprint Price Code A

Plans H-881-1 & H-881-1A

REAR VIEW

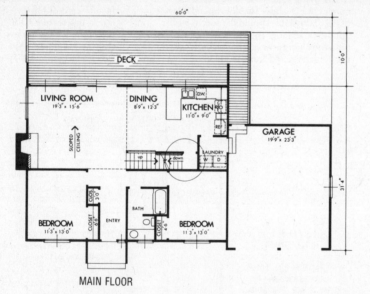

PLAN H-877-4
WITH BASEMENT

PLAN H-877-4A
WITHOUT BASEMENT

PLAN H-877-4B
WITH DAYLIGHT BASEMENT

DECK

LIVING ROOM
19'3" x 15'6"

DINING
8'9" x 12'3"

KITCHEN
11'0" x 9'0"

GARAGE
19'9" x 23'3"

LAUNDRY
W D

BEDROOM
11'3" x 13'0"

BATH

ENTRY

BEDROOM
11'3" x 13'0"

CLOSET

MAIN FLOOR

DECK

BEDROOM
13'9" x 12'3"

WALK IN
CLOSET
5'3" x 6'9"

LIVING ROOM
BELOW

BATH

down

UPPER FLOOR

Hillside Design Fits Contours

- Split-level design perfect for hillside lot.
- Excellent separation of living and sleeping areas.
- Corner kitchen features eating counter and handy laundry facilities.
- Rear wrap-around deck is seen from spacious living room and adjoining dining room; living room features sloped ceiling and corner fireplace.
- Upstairs master suite offers walk-in closet, private bath, and sun deck accessible through sliding glass doors.

Plans H-877-4, -4A & -4B

Bedrooms: 3	Baths: 2

Space:

Upper floor:	333 sq. ft.
Main floor:	1,200 sq. ft.
Total living area:	**1,533 sq. ft.**
Basement:	741 sq. ft.
Garage:	459 sq. ft.

Exterior Wall Framing:	2x6

Foundation options:
Daylight basement (Plan H-877-4B).
Standard basement (Plan H-877-4).
Crawlspace (Plan H-877-4A).
(Foundation & framing conversion diagram available — see order form.)

Blueprint Price Code:	B

Plans H-877-4, -4A & -4B

A Home for Sun Lovers

This open plan home, brightened by a landscaped atrium, also has a vaulted, glass-ceiling solarium with an optional spa, offering a sunny garden room for sitting or soaking — a bonus in a three-bedroom home of only 1,621 sq. ft.

Intersecting hip roofs with corner notches, a clerestory dormer, vertical board siding and a covered front walkway add design interest and set the house apart from its neighbors. Inside the vaulted, skylighted entry, the hallway angles left past the atrium into the vaulted great room, which has a fireplace and a door leading out to a wood deck or patio.

The spacious L-shaped kitchen also overlooks the atrium and has an adjacent vaulted nook with solarium window and a door to the garage.

To the right of the entry hall is the bedroom wing. Double doors open into the master bedroom, with a private bath and walk-in closet. Doors lead to the solarium and the front courtyard. A second bathroom serves the other two bedrooms, one of which can double as a den and has doors opening into the great room.

In the daylight basement version of the plan, a stairway replaces the atrium.

Main floor:	1,497 sq. ft.
Solarium:	124 sq. ft.
Total living area:	1,621 sq. ft.
(Not counting basement or garage)	
Basement:	1,514 sq. ft.

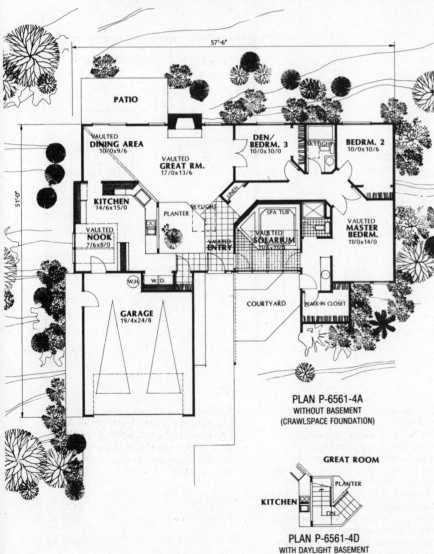

PLAN P-6561-4A
WITHOUT BASEMENT
(CRAWLSPACE FOUNDATION)

GREAT ROOM

PLAN P-6561-4D
WITH DAYLIGHT BASEMENT

Blueprint Price Code B

Plans P-6561-4A & -4D

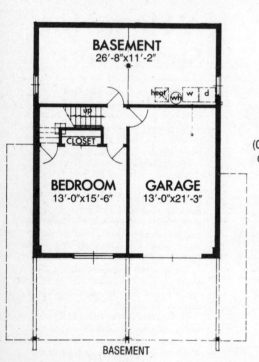

BASEMENT
26'-8"x11'-2"

heat [wh] w d

up

CLOSET

BEDROOM
13'-0"x15'-6"

GARAGE
13'-0"x21'-3"

BASEMENT

(Concrete block construction)

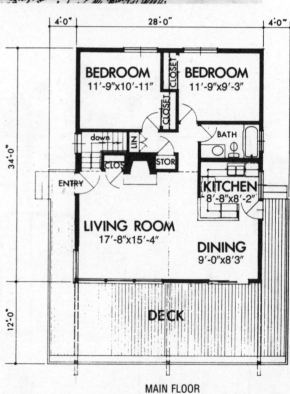

4'-0" 28'-0" 4'-0"

BEDROOM
11'-9"x10'-11"

CLOSET

BEDROOM
11'-9"x9'-3"

CLOSET

down LIN

BATH

34'-0"

CLOS STOR

ENTRY

KITCHEN
8'-8"x8'-2"

LIVING ROOM
17'-8"x15'-4"

DINING
9'-0"x8'3"

12'-0"

DECK

MAIN FLOOR

Economical Recreational Home

A huge wrap-around deck suggests recreational use for this compact two- or three-bedroom home. However, the completeness of detail affords the opportunity for use as a year around residence. As the illustration shows, it is best adapted to an uphill site.

A heavy "shake-style" concrete roof provides virtually carefree lifetime protection for both indoor and outdoor living areas. This is important in rural forested areas where the elements are especially destructive to conventional wood products. Solid block exterior walls laid in a distinctive 8x8 grid pattern are equally impervious to natural deterioration.

The floor plan is a model of efficiency and utility as evidenced by the small but completely adequate kitchen area. Dining and living combine to form a visual concept of much larger rooms. The central

fireplace is located in a convenient spot for refueling either from basement or outdoors. The downstairs room marked "bedroom" is admittedly a room with many other potential uses such as shop, hobby or recreational.

Main floor:	952 sq. ft.
Basement:	676 sq. ft.
Total living area: (Not counting garage)	1,628 sq. ft.
Garage:	276 sq. ft.

Blueprint Price Code B
Plan H-806-M3

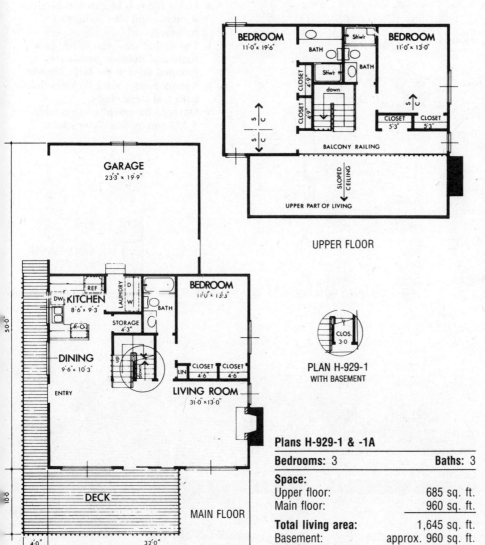

UPPER FLOOR

PLAN H-929-1
WITH BASEMENT

MAIN FLOOR

Contemporary Retreat

- Main floor plan revolves around an open, centrally located stairway.
- Spaciousness prevails throughout entire home with open kitchen and combination dining/living room.
- Living room features a great-sized fireplace and access to two-sided deck.
- Separate baths accommodate each bedroom.
- Upstairs hallway reveals an open balcony railing to oversee activities below.

Plans H-929-1 & -1A			
Bedrooms: 3		**Baths:** 3	
Space:			
Upper floor:		685 sq. ft.	
Main floor:		960 sq. ft.	
Total living area:		1,645 sq. ft.	
Basement:		approx. 960 sq. ft.	
Garage:		459 sq. ft.	

Exterior Wall Framing: 2x6

Foundation options:
Daylight basement (Plan H-929-1).
Crawlspace (Plan H-929-1A).
(Foundation & framing conversion diagram available — see order form.)

Blueprint Price Code: B

Plans H-929-1 & -1A

Exciting Interior Angles

- A relatively modest-looking exterior encloses an exciting interior design that's loaded with surprises.
- The Y-shaped entry directs traffic to the more formal living/dining area or to the family room or bedroom wing.
- Family room features unusual shape, a vaulted ceiling and a fireplace.
- Living room is brightened by a bay window, and also includes a fireplace.
- The dining area, sun room, family room and outdoor patios are grouped around the large kitchen.
- Roomy master suite includes deluxe bath and large closet.
- Daylight basement version adds 1,275 square feet more space.

MAIN FLOOR
PLAN P-7661-3A
WITHOUT BASEMENT

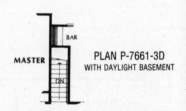

PLAN P-7661-3D
WITH DAYLIGHT BASEMENT

Plans P-7661-3A & -3D	
Bedrooms: 2-3	**Baths:** 2

Space:
Main floor:	1,693 sq. ft.
Basement:	1,275 sq. ft.
Garage:	462 sq. ft.

Exterior Wall Framing:	2x4

Foundation options:
Daylight basement (Plan P-7661-3D).
Crawlspace (Plan P-7661-3A).
(Foundation & framing conversion diagram available — see order form.)

Blueprint Price Code:	B

TO ORDER THIS BLUEPRINT,
CALL TOLL-FREE 1-800-547-5570
158 (Prices and details on pp. 12-15.)

Plans P-7661-3A & -3D

Solar Berm Offers Innovative Living

When viewed from the front road side, this home will match other conventional dwellings in its neighborhood. The approach to the garage is at street level and the covered entry protects a double door that serves a 12'-3" x 9'-6" entry hall.

At this point the plan introduces an innovative concept in construction. The main floor level drops 6' below the entry hall and is connected by eight staircase treads and separated by a 3' open railing.

Open planning that incorporates the family living area with the kitchen is the heart of this home. Extensions on either side provide abundant spaces for bedrooms, laundry, storage and baths.

Surrounded on three sides by the tempering affects of the earth, this bermed home takes maximum advantage of nature for heating and cooling.

The numerous double-paned sun-faced windows are oriented to shower the masonry massed floors and wall with passive solar warmth. Openable clerestories provide cooling and control overheating.

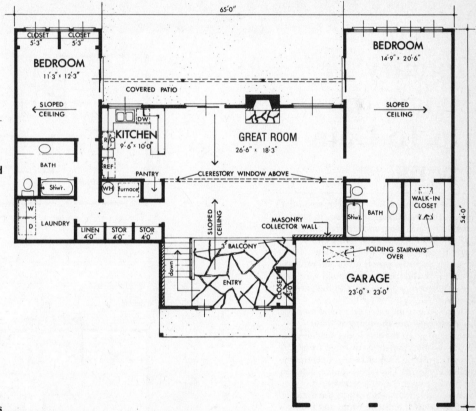

PLAN H-938-1A
WITHOUT BASEMENT
(SLAB-ON-GRADE FOUNDATION)

Total living area: 1,789 sq. ft.
(Not counting garage)

(EXTERIOR WALLS FRAMED
IN 2X6 STUDS)

Blueprint Price Code B
Plan H-938-1A

**TO ORDER THIS BLUEPRINT,
CALL TOLL-FREE 1-800-547-5570**
(Prices and details on pp. 12-15.)

Country Styling for Up-To-Date Living

Nearly surrounded by a covered wood-deck porch, this traditional, 1,860 sq. ft. farm style home has been modernized for an active, up-to-date family, living either in the city or in a rural area. Exterior detailing includes porch posts and railings, a tall brick chimney, multi-paned windows with shutters, and fan lights in the garage doors.

Inside the front entry door, you move easily throughout the home without cross-traffic. To the left is the spacious living room/dining area, warmed by a fireplace with a stone hearth. A central hall leads to the U-shaped country kitchen and family room, with a woodstove. Sliding glass doors lead out to the deck and patio off the dining room and family room.

Stairs also lead off the front entry hall to the upper floor. The front half is devoted to the master bedroom suite, with a dressing area, walk-in wardrobe and a private bathroom. The other two bedrooms share the hall bathroom.

Main floor:	1,035 sq. ft.
Upper floor:	825 sq. ft.
Total living area:	1,860 sq. ft.
(Not counting basement or garage)	
Basement level:	1,014 sq. ft.

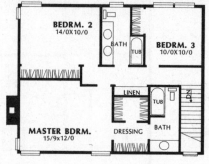

PLAN P-7677-2D
WITH DAYLIGHT BASEMENT

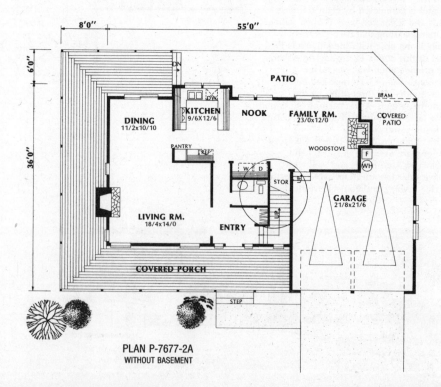

PLAN P-7677-2A
WITHOUT BASEMENT

Blueprint Price Code B
Plans P-7677-2A & -2D

Dramatic and Affordable Chalet

This year-round vacation home is an "upside-down" house, with the main living areas on the upper floor and the sleeping quarters at the ground level. The main entrance on the side of the house opens into a two-story foyer, conveying the feel of being part of the main level, which is just a few steps up.

Once in the living room, one immediately experiences the drama of the open planning and the views beyond. The large front deck has a stairway that can be used as a secondary entrance way. The U-shaped kitchen is illuminated by an operable skylight. A railing in the living room overlooks the foyer below.

Lower level includes two bedrooms and a den which can become a third bedroom. Total living area is 488 sq. ft. on the first floor and 492 sq. ft. on the second.

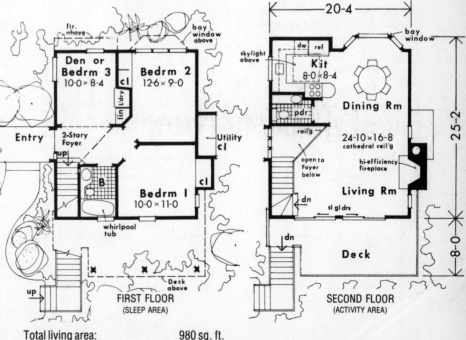

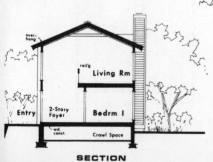

SECTION

FIRST FLOOR
(SLEEP AREA)

SECOND FLOOR
(ACTIVITY AREA)

Total living area: 980 sq. ft.

Plan K-532-L

Compact Chalet

- Three-sided wrap-around deck on main level.
- Large living room with centered pre-fab fireplace and sliding glass doors for entrance to adjoining deck.
- Second-story deck overlooks the outdoors.
- Convenient washer/dryer area in central location.
- Generous storage space flanking upper level bedrooms, one with private sun deck.

BEDROOM 13'-8" × 10'-0"

STORAGE

STORAGE

down

CLOSET

LAV

BEDROOM 13'-8" × 9'-6"

STORAGE

STORAGE

DECK

UPPER FLOOR

Plans H-103-A & -B	
Bedrooms: 3	**Baths: 1½**
Space:	
Upper floor:	378 sq. ft.
Main floor:	624 sq. ft.
Total living area:	1,002 sq. ft.
Basement:	approx. 624 sq. ft.
Garage:	275 sq. ft.
Exterior Wall Framing:	2x4

Foundation options:
Daylight basement (Plan H-103-B).
Crawlspace (Plan H-103-A).
(Foundation & framing conversion diagram available — see order form.)

Blueprint Price Code:	A

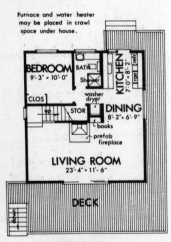

Furnace and water heater may be placed in crawl space under house.

BEDROOM 9'-3" × 10'-0"

BATH Shower

KITCHEN 7'-0" × 8'-2"

CLOS

washer dryer

STOR

DINING 8'-2" × 6'-9"

books

prefab fireplace

LIVING ROOM 23'-4" × 11'-6"

DECK

down

MAIN FLOOR
PLAN H-103-A
WITHOUT BASEMENT

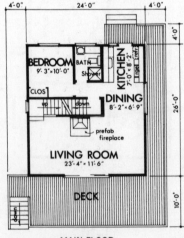

4'-0" 24'-0" 4'-0"

4'-0"

BEDROOM 9'-3" × 10'-0"

BATH Shower

KITCHEN 7'-0" × 8'-2"

CLOS

down

DINING 8'-2" × 6'-9"

26'-0"

prefab fireplace

LIVING ROOM 23'-4" × 11'-6"

DECK

down

10'-0"

MAIN FLOOR
PLAN H-103-B
WITH BASEMENT

LAUNDRY 10'-0" × 11'-2"

dry wash heat

RECREATION 11'-2" × 11'-6"

GARAGE 11'-2" × 24'-8"

BASEMENT

Plans H-103-A & -B

Affordable Relaxation

- An efficient shape for ease of construction offers an affordable vacation home alternative with this plan.
- The main living/dining areas flow together, well lit by transom windows above, highlighting the open-feeling sloped ceiling.
- The island kitchen overlooks the living room with stone fireplace.
- Two bathrooms are located on the main floor, flanking a full bath.
- Additional space can be developed now or later in the full basement.

Plan CPS-1096-B

Bedrooms: 2	Bath: 1

Space:

Total living area:	1,024 sq. ft.
Basement:	1,024 sq. ft.

Exterior Wall Framing:	2x6

Foundation options:
Standard basement.
(Foundation & framing conversion diagram available — see order form.)

Blueprint Price Code:	A

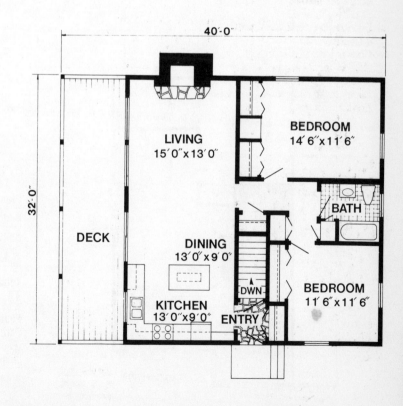

Plan CPS-1096-B

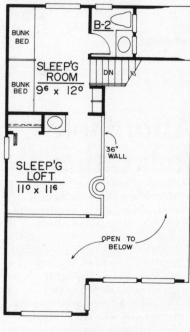

UPPER FLOOR

Casual Flexibility

- This beautifully designed vacation or year-round suite incorporates flexibility in its space and style of living.
- The abundance of windows offers stained glass opportunities as well as a bright interior.
- The open, vaulted living room boasts a central fireplace that makes a great conversation place

or a cozy spot for cold winter evenings.
- The kitchen opens to the dining room and beyond through the dramatic window-wall with half-round transom.
- The sleeping rooms and loft upstairs will adequately accommodate eight, or you may use the space for other activities.

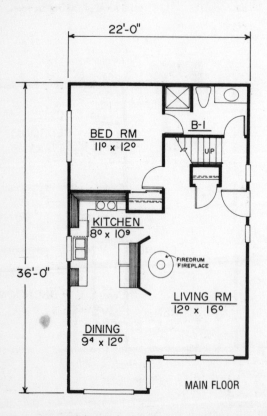

MAIN FLOOR

Plan I-1032-A

Bedrooms: 2-3	Baths: 1½
Space:	
Upper floor:	288 sq. ft.
Main floor:	744 sq. ft.
Total living area:	1,032 sq. ft.
Exterior Wall Framing:	2x6

Foundation options:
Partial basement.
(Foundation & framing conversion diagram available — see order form.)

Blueprint Price Code:	A

Plan I-1032-A

FRONT VIEW

Compact, Economical A-Frame

A huge living room with cathedral-like vaulted ceilings charmingly interrupted midway by an overhanging balcony provides a breath-taking introduction to this home — after you finish marvelling over the expansive entry deck. Furniture arranges itself naturally around the cozy warmth of the free-standing prefabricated fireplace or wood stove. A functional U-shaped kitchen area occupies one open corner of this great room.

This A-Frame boasts a laundry space, complete with washer and dryer. The practical-minded will surely note the central location of the water heater within fuel-saving inches of every hot water tap. A small but functional bathroom is also located in this area. Placement near the rear door allows easy daytime use by children without forcing them to track through the rest of the house with muddy feet.

Two large sleeping areas are located upstairs. One is a balcony room, which might also serve as a charming studio for indoor projects. It should be noted that in none of the rooms except the balcony do the slanting exterior walls intersect directly with the floor to create areas that are useless because of restricted head room. All rooms have a five foot high "knee-wall" located a few feet inboard to assure head space.

If you prefer a home with a basement, Plan H-6B is shown as an alternate, offering garage and recreation space as well as additional plumbing facilities.

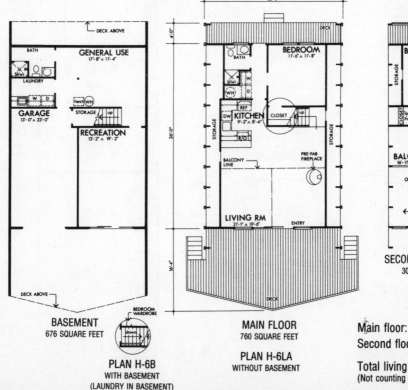

BASEMENT
676 SQUARE FEET

PLAN H-6B
WITH BASEMENT
(LAUNDRY IN BASEMENT)

MAIN FLOOR
760 SQUARE FEET

PLAN H-6LA
WITHOUT BASEMENT

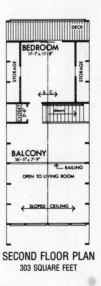

SECOND FLOOR PLAN
303 SQUARE FEET

Main floor:	760 sq. ft.
Second floor:	303 sq. ft.
Total living area: (Not counting basement or garage)	1,063 sq. ft.

Blueprint Price Code A

Plans H-6LA & H-6B

TO ORDER THIS BLUEPRINT, CALL TOLL-FREE 1-800-547-5570 (Prices and details on pp. 12-15.) **165**

Lattice Charm

- Arched transom glass, stucco and lattice trim give style and grace to this narrow-lot design.
- A lattice-clad entry portico and fenced-in patio soften the impact of the long garage wall approaching the front door.
- A vaulted ceiling with skylight provides impact inside the entry, as does the view into the living/dining room with fireplace and sliders to the rear patio.
- The interesting, angled kitchen serves the dining room and overlooks the front patio through the vaulted breakfast nook.
- The spacious master bedroom offers plenty of closet space, double vanities and a compartmented toilet/shower.
- The second and third bedrooms share the second full bathroom with access screened from the living room for privacy.

Plans P-6612-4A,-4D

Bedrooms: 3	Baths: 2

Space:

Main floor without basement:	1,521 sq. ft.
Main floor with basement:	1,598 sq. ft.
Basement:	1,598 sq. ft.

Exterior Wall Framing:	2x6

Foundation options:
Daylight basement. (P-6612-4D)
Crawlspace. (P6612-4A)
(Foundation & framing conversion diagram available — see order form.)

Blueprint Price Code:	B

TO ORDER THIS BLUEPRINT,
CALL TOLL-FREE 1-800-547-5570

(Prices and details on pp. 12-15.)

LOCATION OF
STAIRS IN DAYLIGHT
BASEMENT VERSION

MASTER

DN

BEDRM. 2
10/0 x 11/0

40' - 0"

72' - 6" W/ BASEMENT
69' - 0"

PATIO

MASTER
11/0 x 16/6

LIVING ROOM
14/0 x 19/2

DINING
8/6 x 10/0

REF

DW PANT

BEDRM. 2
10/0 x 11/0

LINEN

VAULT
ENTRY

SKYLIGHT

KITCHEN
11/10 x 14/2

CLG. LINE

EATING
BAR

CEILING LINE

VAULTED
NOOK
9/0 x 10/0

BEDRM. 3
10/0 x 11/0

W   D

STEPS

F   WH

PATIO

GARAGE
21/4 x 22/8

FENCE

Plans P-6612-4A,-4D

Floating Sunspace

Designed to take advantage of narrow and sometimes "left-over" lots, whether urban or rural, this compact dwelling is intended to attract the economy-minded small family. Though it boasts a private, traffic-directing entry hall, all other rooms, especially baths and kitchen, are scaled down to suit the more modest pocketbook. An exception is the beautiful passive sun room (every home should have at least one unique feature). Besides the practical advantage of collecting and storing the free heat of the sun, the room will act as a solarium, for relaxation, or a greenhouse for botanical buffs. In any case it will allow full enjoyment of nature's gifts in an otherwise limited location.

First floor: 1,075 sq. ft.
Sun room: 100 sq. ft.

Total living area: 1,175 sq. ft.
(Not counting basement or garage)

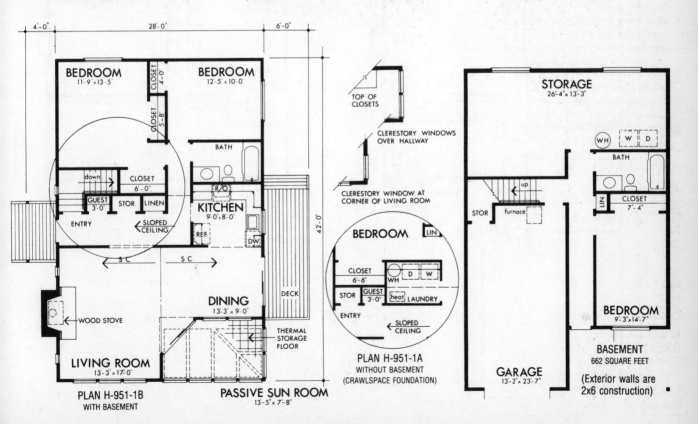

PLAN H-951-1B
WITH BASEMENT

PASSIVE SUN ROOM
13'-5" x 7'-8"

PLAN H-951-1A
WITHOUT BASEMENT
(CRAWLSPACE FOUNDATION)

BASEMENT
662 SQUARE FEET

(Exterior walls are 2x6 construction)

Blueprint Price Code A

Plans H-951-1A & H-951-1B

TO ORDER THIS BLUEPRINT,
CALL TOLL-FREE 1-800-547-5570
(Prices and details on pp. 12-15.)

FRONT VIEW

Compact Plan Fits Narrow Building Site

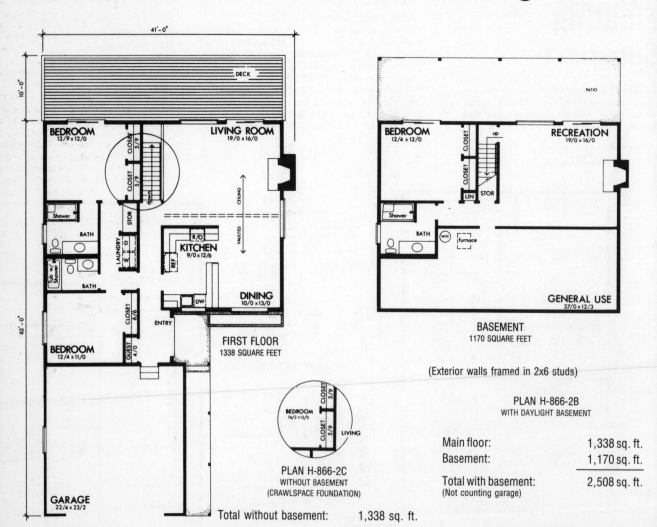

41'-0"

10'-0"

DECK

BEDROOM
12/9 x 12/0

LIVING ROOM
19/0 x 16/0

CLOSET 5/9
CLOSET 5/9

down

STOR

VAULTED CEILING

Shower

BATH

LAUNDRY
W D

R/O

KITCHEN
9/0 x 12/6

REF

Tub w/ Shower

BATH

DINING
10/0 x 13/0

DW

62'-0"

CLOSET 6/6

ENTRY

FIRST FLOOR
1338 SQUARE FEET

BEDROOM
12/4 x 11/0

GUEST 4/0

GARAGE
22/4 x 23/2

PATIO

BEDROOM
12/4 x 12/0

RECREATION
19/0 x 16/0

up

CLOSET
CLOSET

LIN
STOR

Shower

BATH

WH
furnace

GENERAL USE
37/0 x 12/3

BASEMENT
1170 SQUARE FEET

(Exterior walls framed in 2x6 studs)

PLAN H-866-2B
WITH DAYLIGHT BASEMENT

Main floor: 1,338 sq. ft.
Basement: 1,170 sq. ft.

Total with basement: 2,508 sq. ft.
(Not counting garage)

CLOSET 5/9

BEDROOM
16/2 x12/0

CLOSET 5/9

LIVING

PLAN H-866-2C
WITHOUT BASEMENT
(CRAWLSPACE FOUNDATION)

Total without basement: 1,338 sq. ft.

Blueprint Price Code D With Basement
Blueprint Price Code A Without Basement

Plans H-866-2B & H-866-2C

Quality Design for a Narrow, Sloping Lot

Multi-pitched rooflines, custom window treatments and beveled board siding add a distinctive facade to this two-level home of only 1,516 sq. ft. Its slim 34' width allows it to fit nicely on a narrow lot while offering ample indoor and outdoor living areas.

The enclosed entry courtyard is a pleasant area for al fresco breakfasts or spill-over entertaining. The wide, high-ceilinged entry hall opens directly into the sweeping Great Room and dining area. This room is warmed by a large fireplace and has a door to a large wood deck. Also off the entry hall is the morning room with a vaulted ceiling and a matching arched window overlooking the courtyard. A half-bath and utility room is on the other side of the entry.

An open-railed stairway leads from the entry to the bedrooms on the second level. The master suite has a high dormer with peaked windows, a walk-in closet and a private bathroom. The larger of the other bedrooms could be used as a den, and it also overlooks the morning room and entry hall. If additional room is required, this plan is available with a daylight basement.

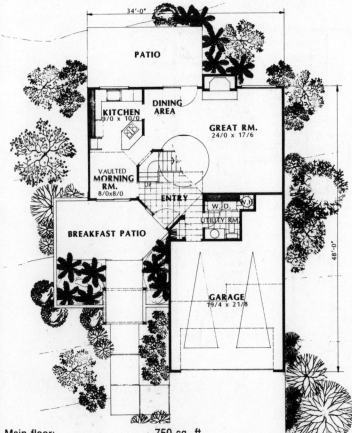

PLAN P-6563-4A
WITHOUT BASEMENT

PLAN P-6563-4D
WITH DAYLIGHT BASEMENT

Main floor:	750 sq. ft.
Upper floor:	766 sq. ft.
Total living area:	1,516 sq. ft.
Basement level:	809 sq. ft.

Blueprint Price Code B

Plans P-6563-4A & P-6563-4D

TO ORDER THIS BLUEPRINT, CALL TOLL-FREE 1-800-547-5570 (Prices and details on pp. 12-15.) **169**

Compact Plan for Small Lot

- Luxury is not forgotten in this lovely, compact ranch.
- Off the entry a vaulted living room with boxed window joins a formal dining area with 3'6" wall to the hallway.
- The kitchen is separated from the rear-oriented family room by a functional eating bar.
- The master bedroom offers generous closet space and dual vanities.

Plan P-7699-2A & -2D

Bedrooms: 3	Baths: 2

Space:

Total living area:	
(without basement)	1,460 sq. ft.
Total living area:	
(with basement)	1,509 sq. ft.
Basement:	1,530 sq. ft.
Garage:	383 sq. ft.

Exterior Wall Framing:	2x4

Foundation options:
Daylight basement.
Crawlspace.
(Foundation & framing conversion diagram available — see order form.)

Blueprint Price Code:

Without basement:	A
With basement:	B

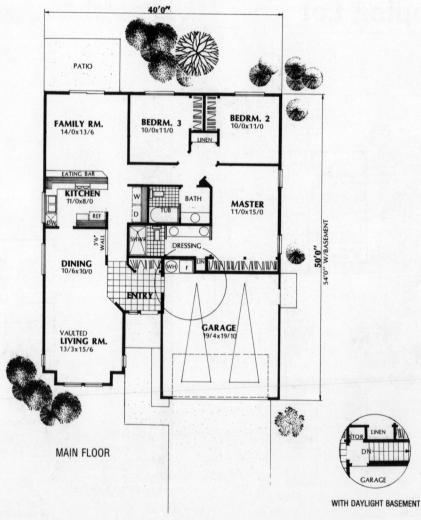

MAIN FLOOR

WITH DAYLIGHT BASEMENT

Plan P-7699-2A & -2D

Fine Example of Post-Modern Design

- Brick columns define entryway, front and rear patios and garage doors.
- Large Great Room and dining room feature raised ceiling for even more spacious look.
- Master suite includes large closet and deluxe bath with skylight over vanity area.
- Breakfast nook in front of kitchen also features raised ceiling.

Plans P-6608-3A & P-6608-3D

Bedrooms: 3	**Baths:** 2

Space: (Plan P-6608-3A)	
Total living area:	1,525 sq. ft.
Space: (Plan P-6608-3D)	
Main floor:	1,618 sq. ft.
Lower floor:	1,618 sq. ft.
Total living area:	3,236 sq. ft.
Garage:	419 sq. ft.

Exterior Wall Framing:	2x6

Foundation options:
Daylight basement P-6608-3D.
Crawlspace P-6608-3A.
(Foundation & framing conversion diagram available — see order form.)

Blueprint Price Code:	B

Floor Plan Labels

44'-0"

60'-0"

66'-6" W/ BASEMENT

MASTER
13/8 x 11/8

BEDRM. 2
10/0 x 10/0

BEDRM. 3
10/0 x 10/0

SKYLIGHT

VAULTED CEILING LINE

RAISED CLG. GREAT RM.
13/0 x 20/4+

RAISED CLG. DINING
10/6 x 10/0

ROOF LINE

PATIO

EXPOSED RAFTERS

LINEN

SHELF ABOVE

WDW ABOVE

ENTRY

CLG. LINE

PANT

CLG. LINE

KITCHEN
13/0 x 14/0+

REF

UTIL.

W
D

F WH

OV

EATING BAR

DW

PATIO

RAISED CLG NOOK
9/6 x 10/0

GARAGE
19/4 x 21/8

MAIN FLOOR

RAIL DN

OV

D W

UTILITY

NOOK

BASEMENT

Plans P-6608-3A & P-6608-3D

TO ORDER THIS BLUEPRINT,
CALL TOLL-FREE 1-800-547-5570
(Prices and details on pp. 12-15.)

Split-Level for Narrow, Sloping Lot

- Front-to-back split level is designed to make good use of a lot sloping down from the street.
- Imposing facade makes home look bigger than it really is.
- Dining room faces front and is well-lighted by three large windows.
- Nice-sized living room includes corner fireplace.
- An upper level den overlooks the living room below.
- Lower level includes large family room, bedroom and full bath.
- Living room features sloped ceiling.

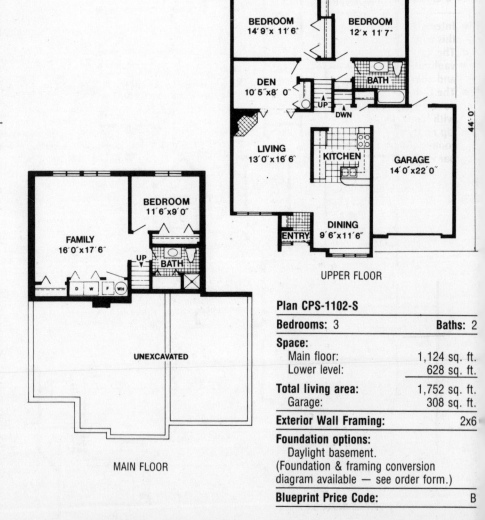

BEDROOM 14'9" x 11'6"

BEDROOM 12' x 11'7"

DEN 10'5" x 8' 0"

BATH

LIVING 13' 0" x 16' 6"

KITCHEN

GARAGE 14' 0" x 22' 0"

ENTRY

DINING 9' 6" x 11' 6"

UPPER FLOOR

38'-0"

44'-0"

UP / DWN

BEDROOM 11'6" x 9'0"

FAMILY 16' 0" x 17' 6"

BATH

UP

D W F WH

UNEXCAVATED

MAIN FLOOR

Plan CPS-1102-S

Bedrooms: 3	Baths: 2

Space:

Main floor:	1,124 sq. ft.
Lower level:	628 sq. ft.
Total living area:	1,752 sq. ft.
Garage:	308 sq. ft.

Exterior Wall Framing:	2x6

Foundation options:
Daylight basement.
(Foundation & framing conversion diagram available — see order form.)

Blueprint Price Code:	B

TO ORDER THIS BLUEPRINT, CALL TOLL-FREE 1-800-547-5570

172 (Prices and details on pp. 12-15.)

Plan CPS-1102-S

Graceful Design for Sloping Lot

- Interesting rooflines add drama to this exciting contemporary.
- The interior boasts a sunken vaulted living room with fireplace and adjoining dining room.
- The L-shaped kitchen overlooks a covered patio and adjacent nook with handy laundry facilities.
- Up multi stairs is the large family room with second fireplace, wet bar and sliders to an attached deck.

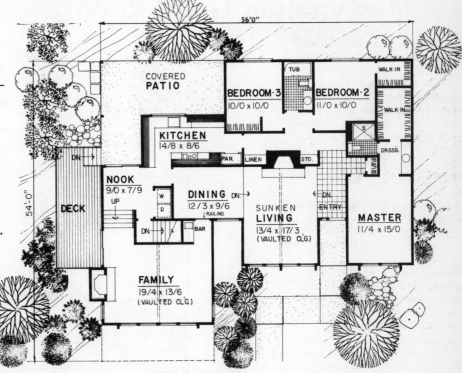

56'0"

COVERED PATIO

BEDROOM·3
10/0 x 10/0

TUB

BEDROOM·2
11/0 x 10/0

WALK·IN

KITCHEN
14/8 x 8/6

PAN. LINEN STO.

WALK·IN

S

DRSSG.

54'0"

DN

DECK

NOOK
9/0 x 7/9
UP

W
D

DINING
12/3 x 9/6
(RAILING)

DN

SUNKEN LIVING
13/4 x 17/3
(VAULTED CL'G)

DN

ENTRY

MASTER
11/4 x 15/0

BAR

DN

FAMILY
19/4 x 13/6
(VAULTED CL'G)

FURN. W.H.

UP

GARAGE
19/4 x 21/6

Plan P-7495-2A

Bedrooms: 3	**Baths:** 2

Space:
Main floor: 1,795 sq. ft.

Total living area: 1,795 sq. ft.
Garage: 416 sq. ft.

Exterior Wall Framing: 2x4

Foundation options:
Crawlspace.
(Foundation & framing conversion diagram available — see order form.)

Blueprint Price Code: B

Plan P-7495-2A

Spacious Vaulted Great Room

- Behind an unpretentious facade lies an exciting and highly livable floor plan.
- A vaulted entry leads visitors to an impressive vaulted Great Room with exposed-beam ceiling.
- The roomy kitchen also boasts a vaulted ceiling, and skylights as well.
- The sunny nook looks out onto a large patio, and includes a built-in desk.
- A first-class master suite includes a large dressing area, enormous walk-in closet and sumptuous bath.
- Bedroom 2 also contains a walk-in closet.
- Also note other details such as the pantry, linen storage and convenient washer/dryer area in the garage entry.

Plans P-6577-3A & -3D

Bedrooms: 3	Baths: 2

Space:

Main floor (crawlspace version):	1,978 sq. ft.
Main floor (basement version):	2,047 sq. ft.
Basement:	1,982 sq. ft.
Garage:	438 sq. ft.

Exterior Wall Framing: 2x4

Foundation options:
Daylight basement (Plan P-6577-3D).
Crawlspace (Plan P-6577-3A).
(Foundation & framing conversion diagram available — see order form.)

Blueprint Price Code:

Without basement:	B
With basement:	C

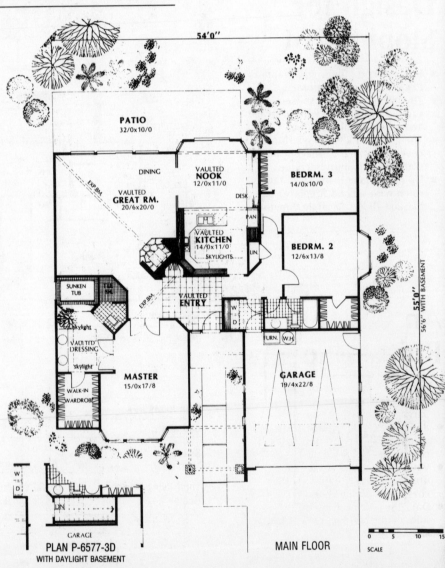

PLAN P-6577-3D
WITH DAYLIGHT BASEMENT

MAIN FLOOR

Plans P-6577-3A & -3D

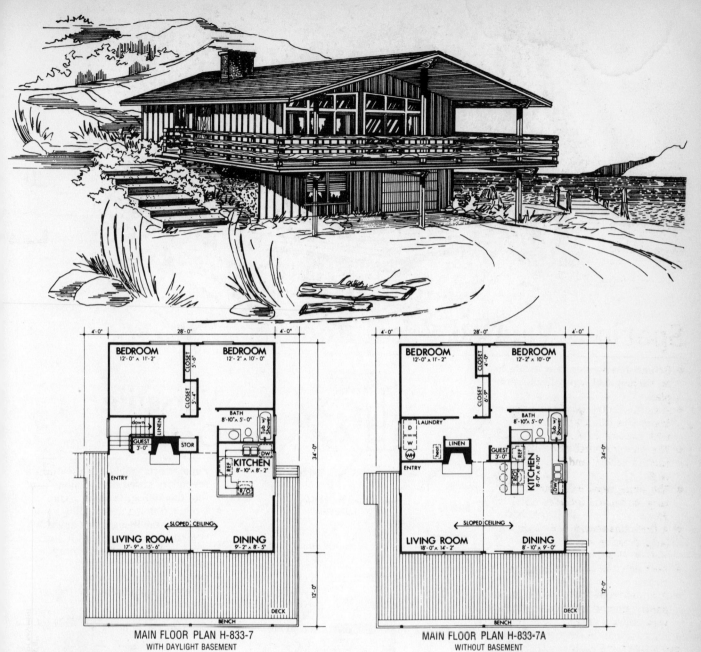

MAIN FLOOR PLAN H-833-7
WITH DAYLIGHT BASEMENT

MAIN FLOOR PLAN H-833-7A
WITHOUT BASEMENT

An Owner-Builder Special

- Everything you need for a leisure or retirement retreat is neatly packaged in just 952 square feet.
- Basic rectangular design features unique wrap-around deck entirely covered by the projecting roof line.
- Vaulted ceilings and central fireplace visually enhances the cozy living-dining room.
- Daylight basement option is suitable for building on a sloping lot.

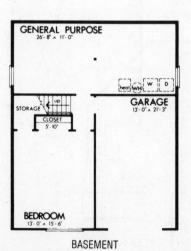

BASEMENT

Plans H-833-7 & -7A

Bedrooms: 2-3	Baths: 1

Space:
Main floor: 952 sq. ft.

Total living area: 952 sq. ft.
Basement: approx. 952 sq. ft.
Garage: 276 sq. ft. (included in basement)

Exterior Wall Framing: 2x6

Foundation options:
Daylight basement (Plan H-833-7).
Crawlspace (Plan H-833-7A).
(Foundation & framing conversion diagram available — see order form.)

Blueprint Price Code:
Without basement A
With basement B

Plans H-833-7 & -7A

TO ORDER THIS BLUEPRINT,
CALL TOLL-FREE 1-800-547-5570
(Prices and details on pp. 12-15.) **175**

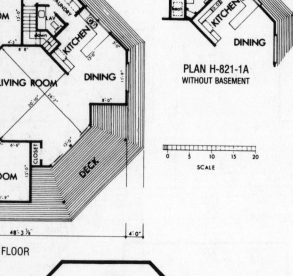

PLAN H-821-1A
WITHOUT BASEMENT

SCALE
0   5   10   15   20

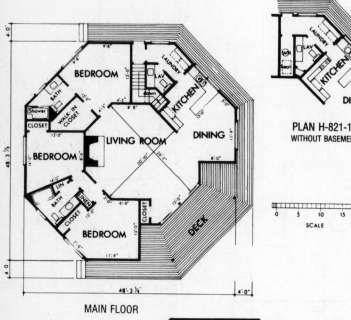

MAIN FLOOR

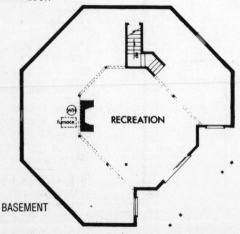

BASEMENT

Versatile Octagon

- Popular octagonal design features a secondary raised roof to allow light into the 500 sq. ft. living room.
- Unique framing design allows you to divide the living space any way you choose: left open, with 3 or more bedrooms, a den, library or other options.
- Large, winding deck can accommodate outdoor parties and guests.
- Optional basement expands recreational opportunities.

Plans H-821-1 & -1A	
Bedrooms: 3	Baths: 2½

Space:	
Main floor:	1,699 sq. ft.

Total living area:	1,699 sq. ft.
Basement:	approx. 1,699 sq. ft.

Exterior Wall Framing:	2x4

Foundation options:
Daylight basement (Plan H-821-1).
Crawlspace (Plan H-821-1A).
(Foundation & framing conversion diagram available — see order form.)

Blueprint Price Code:	
Without basement	B
With basement	E

Plans H-821-1 & -1A

Angled Excitement

- An efficient, economical leisure home is lifted out of the ordinary by soaring cathedral ceilings with angled transom windows and an eyebrow clerestory.
- Guests enter a bright ground level foyer with windowed stair tower leading up to the Great Room.
- The cathedral ceiling opens up the Great Room, dining area and kitchen to give a light, airy vacation feel to the main living space. A wood stove, wet bar and sliders to the view deck highlight the Great Room.
- The vaulted master bedroom has its own bath.
- The second bedroom is privately situated with another full bath on the lower level.

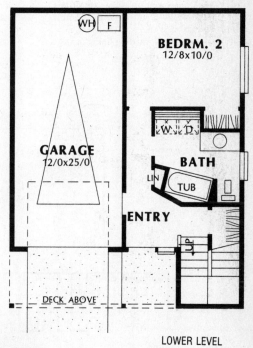

LOWER LEVEL

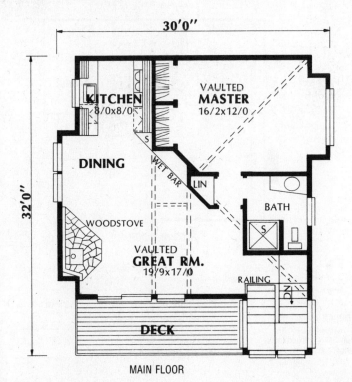

MAIN FLOOR

Plan P-535	
Bedrooms: 2	**Baths: 2**
Space:	
Lower floor:	390 sq. ft.
Main floor:	770 sq. ft.
Total living area:	1,160 sq. ft.
Garage:	300 sq. ft.
Exterior Wall Framing	2x4
Foundation options: Slab. (Foundation & framing conversion diagram available — see order form.)	
Blueprint Price Code:	A

Plan P-535-4D

Contemporary Blends with Site

The striking contemporary silhouette of this home paradoxically blends with the rustic setting. Perhaps it is the way the shed rooflines repeat the spreading limbs of the surrounding evergreens, or the way the foundation conforms to the grade much as do the rocks in the foreground. Whatever the reason, the home "belongs."

Aesthetics aside, one must examine the floor plan to determine genuine livability. From the weather-protected entry there is access to any part of the house without annoying cross traffic. Kitchen, dining and living room, the active "waking-hours" section of the residence, are enlarged and enhanced by the convenient outdoor deck. Laundry and bath are located inconspicuously along the hall leading to the main floor bedroom. A huge linen closet is convenient to this area. The additional bedrooms are located upstairs on the 517 sq. ft. second level. A romantic feature of the second floor is the balcony overlooking the living area.

Plans including a full basement are available at your option. A large double garage completes the plan and is an important adjunct, especially if the home is built without a basement, because it can provide much needed storage space.

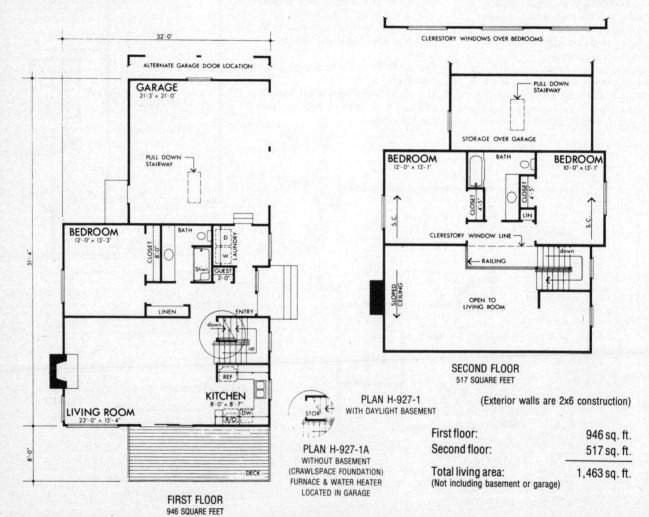

FIRST FLOOR
946 SQUARE FEET

PLAN H-927-1
WITH DAYLIGHT BASEMENT

PLAN H-927-1A
WITHOUT BASEMENT
(CRAWLSPACE FOUNDATION)
FURNACE & WATER HEATER
LOCATED IN GARAGE

SECOND FLOOR
517 SQUARE FEET

(Exterior walls are 2x6 construction)

First floor: 946 sq. ft.
Second floor: 517 sq. ft.

Total living area: 1,463 sq. ft.
(Not including basement or garage)

TO ORDER THIS BLUEPRINT,
CALL TOLL-FREE 1-800-547-5570

Blueprint Price Code A
Plans H-927-1 & H-927-1A

Eye-Catching Prow-Shaped Chalet

- Steep pitched roof lines and wide cornices give this chalet a distinct alpine appearance.
- Prowed shape, large windows, and 10' deck provide view and enhancement of indoor/outdoor living.
- Functional division of living and sleeping areas by hallway and first floor full bath.
- Laundry facilities conveniently located near bedroom wing.
- U-shaped kitchen and spacious dining/living areas make the main floor perfect for entertaining.

BEDROOM 12'-11" x 13'-10"
STORAGE
STORAGE
Shower
LIN
BATH
CLOSET 7'-9"
down
STORAGE
BALCONY 12'-10" x 9'-7"
STORAGE
Handrail

UPPER FLOOR

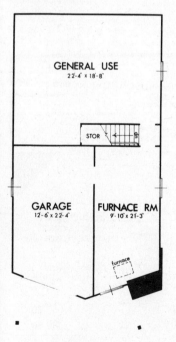

23'-8"

4'-0"

GENERAL USE 22'-4" x 18'-8"

STOR

GARAGE 12'-6" x 22'-4"

FURNACE RM 9'-10" x 21'-3"

furnace

BASEMENT

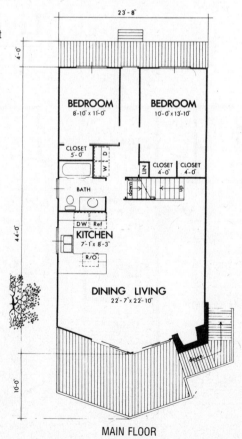

44'-0"

BEDROOM 8'-10" x 11'-0"
BEDROOM 10'-0" x 13'-10"

CLOSET 5'-0"
W D
CLOSET 4'-0"
CLOSET 4'-0"
LIN
down

BATH

DW Ref
KITCHEN 7'-1" x 8'-3"
R/O

DINING LIVING 22'-7" x 22'-10"

10'-0"

MAIN FLOOR

Plans H-886-3 & -3A

Bedrooms: 3	Baths: 2

Space:

Upper floor:	486 sq. ft.
Main floor:	994 sq. ft.
Total without basement:	1,480 sq. ft.
Basement:	approx. 715 sq. ft.
Total with basement:	2,195 sq. ft.
Garage:	279 sq. ft.

Exterior Wall Framing:	2x6

Foundation options:
Daylight basement (Plan H-886-3).
Crawlspace (Plan H-886-3A).
(Foundation & framing conversion diagram available — see order form.)

Blueprint Price Code:

Without basement:	A
With basement:	C

Plans H-886-3 & -3A

Indoor/Outdoor Living At Its Best

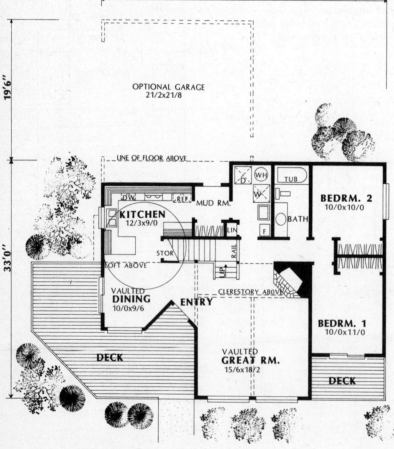

41'0"

19'6"

33'0"

OPTIONAL GARAGE
21/2x21/8

LINE OF FLOOR ABOVE

DW

REF.

MUD RM.

KITCHEN
12/3x9/0

LIN

STOR

LOFT ABOVE

VAULTED
DINING
10/0x9/6

ENTRY

CLERESTORY ABOVE

UP RAIL

WH

TUB

W

BATH

F

BEDRM. 2
10/0x10/0

BEDRM. 1
10/0x11/0

VAULTED
GREAT RM.
15/6x18/2

DECK

DECK

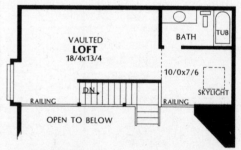

VAULTED
LOFT
18/4x13/4

BATH

TUB

10/0x7/6

SKYLIGHT

RAILING

DN

RAILING

OPEN TO BELOW

KITCHEN

DN

DINING

PLAN P-539-3A
WITHOUT BASEMENT
(CRAWLSPACE FOUNDATION)

PLAN P-539-3D
WITH DAYLIGHT BASEMENT

Main floor:	1,095 sq. ft.
Upper floor:	390 sq. ft.
Total living area:	1,485 sq. ft.
(Not counting basement or garage)	
Basement level:	1,065 sq. ft.

Blueprint Price Code A

Plans P-539-3A & -3D

Split Entry in Western Contemporary Style

- Interior design emphasizes openness in activity areas.
- Living/dining combination makes great space for gathering family and friends.
- Recreation room and living room both include fireplaces.
- Bedrooms are grouped in quiet zone above garage.

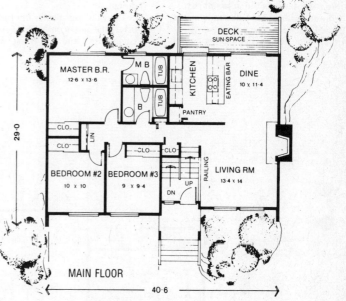

MAIN FLOOR

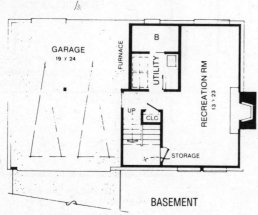

BASEMENT

Plan S-45581

Bedrooms: 3	Baths: 2

Space:

Main floor:	1,073 sq. ft.
Lower level:	437 sq. ft.
Total living area:	**1,510 sq. ft.**
Garage:	456 sq. ft.

Exterior Wall Framing:	2x4

Foundation options:
Daylight basement only.
(Foundation & framing conversion diagram available — see order form.)

Blueprint Price Code:	B

Plan S-45581

Split-Level Vacation Home

By opting for a smaller than average lot, a family choosing a split-level design such as this will benefit from the space-savings and their attending cost savings. Notice, for example, the overall width of 68' includes the projection of the double-sized garage on one side and the location of a sun deck that flanks the sliding doors of the den. Since most leisure home building sites have some slope, the three-level design of this dwelling will fit many situations.

This plan is an example of a design for seclusion, with all the primary living areas oriented to the rear of the home. Notice how the living room, dining area and U-shaped kitchen face the rear wall and have access to the spacious raised deck. The recreation room at the basement level and a third bedroom also face the rear garden.

The main floor area of 1,200 sq. ft. is actually on two elevations. The entry hall is on the same level as the adjacent den and bedroom with bath. A dramatic effect is achieved by the placement of the living room four steps below. The soaring height

of the vaulted ceiling, with exposed beams extending from the central ridge to the exterior wall, adds to the feeling of openness to the outdoors, framed by the window wall and sliding glass doors.

The kitchen itself is convenient to both the dining area and informal portions of the home, and has a work-saving U-shaped design.

The spacious master bedroom suite offers the unencumbered view of an eagle's nest, and also boasts a walk-in

closet and private bath with shower stall. Another added luxury is the 4' cantilevered sun deck, accessible through sliding glass doors. This raised portion of the home that includes the master bedroom contains 320 additional sq. ft.

Other features which should be pointed out include the two massive fireplaces. One is located in the recreation room and the other is the focal point of the end wall of the living room. A third full bath is also placed at the basement level.

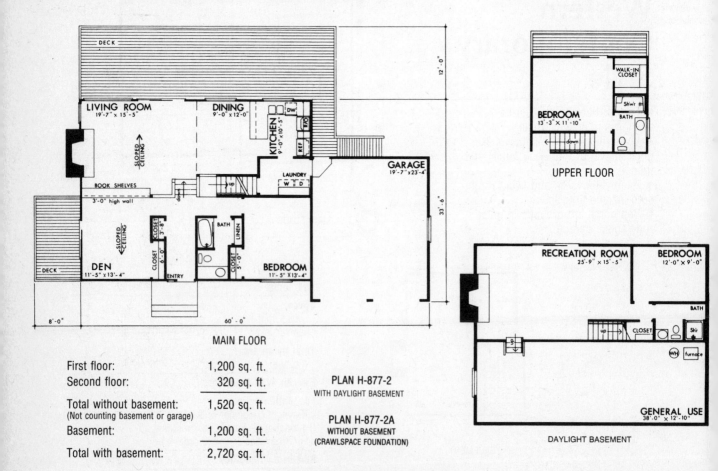

MAIN FLOOR

First floor:	1,200 sq. ft.
Second floor:	320 sq. ft.
Total without basement:	1,520 sq. ft.
(Not counting basement or garage)	
Basement:	1,200 sq. ft.
Total with basement:	2,720 sq. ft.

PLAN H-877-2
WITH DAYLIGHT BASEMENT

PLAN H-877-2A
WITHOUT BASEMENT
(CRAWLSPACE FOUNDATION)

UPPER FLOOR

DAYLIGHT BASEMENT

Blueprint Price Code D With Basement
Blueprint Price Code B Without Basement

Plans H-877-2 & -2A

TRADITIONAL VERSION

Bonus Value

The special values of the split level home continue to offer a nicely furnished initial house package, plus the appeal of an optionally finished bonus work or hobby space or family room. This house is designed to bring high-level exterior appeal and character to a modest plan package. Whether you choose the Traditional or the Contemporary elevation, your home will look good and live well.

PLAN B-8321
WITH BASEMENT

CONTEMPORARY VERSION

Total living area: 1,096 sq. ft.
(Not counting basement, garage or bonus space)

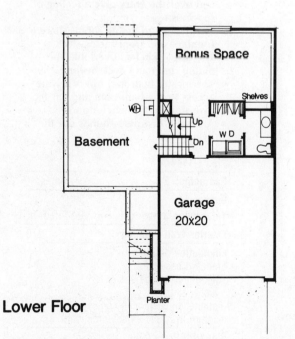

Lower Floor

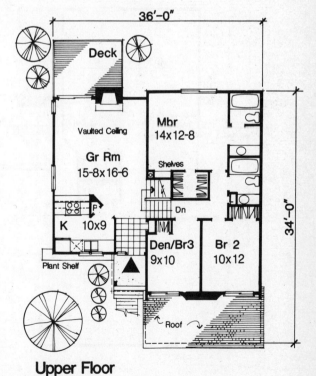

Upper Floor
1096 Sq.Ft.

Blueprint Price Code A
Plan B-8321

Small Pleasures

- A raised living area over a tuck-under garage gives improved views with multiple decks and windows aplenty.
- Vaulted ceilings in the living area and over the entry give a feeling of spaciousness.
- The living and dining rooms share a fireplace and front-facing deck.
- The bright kitchen overlooks the dining room and deck beyond.
- The master bedroom offers private access to the bathroom and has its own deck with French doors.
- A second bedroom rounds out the living floor.

Plan I-1144-A

Bedrooms: 2	Baths: 1
Space:	
Total living area:	1,144 sq. ft.
Exterior Wall Framing:	2x6

Foundation options:
Standard basement.
Tuck-under garage and
   utility space.
(Foundation & framing conversion
diagram available — see order form.)

Blueprint Price Code:	A

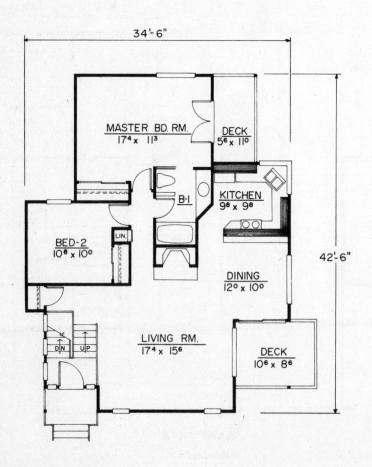

Plan I-1144-A

Simple and Economical Chalet

- This home away from home is relatively simple to construct; it is also an enjoyable reason to spend your weekends in the mountains or at the beach.
- The main level is largely devoted to open living space, other than the kitchen and master bedroom, which could also be used as a study or hobby room.
- Second-floor bedrooms are larger and share a full bath and large storage areas.

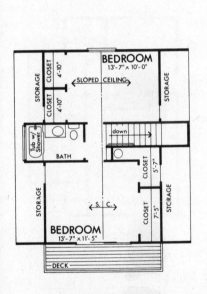

UPPER FLOOR

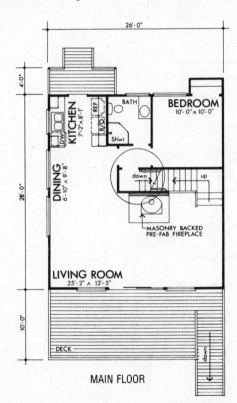

MAIN FLOOR

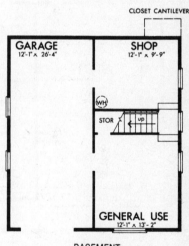

BASEMENT
PLAN H-26-1
DAYLIGHT BASEMENT

PLAN H-26-1A
WITHOUT BASEMENT

Plans H-26-1 & -1A

Bedrooms: 3	Baths: 2

Space:

Upper floor:	476 sq. ft.
Main floor:	728 sq. ft.
Total living area:	**1,204 sq. ft.**
Basement:	approx. 728 sq. ft.
Garage: (included in basement)	318 sq. ft.

Exterior Wall Framing:	2x4

Foundation options:
Daylight basement (Plan H-26-1).
Crawlspace (Plan H-26-1A).
(Foundation & framing conversion diagram available — see order form.)

Blueprint Price Code:	A

Plans H-26-1 & -1A

Hillside Views

- For the sloping or hillside vacation lot with side-oriented views, this design will take full advantage of the beautiful surroundings.
- The wrap-around deck is overlooked and accessed by the spacious living and dining rooms through two sets of glass doors.
- The living room features a fireplace soaring up to the peak of a high sloped ceiling with balcony overhead, accessing the two upstairs bedrooms.
- The kitchen has open sight-lines over the dining room, out to the deck and beyond.
- The main floor master bedroom saves climbing steps and has private access to the bathroom.

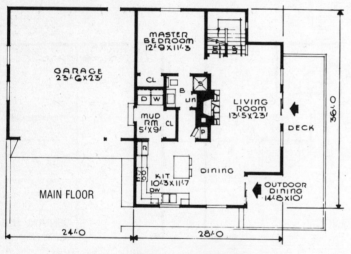

MAIN FLOOR

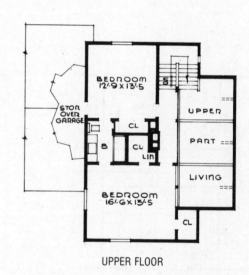

UPPER FLOOR

BASEMENT

Plan CPS-1060-S

Bedrooms: 3		**Baths:** 2

Space:	
Upper floor:	648 sq. ft.
Main floor:	928 sq. ft.

Total living area:	1,576 sq. ft.
Basement:	928 sq. ft.
Garage:	541 sq. ft.

Exterior Wall Framing:	2x6

Foundation options:
Daylight basement.
(Foundation & framing conversion diagram available — see order form.)

Blueprint Price Code:	B

TO ORDER THIS BLUEPRINT,
CALL TOLL-FREE 1-800-547-5570

Plan CPS-1060-S

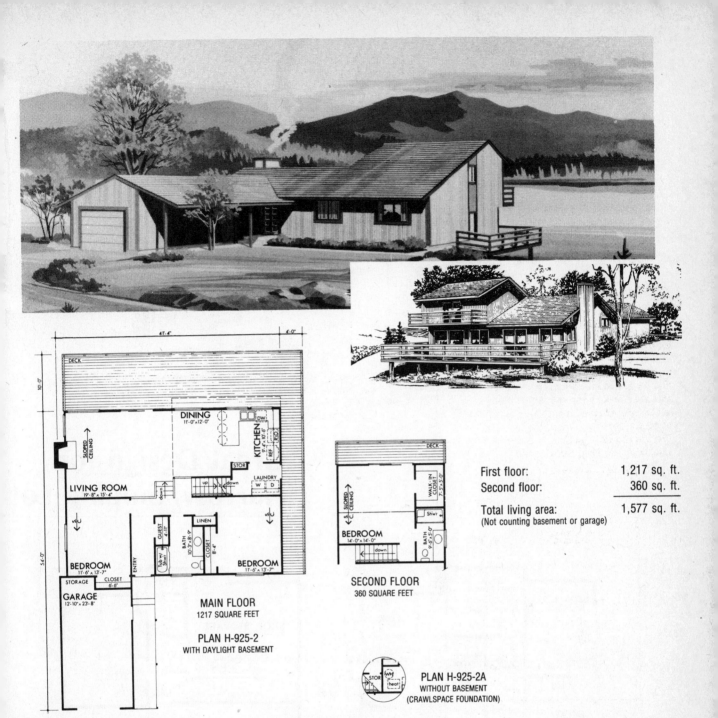

First floor: 1,217 sq. ft.
Second floor: 360 sq. ft.

Total living area: 1,577 sq. ft.
(Not counting basement or garage)

MAIN FLOOR
1217 SQUARE FEET

PLAN H-925-2
WITH DAYLIGHT BASEMENT

SECOND FLOOR
360 SQUARE FEET

PLAN H-925-2A
WITHOUT BASEMENT
(CRAWLSPACE FOUNDATION)

Economical and Convenient

In an effort to merge the financial possibilities and the space requirements of the greatest number of families, the designers of this home restricted themselves to just over 1,200 sq. ft. of ground cover (exclusive of garage), and still managed to develop a superior three-bedroom design.

From a covered walkway, one approaches a centralized entry hall which effectively distributes traffic throughout the home without causing interruptions. Two main floor bedrooms and bath as well as the stairway to the second floor master suite are immediately accessible to the entry. Directly forward and four steps down finds one in the main living area, consisting of a large living room with vaulted ceiling and a dining-kitchen combination with conventional ceiling height. All these rooms have direct access to an outdoor living deck of over 400 sq. ft. Thus, though modest and unassuming from the street side, this home evolves into eye-popping expansion and luxury toward the rear.

To ease homemaking chores, whether this is to be a permanent or vacation home, the working equipment, including laundry space, is all on the main floor. Yet the homemaker remains part of the family scene because there is only a breakfast counter separating the work space from the living area.

Tucked away upstairs, in complete privacy, one finds a master bedroom suite equipped with separate bath, walk-in wardrobe and a romantic private deck.

The plan is available with or without a basement and is best suited to a lot that slopes gently down from the road.

Blueprint Price Code B

Plans H-925-2 & H-925-2A

TO ORDER THIS BLUEPRINT,
CALL TOLL-FREE 1-800-547-5570
(Prices and details on pp. 12-15.) **187**

Great Design for Narrow, Sloping Lot

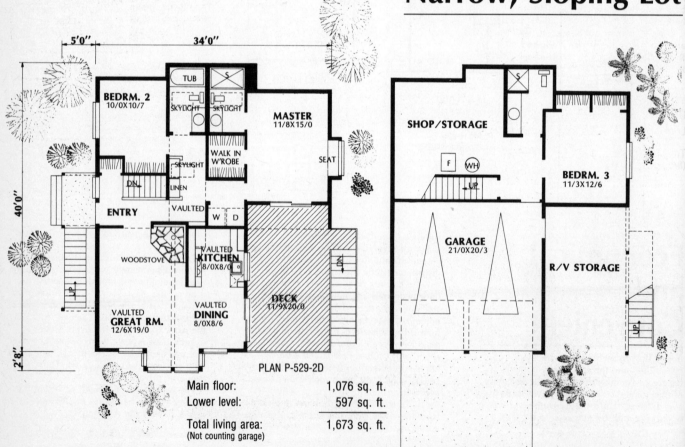

PLAN P-529-2D

Main floor:	1,076 sq. ft.
Lower level:	597 sq. ft.
Total living area:	1,673 sq. ft.
(Not counting garage)	

Blueprint Price Code B
Plan P-529-2D

Sun Room Adds Warmth to "Switched-Level" Contemporary

Solar warmth abounds in this dining area sun room, bolstered by a nearby free-standing wood fireplace and heat-storing masonry. An unusual feature of this design is that the active areas are on the second floor for a better view, and the sleeping rooms on the lower floor.

The spacious entry hall, with a door in from the double garage, has stairs with an open balcony railing leading up to the living-dining-kitchen floor, or down to the bedrooms, for complete traffic separation.

The open-plan upper floor, with vaulted ceiling, has an eight-foot wall screening the dining area from the stairway and the half-bath that is adjacent to the kitchen.

The glass roof and windows over and around the dining area are passive solar collectors and a brick or slate floor provides a storage mass.

A sliding glass door in the living room window wall opens onto the large wood deck, enhancing the view orientation of the house. Another small deck is reached by a French door next to the woodstove.

Downstairs, a hallway from the stairs leads to the master bedroom, with its own bath and large closets, and to the other two bedrooms, second bath and utility room.

The upper floor has 886 sq. ft., and there are 790 sq. ft. downstairs. Ceilings have R-30 insulation and the 2x6 stud walls hold R-19 batts.

Upper floor:	886 sq. ft.
Lower floor:	790 sq. ft.
Total living area: (Not counting garage)	1,676 sq. ft.

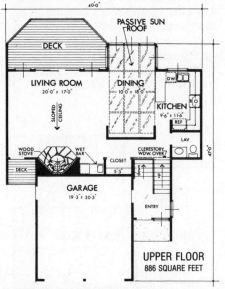

UPPER FLOOR
886 SQUARE FEET

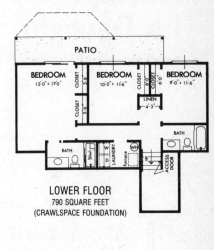

LOWER FLOOR
790 SQUARE FEET
(CRAWLSPACE FOUNDATION)

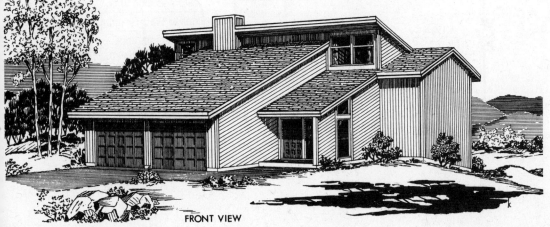

FRONT VIEW

Blueprint Price Code B

Plan H-945-1A

Western Contemporary with Daylight Basement

- Living room includes fireplace and vaulted ceiling.
- Vaulted family room adjoins kitchen and has easy access to patio.
- Master suite includes large closet and private bath.
- Both secondary bedrooms include window seats.
- Daylight basement option virtually doubles the size of the plan.

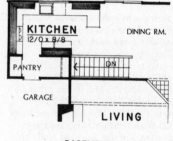

BASEMENT

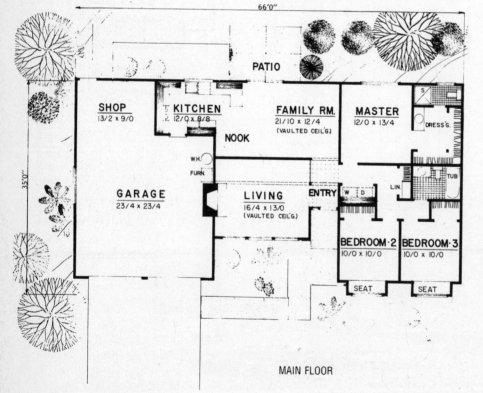

MAIN FLOOR

Plans P-7490-2A & P-7490-2D

Bedrooms: 3	Baths: 2

Total living area:	1,297 sq. ft.
Basement: +/–	1,200 sq. ft.
Garage:	544 sq. ft.
Storage/shop area:	118 sq. ft.

Exterior Wall Framing:	2x4

Foundation options:
Daylight basement, Plan P-7490-2D.
Crawlspace, Plan P-7490-2A.
(Foundation & framing conversion diagram available — see order form.)

Blueprint Price Code:	A

Plans P-7490-2A & -2D

Panoramic Prow View

- A glass-filled prow gable design is almost as spectacular as the panoramic view from inside. The two-story window-wall floods the living room with light and views.
- The open-feeling corner kitchen has the right angle to enjoy the dining room and the family room, including views of the front and rear decks.
- Two main level bedrooms share a full bath.
- The entire upper floor is a private master bedroom suite with large bath, dressing area and balcony opening to the two-story glass wall, a real "good morning" view.

Plan NW-196	
Bedrooms: 3	**Baths:** 2

Space:	
Upper floor	394 sq. ft.
Main floor:	1,317 sq. ft.
Total living area:	1,711 sq. ft.
Exterior Wall Framing:	2x6

Foundation options:
Crawlspace.
(Foundation & framing conversion diagram available — see order form.)

Blueprint Price Code:	B

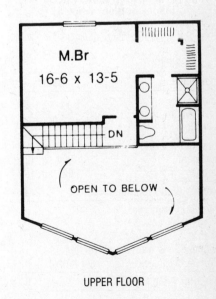

48'-0"

27'-0"

Br #2
11-6 x 11

Br #3
11 x 11-3

Util.

Deck   DN

Family
15-4 x 13-6

DN
UP

Living Rm.
25-8 x 14-6

Dining
12 x 10-6

Kit.

DN

Deck

MAIN FLOOR

M.Br
16-6 x 13-5

DN

OPEN TO BELOW

UPPER FLOOR

Plan NW-196

TO ORDER THIS BLUEPRINT,
CALL TOLL-FREE 1-800-547-5570
(Prices and details on pp. 12-15.) **191**

Spectacular Sloping Design

- For the lake or mountain-view sloping lot, this spectacular design hugs the hill and takes full advantage of the views.
- A three-sided wrap-around deck makes indoor-outdoor living a pleasure.

- The sunken living room, with cathedral ceiling, skylight, fireplace, and glass galore, is the heart of the plan.
- The formal dining room and the kitchen/breakfast room both overlook the living room and deck

views beyond.
- The main-floor master bedroom has private access to the deck and the bath.
- Two more bedrooms upstairs share a skylit bath and flank a dramatic balcony sitting area overlooking the living room below.

Plan AX-98607

Bedrooms: 3	Baths: 2

Space:	
Upper floor:	531 sq. ft.
Main floor:	1,098 sq. ft.

Total living area:	1,629 sq. ft.
Basement:	894 sq. ft.
Garage:	327 sq. ft.

Exterior Wall Framing:	2x4

Foundation options:
Standard basement.
Slab.
(Foundation & framing conversion diagram available — see order form.)

Blueprint Price Code:	B

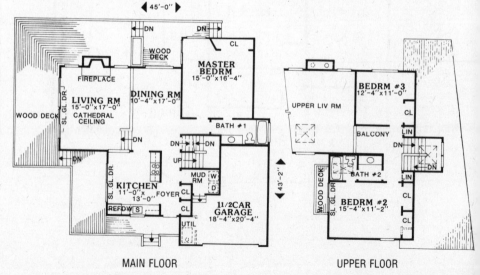

MAIN FLOOR

UPPER FLOOR

Plan AX-98607

Modern Country Cottage for Small Lot

This drive-under garage design is great for smaller lots. But even though the home is relatively compact, it's still loaded with modern features. The deluxe master bedroom has a large bath with garden tub and shower. The country kitchen/dining room combination has access to a deck out back. The large living room with fireplace is accessible from the two story foyer.

The upper floor has two large bedrooms and a full bath, and the large basement has room for two cars and expandable living areas.

This plan is available with basement foundation only.

Main floor:	1,100 sq. ft.
Second floor:	664 sq. ft.
Total living area:	1,764 sq. ft.
(Not counting basement or garage)	
Basement:	1,100 sq. ft.

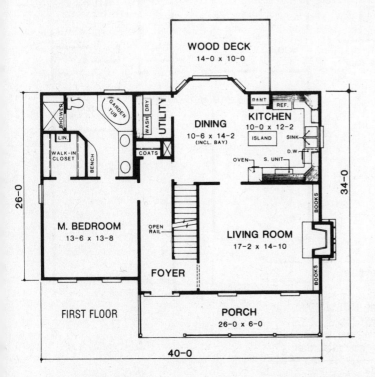

Blueprint Price Code B

Plan C-8870

Contemporary for Today's Small Lot

- Crisp contemporary styling makes this a design that will fit just about anywhere.
- Use of vaulted ceilings in the dining, living and family rooms increases the feeling of spaciousness found in this home.
- Living room and dining area flow together to create ample space for entertaining.
- Open-ended, U-shaped kitchen blends together with the nook for informal dining and food preparation.
- The family room features a fireplace and easy access to a patio in the rear.
- The master suite includes a private bath and large closet area.
- Note the washer and dryer tucked into the garage entry area.

Plans P-7651-2A & -2D

Bedrooms: 3	Baths: 2

Space:

Main floor
(non-basement version): 1,700 sq. ft.
Main floor
(basement version): 1,765 sq. ft.
Basement: 1,780 sq. ft.
Garage: 547 sq. ft.

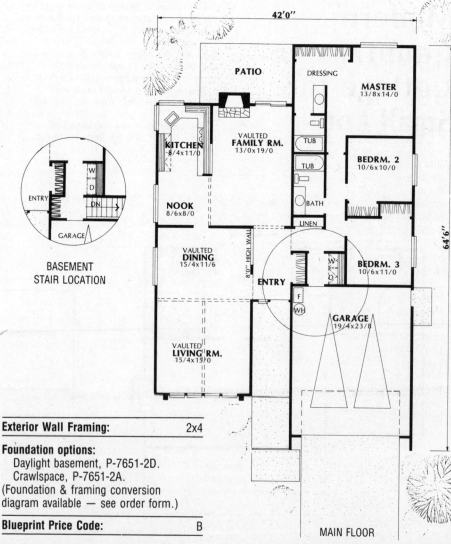

BASEMENT
STAIR LOCATION

MAIN FLOOR

Exterior Wall Framing: 2x4

Foundation options:
Daylight basement, P-7651-2D.
Crawlspace, P-7651-2A.
(Foundation & framing conversion diagram available — see order form.)

Blueprint Price Code: B

Plans P-7651-2A & -2D

Multi-Level Ideal for Difficult Lot

- This compact design is well suited for a lot that slopes steeply up to the rear.
- Massive open spaces and windows create a light and airy feeling inside.
- A mid-level landing at the entry takes you to the vaulted living room, which offers a pass-through to the kitchen; completing the main level are a dining room, two bedrooms and a bath.
- The master bedroom is an upper level loft arrangement. The attached master bath is entered through double doors and features dual vanities, large tub and separate toilet.
- The basement/lower level houses the garage, utility room and fourth bedroom.

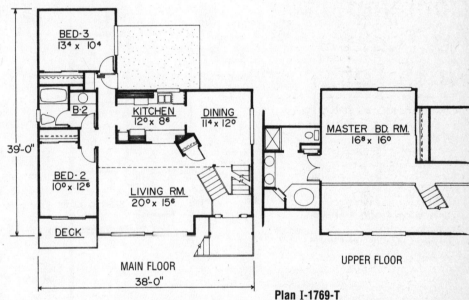

BED-3
13⁴ x 10⁴

B-2

KITCHEN
12⁰ x 8⁶

DINING
11⁴ x 12⁰

MASTER BD. RM.
16⁸ x 16⁰

39'-0"

BED-2
10⁰ x 12⁶

LIVING RM.
20⁰ x 15⁶

DECK

MAIN FLOOR
38'-0"

UPPER FLOOR

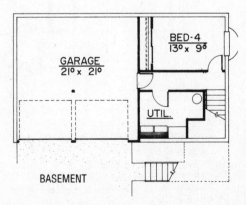

GARAGE
21⁰ x 21⁰

BED-4
13⁰ x 9⁶

UTIL.

BASEMENT

Plan I-1769-T

Bedrooms: 4	Baths: 2

Space:	
Upper floor:	418 sq. ft.
Main floor:	1,021 sq. ft.
Lower floor:	330 sq. ft.
Total living area:	**1,769 sq. ft.**
Garage:	441 sq. ft.

Exterior Wall Framing:	2x6

Foundation options:
Daylight basement.
(Foundation & framing conversion diagram available — see order form.)

Blueprint Price Code:	B

Plan I-1769-T

TO ORDER THIS BLUEPRINT,
CALL TOLL-FREE 1-800-547-5570
(Prices and details on pp. 12-15.) **195**

Stately Character

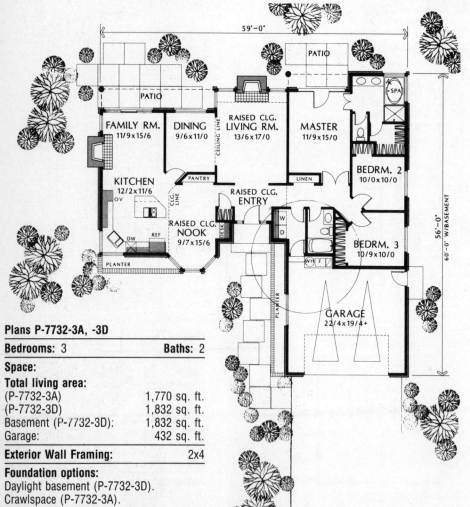

59'-0"

PATIO

RAISED CLG.
LIVING RM.
13/6 x 17/0

MASTER
11/9 x 15/0

FAMILY RM.
11/9 x 15/6

DINING
9/6 x 11/0

SPA

KITCHEN
12/2 x 11/6

PANTRY

BEDRM. 2
10/0 x 10/0

LINEN

OV

CLG. LINE

RAISED CLG.
ENTRY

RAISED CLG.
NOOK
9/7 x 15/6

DESK

W
D

BEDRM. 3
10/9 x 10/0

DW

REF

WH F

PLANTER

PLANTER

GARAGE
22/4 x 19/4+

56'-0" W/BASEMENT
60'-0" W/BASEMENT

- Brick with kneewall planters, stylish hip rooflines and a covered entry with transom glass give a stately character to this exciting one-story design.
- A raised ceiling at the entry and on into the living room enhances the feeling of spaciousness.
- The formal dining room flows into the living room and enjoys the fireplace view.
- The island kitchen opens to both the raised ceilinged breakfast bay with built-in desk and to the family room with second fireplace and sliders to the rear patio.
- The master suite enjoys double doors, private patio access, walk-in closet and spa bath.

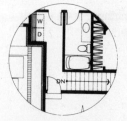

LOCATION OF STAIRS IN
BASEMENT VERSION.

Plans P-7732-3A, -3D

Bedrooms: 3	Baths: 2

Space:

Total living area:

(P-7732-3A)	1,770 sq. ft.
(P-7732-3D)	1,832 sq. ft.
Basement (P-7732-3D):	1,832 sq. ft.
Garage:	432 sq. ft.

Exterior Wall Framing:	2x4

Foundation options:
Daylight basement (P-7732-3D).
Crawlspace (P-7732-3A).
(Foundation & framing conversion diagram available — see order form.)

Blueprint Price Code:	B

TO ORDER THIS BLUEPRINT,
CALL TOLL-FREE 1-800-547-5570
196 (Prices and details on pp. 12-15.)

Plans P-7732-3A, -3D

Dramatic Visual Impact Inside

Rich brick accents this unique hillside home. The family room is sequestered on the lower level for informal, relaxed living and is overlooked not only by the nook and entry but the stairway landing above as well. The added height creates a dramatic visual impact and opens up the core of the house.

The landing itself presents an unusual decorating opportunity. It is light and spacious enough for plants, handsome book shelves, or perhaps your own art collection!

Upstairs, double doors lead into a spacious master suite getaway featuring a large walk-in closet.

Main floor:	1,048 sq. ft.
Upper floor:	726 sq. ft.
Total living area:	1,774 sq. ft.
(Not counting garage)	

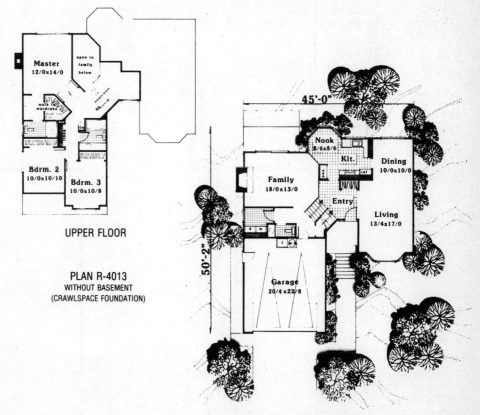

UPPER FLOOR

Master 12/0x14/0
open to family below
walk wardrobe
Bdrm. 2 10/0x10/10
Bdrm. 3 10/0x10/8

PLAN R-4013
WITHOUT BASEMENT
(CRAWLSPACE FOUNDATION)

45'-0"
50'-2"
Nook 8/6x8/6
Kit.
Dining 10/0x10/0
Family 18/0x13/0
Entry
Living 13/4x17/0
Garage 20/4x22/8

MAIN FLOOR

Blueprint Price Code B
Plan R-4013

TO ORDER THIS BLUEPRINT, CALL TOLL-FREE 1-800-547-5570
(Prices and details on pp. 12-15.)

The Simple & Economical Housing Solution

- This compact plan could serve as a second home or a primary residence for a small family.
- Spacious Great Room features woodstove and a large adjoining deck.
- Efficent kitchen is close to storage and laundry area.
- Large, overlooking loft offers infinite possibilities, such as extra sleeping quarters, a home office, art studio, or recreation room.
- Clerestory window arrangement and sloped-ceilings top the loft for added light.

Plan H-963-2A

Bedrooms: 1	Baths: 1
Space:	
Loft:	432 sq. ft.
Main floor:	728 sq. ft.
Total living area:	1,160 sq. ft.
Lower level/garage:	728 sq. ft.
Exterior Wall Framing:	2x4
Foundation options: Slab. (Foundation & framing conversion diagram available — see order form.)	
Blueprint Price Code:	A

LOFT
25'-3" x 16'-2"

CLERESTORY WINDOWS OVER LOFT AND STAIRS

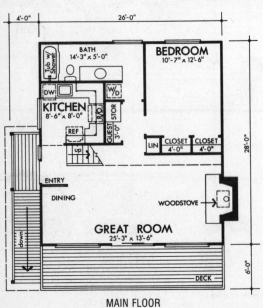

MAIN FLOOR

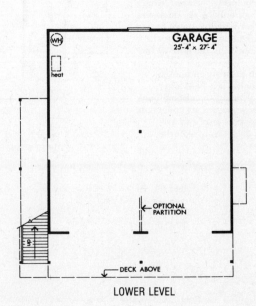

LOWER LEVEL

Plan H-963-2A

Lake Home for Sloping Lot

- Large expanses of glass at the rear of this beautiful rustic recreational home allow views to the outdoors through the dining room, kitchen, living room, master bedroom and upper loft.
- The huge living room is flanked by decks; an eating bar separates it from the adjoining kitchen and dining area. The large fireplace and circular staircase are points of interest.
- The spacious master bedroom has its own fireplace, bath and private deck.
- A second bedroom on the main level and an optional third on the upper level with its own fireplace offer additional sleeping arrangements.

Plan DD-1736

Bedrooms: 2-3	Baths: 2
Space:	
Upper floor:	453 sq. ft.
Main floor:	1,376 sq. ft.
Total living area:	1,829 sq. ft.
Carport:	360 sq. ft.
Exterior Wall Framing:	2x4

Foundation options:
Crawlspace.
(Foundation & framing conversion diagram available — see order form.)

Blueprint Price Code:	B

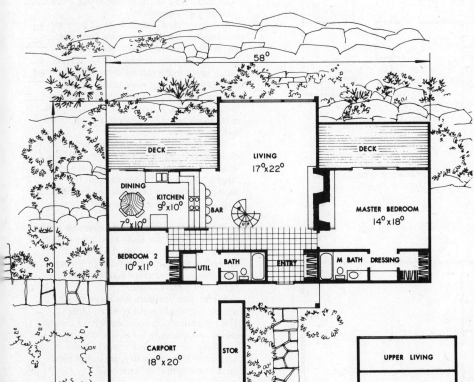

MAIN FLOOR

UPPER FLOOR

Plan DD-1736

Economical Hillside Design

The solid, expansive, well-to-do appearance of this home plan belies the fact that it contains only 1,262 sq. ft. on the main floor and 1,152 sq. ft. on the lower level, including garage space.

This plan has a simple framing pattern, rectangular shape and straight roof line, and it lacks complicated embellishments. Even the excavation, only half as deep as usual, helps make this an affordable and relatively quick and easy house to build.

A split-level entry opens onto a landing between floors, providing access up to the main living room or down to the recreation and work areas.

The living space is large and open. The dining and living rooms combine with the stairwell to form a large visual space. A large 8'x20' deck, visible through the picture window in the dining room, adds visual expansiveness to this multi-purpose space.

The L-shaped kitchen and adjoining nook are perfect for daily food preparation and family meals, and the deck is also accessible from this area through sliding glass doors. The kitchen features a 48 cubic foot pantry closet.

The master bedroom has a complete private bathroom and oversized closet. The remaining bedrooms each have a large closet and access to a full-size bathroom.

A huge rec and game room is easily accessible from the entry, making it ideal for a home office or business.

Main floor:	1,262 sq. ft.
Lower level:	576 sq. ft.
Total living area:	1,838 sq. ft.
(Not counting garage)	

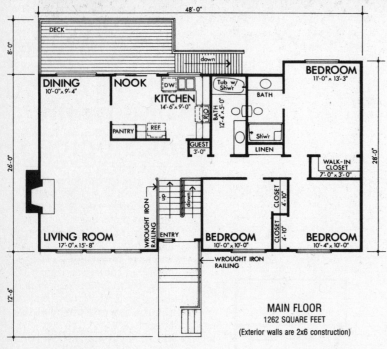

MAIN FLOOR
1262 SQUARE FEET
(Exterior walls are 2x6 construction)

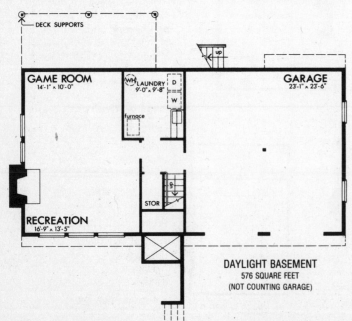

DAYLIGHT BASEMENT
576 SQUARE FEET
(NOT COUNTING GARAGE)

Blueprint Price Code B
Plan H-1332-5

Three Bedrooms in Daylight Basement

- Front porch offers warm welcome to vaulted entry area.
- Main floor offers plenty of space for family living and entertaining.
- Lower level provides three bedrooms, with the master suite including a private bath and walk-in closet.

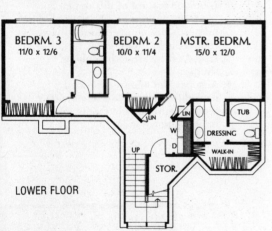

LOWER FLOOR

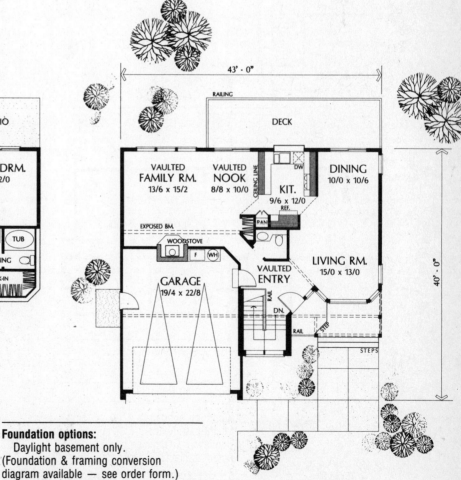

MAIN FLOOR

Plan P-7725-2D

Bedrooms: 3	Baths: 2½

Space:

Main floor:	921 sq. ft.
Lower floor:	921 sq. ft.
Total living area:	**1,842 sq. ft.**
Garage:	438 sq. ft.
Exterior Wall Framing:	**2x6**

Foundation options:
Daylight basement only.
(Foundation & framing conversion diagram available — see order form.)

Blueprint Price Code: B

Plan P-7725-2D

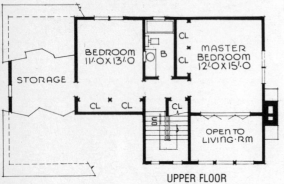

UPPER FLOOR

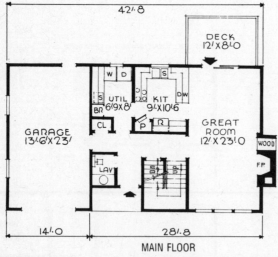

Three Living Levels

- This distinctive three-level home packs a lot of living space into a compact frame.
- The large Great Room houses a fireplace and wood storage area, plus it offers an exciting windowwall to view the front yard and sliding glass doors for gazing at the back yard scenery.
- A unique feature of this design is the front portion of the upstairs master bedroom open to the living room below; if desired, it can be closed off by attractive folding shutters.
- A sloping lot allows a finished daylight basement to accommodate a third bedroom and family room or recreational area.

MAIN FLOOR

BASEMENT

Plan CPS-1029

Bedrooms: 3	Baths: 1 + 2	Exterior Wall Framing:	2x6

Space:			
Upper floor:	512 sq. ft.	**Foundation options:**	
Main floor:	656 sq. ft.	Daylight basement.	
Lower level:	688 sq. ft.	(Foundation & framing conversion diagram available — see order form.)	
Total living area:	1,856 sq. ft.		
Garage:	311 sq. ft.	**Blueprint Price Code:**	B

TO ORDER THIS BLUEPRINT,
CALL TOLL-FREE 1-800-547-5570
(Prices and details on pp. 12-15.)

Plan CPS-1029

"A-One" A-Frame

- Open, dramatic, rustic, and relaxing are all words you might use to describe your image of an A-frame vacation home. This design fits all of those words and more!
- An open entryway houses a spiral stairway that leads to the upper loft.
- The living room is open at the back for a dramatic view from the balcony above; an 11'-long dining bar off the adjoining kitchen makes serving and entertaining a breeze! A deck at the rear extends entertainment accommodations outdoors.
- One bedroom and 2-3 additional sleeping rooms in the loft area are also provided.

Plan DD-1026

Bedrooms: 1-4	Baths: 1½

Space:	
Upper floor:	843 sq. ft.
Main floor:	1,026 sq. ft.
Total living area:	**1,869 sq. ft.**

Exterior Wall Framing:	2x4

Foundation options:
Crawlspace.
(Foundation & framing conversion diagram available — see order form.)

Blueprint Price Code:	B

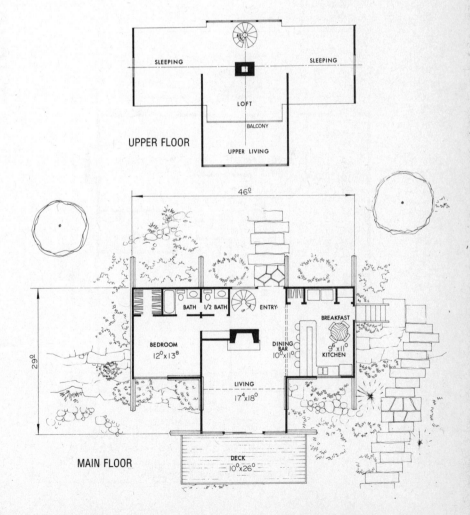

UPPER FLOOR

MAIN FLOOR

Plan DD-1026

TO ORDER THIS BLUEPRINT,
CALL TOLL-FREE 1-800-547-5570
(Prices and details on pp. 12-15.)

Stunning Split-Level for Sloping Lots

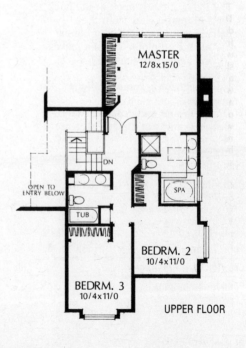

PLAN P-7717-2A

PATIO
FLOOR LINE ABOVE

DINING
10/0x10/0

VAULTED
NOOK
8/0x9/2

FAMILY RM.
16/8x14/8

KITCHEN
9/0x12/8

STEP

REF

CEILING LINE

DN
UP

RAIL

UTIL.

VAULTED/SUNKEN
LIVING RM.
17/0x18/0

VAULTED
ENTRY

DN

W D

F WH

GARAGE
21/0x21/6

45'-0"

44'-0"

MAIN FLOOR

MASTER
12/8x15/0

DN

SPA

OPEN TO
ENTRY BELOW

TUB

BEDRM. 2
10/4x11/0

BEDRM. 3
10/4x11/0

UPPER FLOOR

Main floor:	1,096 sq. ft.
Upper floor:	780 sq. ft.
Total living area: (Not counting garage)	1,876 sq. ft.

TO ORDER THIS BLUEPRINT,
CALL TOLL-FREE 1-800-547-5570
204 (Prices and details on pp. 12-15.)

Blueprint Price Code B
Plan P-7717-2A

P-524-5D Exterior

P-524-2D Exterior

Spacious Great Room

This floor plan is available with two different exterior treatments, as illustrated. In both versions, a spacious Great Room with vaulted-ceiling, wide windows and sliding glass doors opens to the view from a covered wood deck spanning the end wall of this economically styled and adaptable second home. With a main floor of just 1,008 sq. ft., the plan is only 28' wide to fit onto a minimum-size lot. A loft room adds 160 sq. ft. and the daylight basement adds another 722 sq. ft. of living space plus a single garage.

The entry doors open to the spacious Great Room, warmed by a wood stove set on a stone hearth. The vaulted ceiling spreads over the dining area and the U-shaped kitchen. Stairs lead to the multi-purpose loft room or to the daylight basement. Down a short hallway are two large bedrooms, one with a window seat and both with long closets.

Main floor:	1,008 sq. ft.
Loft:	160 sq. ft.
Lower level:	722 sq. ft.
Total living area:	1,890 sq. ft.
(Not counting garage)	

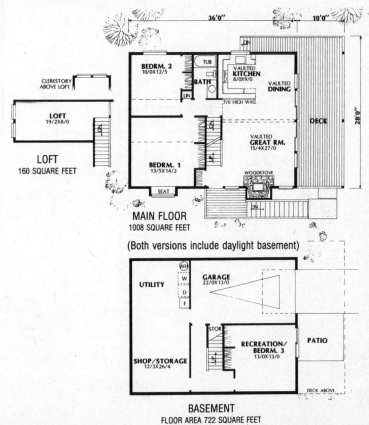

LOFT
LOFT 19/2X8/0
160 SQUARE FEET
CLERESTORY ABOVE LOFT

MAIN FLOOR
1008 SQUARE FEET
BEDRM. 2 10/0X12/5
TUB
BATH
VAULTED KITCHEN 8/0X9/0
VAULTED DINING
LN
7/0 HIGH WALL
DECK
VAULTED GREAT RM. 15/4X27/0
BEDRM. 1 13/5X14/2
WOODSTOVE
SEAT
36'0"
10'0"
28'0"

(Both versions include daylight basement)

BASEMENT
FLOOR AREA 722 SQUARE FEET
(Not counting garage)
UTILITY
WH
W D F
GARAGE 22/0X13/0
SHOP/STORAGE 12/3X26/4
STOR.
UP
RECREATION/ BEDRM. 3 13/0X13/0
PATIO
DECK ABOVE

Blueprint Price Code B

Plans P-524-2D & -5D

TO ORDER THIS BLUEPRINT, CALL TOLL-FREE 1-800-547-5570
(Prices and details on pp. 12-15.) **205**

Massive, Windowed Great Room

- This attractive, open design can function as a cabin, mountain retreat or permanent residence.
- The kitchen and Great Room merge to form a large family activity area; an open balcony loft above offers an elevated view of the massive front window wall.
- A third sleeping room upstairs could be split into two smaller bedrooms.
- The main level of the home is entered via a split-landing deck off the Great Room.

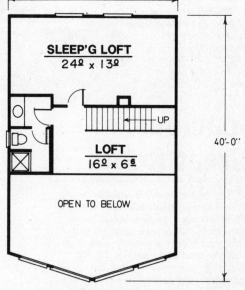

UPPER FLOOR

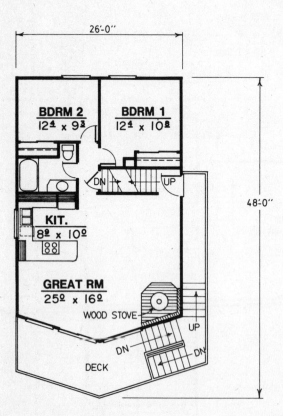

MAIN FLOOR

Plan I-1354-B

Bedrooms: 2-3	Baths: 2

Space:	
Upper floor:	366 sq. ft.
Main floor:	988 sq. ft.

Total living area:	1,354 sq. ft.
Garage and basement:	1,000 sq. ft.

Exterior Wall Framing:	2x6

Foundation options:
Standard basement.
Slab.
(Foundation & framing conversion diagram available — see order form.)

Blueprint Price Code:	A

Plan I-1354-B

FRONT VIEW

Versatile, Open Plan

One enters this home from a side entry approached by the elevated deck and gains access to a spacious entry that controls traffic to all portions of the home. The entrance immediately reveals the open character of the home where you can see the spacious living room with central fireplace located at one end of the building.

Besides an expansive view through clerestory windows, one will notice the sliding glass doors that flank each side of the log-sized fireplace.

Connected to the living room by a 10' wide opening, a dining area is located in such manner as to provide an expandable dining table arrangement. Combination living-dining area opens all living space for entertaining.

First floor:	1,056 sq. ft.
Second floor:	336 sq. ft.
Total living area:	1,392 sq. ft.

(Not counting basement or garage)

FOR PLAN WITH NO BASEMENT
AND BEDROOM/BATH ON SECOND FLOOR, ORDER
PLAN H-893-1A

FOR PLAN WITH NO BASEMENT
AND DORMITORY ON SECOND FLOOR, ORDER
PLAN H-893-2A

FOR PLAN WITH STANDARD BASEMENT
AND BEDROOM/BATH ON SECOND FLOOR, ORDER
PLAN H-893-1B

FOR PLAN WITH STANDARD BASEMENT
AND DORMITORY ON SECOND FLOOR, ORDER
PLAN H-893-2B

FOR PLAN WITH DAYLIGHT BASEMENT
AND BEDROOM/BATH ON SECOND FLOOR, ORDER
PLAN H-893-1C

FOR PLAN WITH DAYLIGHT BASEMENT
AND DORMITORY ON SECOND FLOOR, ORDER
PLAN H-893-2C

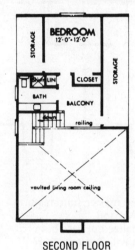

SECOND FLOOR
WITH BATHROOM
336 SQUARE FEET

(NON-BASEMENT VERSIONS
HAVE CRAWLSPACE
FOUNDATIONS)

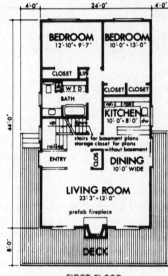

FIRST FLOOR
1056 SQUARE FEET

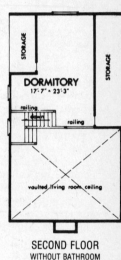

SECOND FLOOR
WITHOUT BATHROOM
336 SQUARE FEET

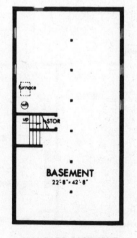

STANDARD BASEMENT

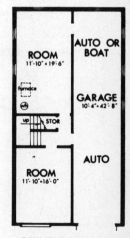

DAYLIGHT BASEMENT

Blueprint Price Code A

Plans H-893-1A, H-893-2A, H-893-1B, H-893-2B, H-893-1C & H-893-2C

TO ORDER THIS BLUEPRINT,
CALL TOLL-FREE 1-800-547-5570
(Prices and details on pp. 12-15.) **207**

Rustic Country Design

- A welcoming front porch, window shutters and a bay window on the exterior of this rustic design are complemented by a comfortable, informal interior.
- A spacious country kitchen includes a bay-windowed breakfast area, center work island and abundant counter and cabinet space.
- Note the large utility room in the garage entry area.
- The large Great Room includes an impressive fireplace and another informal eating area with double doors opening to a deck, patio or screened porch. Also note the half-bath.

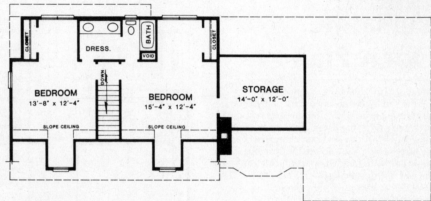

- The main floor master suite features a walk-in closet and compartmentalized private bath.
- Upstairs, you will find two more bedrooms, another full bath and a large storage area.

UPPER FLOOR

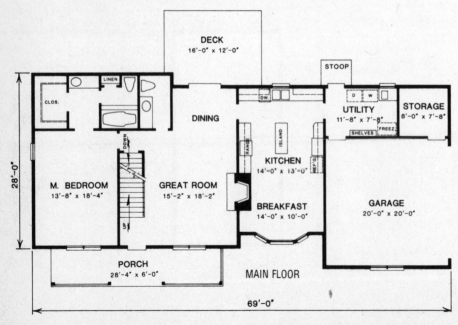

MAIN FLOOR

Plan C-8476

Bedrooms: 3	Baths: 2½

Space:

Upper floor:	720 sq. ft.
Main floor:	1,277 sq. ft.

Total living area:	**1,997 sq. ft.**
Basement:	approx. 1,200 sq. ft.
Garage:	400 sq. ft.
Storage:	(in garage) 61 sq. ft.

Exterior Wall Framing:	2x4

Foundation options:
Daylight basement.
Standard basement.
Crawlspace.
Slab.
(Foundation & framing conversion diagram available — see order form.)

Blueprint Price Code:	B

Plan C-8476

Exciting, Economical Design

Exciting but economical, this 1,895 sq. ft., three-bedroom house is arranged carefully for maximum use and enjoyment on two floors, and is only 42 feet wide to

minimize lot size requirements. The multi-paned bay windows of the living room and an upstairs bedroom add contrast to the hip rooflines and lead you to the sheltered front entry porch.

The open, vaulted foyer is brightened by a skylight as it sorts traffic to the downstairs living areas or to the upper bedroom level. A few steps to the right puts you in the vaulted living room and the adjoining dining area. Sliding doors in the dining area and the nook, and a pass-through window in the U-shaped

kitchen, make the patio a perfect place for outdoor activities and meals.

A large fireplace warms the spacious family room, which has a corner wet bar for efficient entertaining. A utility room leading to the garage and a powder room complete the 1,020 sq. ft. main floor.

An open stairway in the foyer leads to the 875 sq. ft. upper level. The master bedroom has a large walk-in wardrobe, twin vanity, shower and bathroom. The front bedroom has a seat in the bay window and the third bedroom has a built-in seat overlooking the vaulted living room. A full bath with twin vanity serves these bedrooms.

The daylight basement version of the plan adds 925 sq. ft. of living space.

Main floor:	1,020 sq. ft.
Upper floor:	875 sq. ft.
Total living area: (Not counting basement or garage)	1,895 sq. ft.

PLAN P-7681-3D
BASEMENT LEVEL: 925 sq. ft.

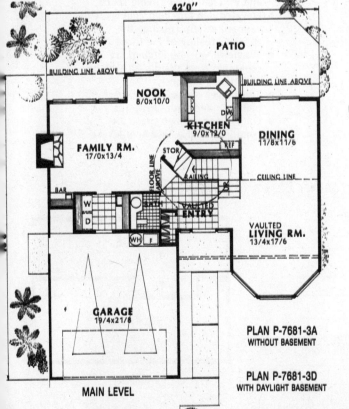

MAIN LEVEL

PLAN P-7681-3A
WITHOUT BASEMENT

PLAN P-7681-3D
WITH DAYLIGHT BASEMENT

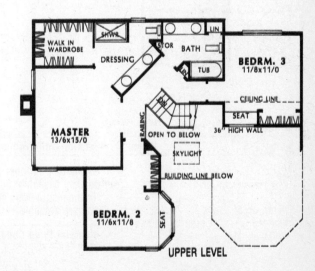

UPPER LEVEL

Blueprint Price Code B

Plans P-7681-3A & P-7681-3D

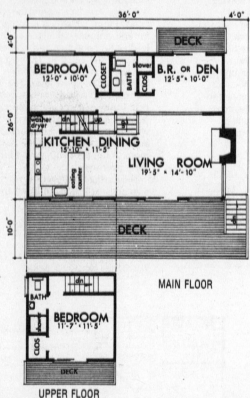

MAIN FLOOR

UPPER FLOOR

Multi-Level Design

- This open and attractive design features multi-level construction and efficient use of living space.
- Elevated den and high ceilings with exposed rafters enhance the spacious feeling of the living room.
- Washer/dryer and kitchen are separated from the dining area by an eating counter.
- Third level comprises the master bedroom and bath.
- Garage and storage space are combined in the basement level.

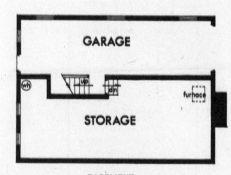

BASEMENT

Plan H-863-2

Bedrooms: 2-3	Baths: 2

Space:

Upper floor:	252 sq. ft.
Main floor:	936 sq. ft.
Total living area:	**1,188 sq. ft.**
Basement: (includes garage)	approx. 936 sq. ft.

Exterior Wall Framing:	2x4

Foundation options:
Daylight basement only.
(Foundation & framing conversion diagram available — see order form.)

Blueprint Price Code:	A

Plan H-863-2

Photo by James Erickson

Rustic Styling, Comfortable Interior

- Front-to-back split level with large decks lends itself to steep sloping site, particularly in a scenic area.
- Compact, space-efficient design makes for economical construction.
- Great Room design concept utilizes the entire 36' width of home for the kitchen/dining/living area.
- Two bedrooms and a bath are up three steps, on the entry level.
- Upper level bedroom includes a compact bath and a private deck.

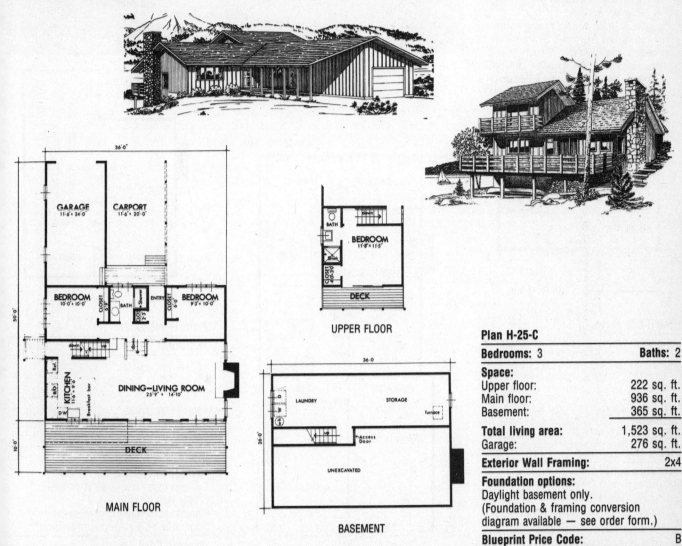

MAIN FLOOR

36'-0"

GARAGE 11'-6" x 24'-0"

CARPORT 11'-6" x 20'-0"

36'-0"

BEDROOM 10'-0" x 10'-0"

CLOSET 6'-9"

BATH

CLOS 2'-3"

Entry

CLOSET

BEDROOM 9'-3" x 10'-0"

KITCHEN 11'-5" x 9'-0"

DW

Breakfast bar

DINING–LIVING ROOM 25'-9" x 14'-10"

10'-0"

DECK

UPPER FLOOR

BATH

BEDROOM 11'-8" x 11'-5"

CLOSET 4'-0" x 3'-0"

DECK

BASEMENT

36'-0

26'-0"

W D

LAUNDRY

STORAGE

furnace

Access Door

UNEXCAVATED

Plan H-25-C

Bedrooms: 3	Baths: 2
Space:	
Upper floor:	222 sq. ft.
Main floor:	936 sq. ft.
Basement:	365 sq. ft.
Total living area:	1,523 sq. ft.
Garage:	276 sq. ft.
Exterior Wall Framing:	2x4

Foundation options:
Daylight basement only.
(Foundation & framing conversion diagram available — see order form.)

Blueprint Price Code:	B

Plan H-25-C

TO ORDER THIS BLUEPRINT,
CALL TOLL-FREE 1-800-547-5570
(Prices and details on pp. 12-15.) **211**

Narrow Lot Solar Design Offers Choice of Upper-Level Bedroom Arrangements

- This design offers your choice of foundation and number of bedrooms, plus it can be built on a narrow, sloping lot.
- Passive solar dining room has windows on three sides and slate floor for heat storage; French door leads to rear deck.
- Living room features sloped ceiling, wood stove in ceiling-high masonry, and its own entrance to the adjoining deck.
- Kitchen is open to the dining room but separated from the living room by a 7½' high wall.
- Upper level variations offer choice of one or two bedrooms. Clerestory windows above the balcony railing exist in both.

UPPER FLOOR

Plans H-946-1A/1B

Bedrooms: 2	Baths: 2
Space:	
Upper floor:	381 sq. ft.
Main floor:	814 sq. ft.
Total living area:	1,195 sq. ft.
Basement	approx. 814 sq. ft.
Garage:	315 sq. ft.
Exterior Wall Framing:	2x6

Foundation options:
Daylight basement (Plan H-946-1B).
Crawlspace (Plan H-946-1A).
Foundation & framing conversion diagram available — see order form.)

Blueprint Price Code:	A

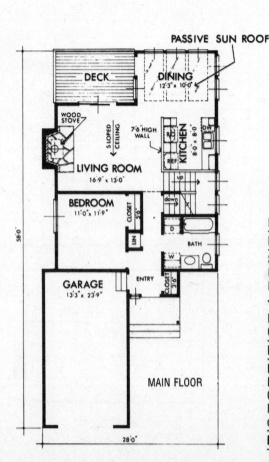

MAIN FLOOR

UPPER FLOOR

Plans H-946-2A/2B

Bedrooms: 3	Baths: 2
Space:	
Upper floor:	290 sq. ft.
Main floor:	814 sq. ft.
Total living area:	1,104 sq. ft.
Basement	approx. 814 sq. ft.
Garage:	315 sq. ft.
Exterior Wall Framing:	2x6

Foundation options:
Daylight basement (Plan H-946-2B).
Crawlspace (Plan H-946-2A).
Foundation & framing conversion diagram available — see order form.)

Blueprint Price Code:	A

Plans H-946-1A/1B & -2A/2B

FRONT VIEW

Wide Open Spaces

This home is applicable to just about any lot and housing need. For year-round residence, the possibilities include a finished basement and an upstairs master bedroom suite. For a second home, the upstairs dormitory can be used as a game room and the basement for storage.

Sliding glass doors and clerestory windows in the living room take advantage of the deck and the view beyond. The stairway to the second floor is flooded with light from another clerestory window.

Like plan H-893, the open kitchen, dining and living rooms are at the heart of the design. What sets this plan apart are the distinctive twin roof peaks over the side entrance.

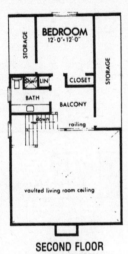

SECOND FLOOR
WITH BATHROOM
336 SQUARE FEET

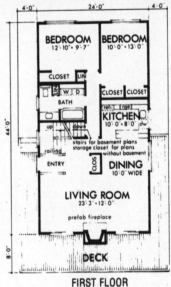

FIRST FLOOR
1056 SQUARE FEET

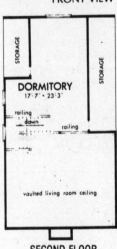

SECOND FLOOR
WITHOUT BATHROOM
336 SQUARE FEET

FOR PLAN WITH NO BASEMENT
AND BEDROOM/BATH ON SECOND FLOOR, ORDER
PLAN H-894-1A

FOR PLAN WITH NO BASEMENT
AND DORMITORY ON SECOND FLOOR, ORDER
PLAN H-894-2A

FOR PLAN WITH STANDARD BASEMENT
AND BEDROOM/BATH ON SECOND FLOOR, ORDER
PLAN H-894-1B

FOR PLAN WITH STANDARD BASEMENT
AND DORMITORY ON SECOND FLOOR, ORDER
PLAN H-894-2B

FOR PLAN WITH DAYLIGHT BASEMENT
AND BEDROOM/BATH ON SECOND FLOOR, ORDER
PLAN H-894-1C

FOR PLAN WITH DAYLIGHT BASEMENT
AND DORMITORY ON SECOND FLOOR, ORDER
PLAN H-894-2C

All Versions:
First floor: 1,056 sq. ft.
Second floor: 336 sq. ft.

Total living area: 1,392 sq. ft.
(Not counting basement)

(NON-BASEMENT VERSIONS
HAVE CRAWLSPACE
FOUNDATIONS)

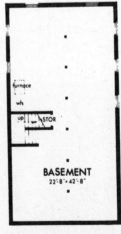

STANDARD BASEMENT

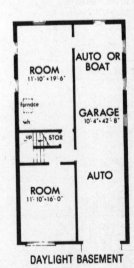

DAYLIGHT BASEMENT

Blueprint Price Code A

Plans H-894-1A, H-894-2A, H-894-1B, H-894-2B, H-894-1C & H-894-2C

Easy Living

- Large, beautiful living area with sloped ceiling and fireplace lies five steps below entry and sleeping areas.
- Attached dining room and kitchen separated by eating bar.
- Convenient main floor laundry near kitchen and side entrance.
- Secluded master suite includes personal bath and private access to sun deck.

Plans H-925-1 & -1A

Bedrooms: 3	Baths: 2

Space:

Upper floor:	288 sq. ft.
Main floor:	951 sq. ft.
Total living area:	**1,239 sq. ft.**
Basement:	approx. 951 sq. ft.
Garage:	266 sq. ft.

Exterior Wall Framing:	2x4

Foundation options:
Daylight basement (Plan H-925-1).
Crawlspace (Plan H-925-1A).
(Foundation & framing conversion diagram available — see order form.)

Blueprint Price Code:	A

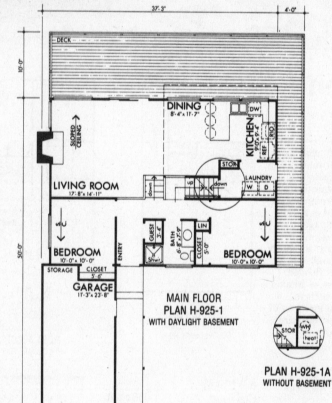

MAIN FLOOR
PLAN H-925-1
WITH DAYLIGHT BASEMENT

PLAN H-925-1A
WITHOUT BASEMENT

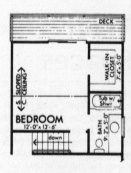

UPPER FLOOR

Plans H-925-1 & -1A

Covered Wrap-
Around Deck Featured

- Covered deck spans home from main entrance to kitchen/side door.
- An over-sized fireplace is the focal point of the living room, which merges into an expandable dining area.
- Kitchen is tucked into one corner, but open counter space allows

visual contact with living areas beyond.
- Good-sized main floor bedrooms furnished with sufficient closet space.
- Basement level adds a third bedroom and an additional 673 sq. ft. of living space.

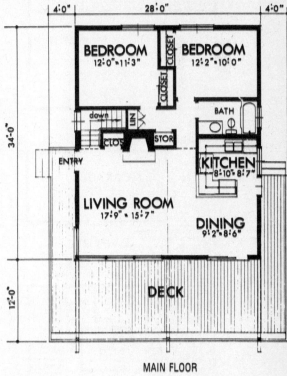

MAIN FLOOR

BASEMENT

Plan H-806-2

Bedrooms: 3		Baths: 1
Space:		
Main floor:		952 sq. ft.
Basement:		673 sq. ft.
Total living area:		1,625 sq. ft.
Garage:		279 sq. ft.

Exterior Wall Framing: 2x6

Foundation options:
Daylight basement only.
(Foundation & framing conversion diagram available — see order form.)

Blueprint Price Code: B

Plan H-806-2

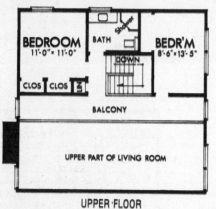

UPPER FLOOR

BEDROOM 11'-0" x 11'-0"
BATH
Shower
BEDR'M 8'-6" x 13'-5"
DOWN
CLOS CLOS
BALCONY
UPPER PART OF LIVING ROOM

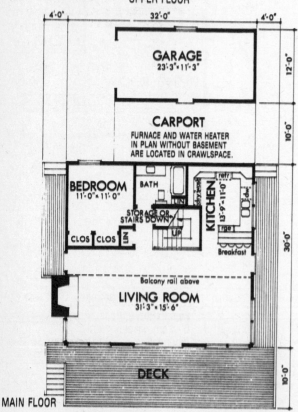

MAIN FLOOR

4'-0" · 32'-0" · 4'-0"

GARAGE 23'-3" x 11'-3" · 12'-0"

CARPORT
FURNACE AND WATER HEATER IN PLAN WITHOUT BASEMENT ARE LOCATED IN CRAWLSPACE. · 10'-0"

BEDROOM 11'-0" x 11'-0"
BATH
KITCHEN 13'-9" x 11'-0"
STORAGE OR STAIRS DOWN
CLOS CLOS
LIN
UP
Breakfast · 30'-0"

Balcony rail above
LIVING ROOM 31'-3" x 15'-6" · 10'-0"

DECK

Surprising Spaces via Beamed Ceilings

- Open and spacious floor plan allows for uninhibited movement.
- Bordering decks beckon you to the outdoors.
- Expansive living room features beamed ceiling open to second level and front window wall at an attractive angle.
- Large, versatile kitchen and breakfast bar make dining a pleasure and laundry an easy chore.
- Inviting balcony adjoins second level bedrooms.

Plans H-876-1 & -1A

Bedrooms: 3	Baths: 2

Space:	
Upper floor:	592 sq. ft.
Main floor:	960 sq. ft.

Total living area:	1,552 sq. ft.
Basement:	approx. 960 sq. ft.
Garage:	262 sq. ft.

Exterior Wall Framing:	2x4

Foundation options:
Standard basement (Plan H-876-1).
Crawlspace (Plan H-876-1A).
(Foundation & framing conversion diagram available — see order form.)

Blueprint Price Code:	B

Plans H-876-1 & -1A

Five-Bedroom Chalet

Realizing that there are situations that require the maximum number of bedrooms, we have created this modest-sized home containing five bedrooms. One of these, especially the one over the garage, would serve very well as a private den, card room or library. The plan is available with or without basement.

This is an excellent example of the classic chalet. Close study will reveal how hall space has been kept at an absolute minimum. As a result, a modest first floor area of 952 sq. ft. and a compact second floor plan of 767 sq. ft. make the five bedrooms possible.

Also notice the abundance of storage space and built-ins with many other conveniences. Plumbing is provided in two complete bathrooms, and a washer and dryer has been tucked into one corner of the central hall on the main floor.

A clever technique has been used in the design of the staircase as it progresses halfway up to a landing midway between the two floors. From here it branches in two directions to a bedroom over the garage and to a hallway common to other rooms.

First floor:	952 sq. ft.
Second floor:	767 sq. ft.
Total living area: (Not counting basement or garage)	1,719 sq. ft.

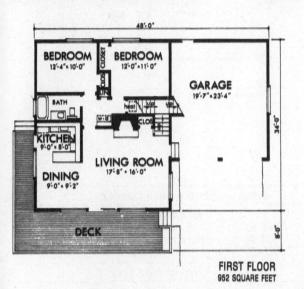

FIRST FLOOR
952 SQUARE FEET

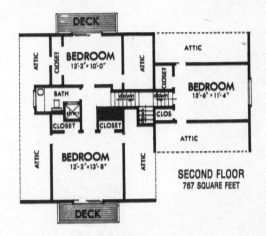

SECOND FLOOR
767 SQUARE FEET

PLAN H-804-2
WITH BASEMENT
PLAN H-804-2A
WITHOUT BASEMENT
(CRAWLSPACE FOUNDATION)

Two Story Impact

- The main, or upper level of this quaint retreat is accessed via a stairway and bordering deck.
- The upper foyer first leads to the Grand room, highlighted by a large fireplace, TV accommodations, sliding glass doors and a snack bar that separates it from the adjoining kitchen.
- The large island kitchen has walk-in pantry and attached morning room brightened by incoming light from three walls of glass.
- The magnificent master suite also has deck access; other amenities include a dressing area, walk-in closet and attached bath with sunken shower and drying area.
- The lower foyer accesses the secondary bedrooms, a second bath, laundry facilities and the two-car garage.

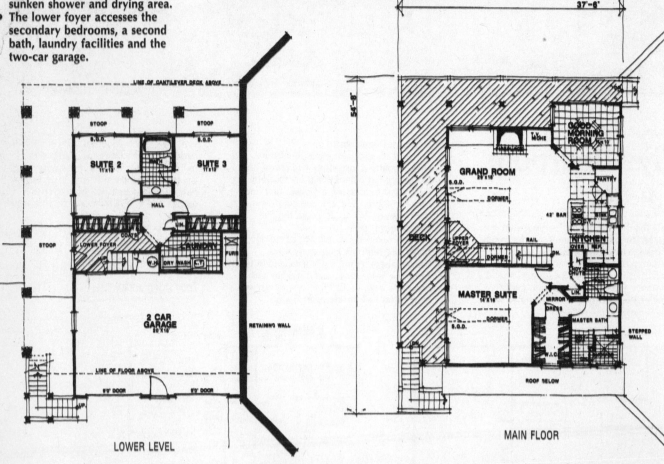

LOWER LEVEL

MAIN FLOOR

Plan EOF-15		
Bedrooms: 3		**Baths:** 2
Space:		
Main floor:		1,193 sq. ft.
Lower level:		593 sq. ft.
Total living area:		1,786 sq. ft.
Garage:		360 sq. ft.

Exterior Wall Framing:	2x4
Foundation options:	
Daylight basement.	
(Foundation & framing conversion diagram available — see order form.)	
Blueprint Price Code:	B

Plan EOF-15

Every Room with a View

- Unique, octagonal design allows an outdoor view from each room.
- Three bordering decks extend first-level living areas.
- Generous living room features dramatic stone fireplace and central skylight open to second floor.
- Second level features circular balcony connecting all bedrooms.
- Alternate second-floor plan replaces one bedroom with a viewing deck.

Plan H-27	
Bedrooms: 3-4	Baths: 2½
Space:	
Upper floor:	1,167 sq. ft.
Main floor:	697 sq. ft.
Total living area:	1,864 sq. ft.
Exterior Wall Framing:	2x4
Foundation options: Crawlspace only. (Foundation & framing conversion diagram available — see order form.)	
Blueprint Price Code:	B

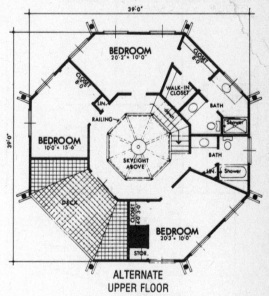

ALTERNATE UPPER FLOOR

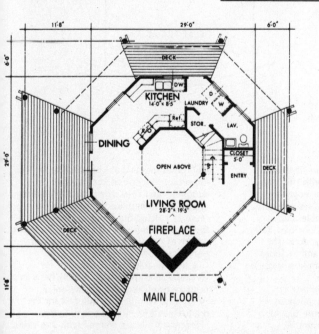

MAIN FLOOR

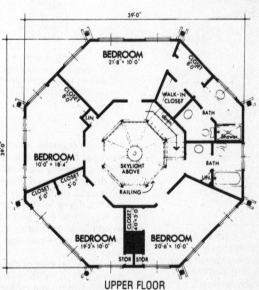

UPPER FLOOR

Plan H-27

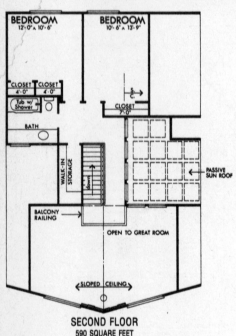

BEDROOM
12'-0" x 10'-6"

BEDROOM
10'-6" x 13'-9"

CLOSET
4'-0"

CLOSET
4'-0"

Tub w/
Shower

BATH

CLOSET
7'-0"

← PASSIVE
SUN ROOF

WALK-IN STORAGE

down

BALCONY
RAILING

OPEN TO GREAT ROOM

← SLOPED CEILING →

SECOND FLOOR
590 SQUARE FEET

First floor:	1,074 sq. ft.
Passive sun room:	136 sq. ft.
Second floor:	590 sq. ft.
Total living area:	1,800 sq. ft.

(Not counting basement or garage)

A Truly Livable Retreat

For a number of years the A-Frame idea has enjoyed great acceptance and popularity, especially in recreational areas. Too often, however, hopeful expectations have led to disappointment because

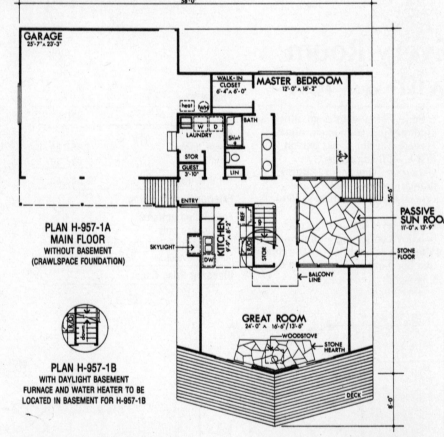

58'-0"

GARAGE
25'-7" x 23'-3"

WALK-IN
CLOSET
6'-4" x 6'-0"

MASTER BEDROOM
12'-0" x 16'-2"

heat   WH

W D
LAUNDRY

BATH

STOR

Sh/wt

GUEST
3'-10"

LIN

ENTRY

PLAN H-957-1A
MAIN FLOOR
WITHOUT BASEMENT
(CRAWLSPACE FOUNDATION)

SKYLIGHT

KITCHEN
9'-9" x 8'-2"

REF

DW

STOR

up

BALCONY
LINE

PASSIVE
SUN ROOM
11'-0" x 13'-9"

STONE
FLOOR

55'-6"

GREAT ROOM
24'-0" x 16'-6"/13'-6"

WOODSTOVE

STONE
HEARTH

DECK

8'-0"

down

PLAN H-957-1B
WITH DAYLIGHT BASEMENT
FURNACE AND WATER HEATER TO BE
LOCATED IN BASEMENT FOR H-957-1B

economic necessity resulted in small and restricted buildings. Not so with this plan. Without ignoring the need for economy, the designers allowed themselves enough freedom to create a truly livable and practical home with a main floor of 1,210 sq. ft., exclusive of the garage area. The second floor has 590 sq. ft., and includes two bedrooms, a bath and ample storage space.

Take special note of the multi-use passive sun room. Its primary purpose is to collect, store and redistribute the sun's heat, not only saving a considerable

amount of money but contributing an important function of keeping out dampness and cold when the owners are elsewhere. Otherwise the room might serve as a delightful breakfast room, a lovely arboretum, an indoor exercise room or any of many other functions limited only by the occupants' ingenuity.

A truly livable retreat, whether for weekend relaxation or on a daily basis as a primary residence, this passive solar A-Frame is completely equipped for the requirements of today's active living.

Exterior walls are framed with 2x6 studs.

Blueprint Price Code B

Plans H-957-1A & -1B

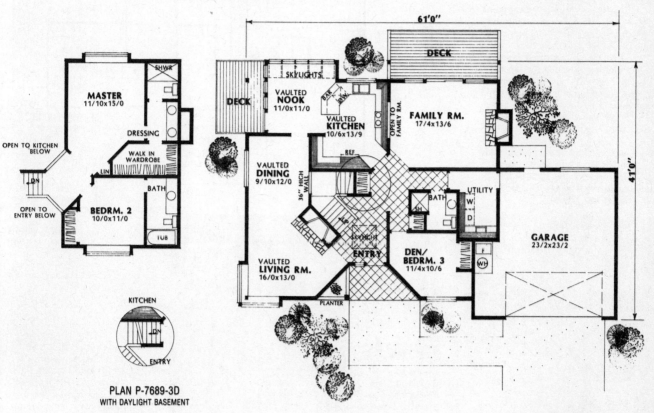

PLAN P-7689-3D
WITH DAYLIGHT BASEMENT

PLAN P-7689-3A
WITHOUT BASEMENT
(CRAWLSPACE FOUNDATION)

Main floor:	1,358 sq. ft.
Upper floor:	576 sq. ft.
Total living area: (Not counting basement or garage)	1,934 sq. ft.
Basement level:	1,358 sq. ft.

Blueprint Price Code B

Plans P-7689-3A & -3D

TO ORDER THIS BLUEPRINT,
CALL TOLL-FREE 1-800-547-5570
(Prices and details on pp. 12-15.)

FRONT VIEW

Sun Chaser

A passive sun room with two fully glazed walls and an all-glass roof offers leeway when siting this comfortable, contemporary leisure home. Orientation is towards the south to capture maximum solar warmth. The window wall in the living room and a bank of clerestory windows high on the master bedroom wall soak up the winter rays for direct heat gain, yet are shaded with overhangs to block out the higher sun in the summer.

The 165 sq. ft. sun room is a focal point from the living and family rooms, through windows and sliding glass doors between these rooms. A dining table in the family room would command a sweeping view, or meals could be enjoyed in the sun room.

Sloping ceilings in the living and sun rooms allow balcony railings to open the master bedroom partially for a view down to these rooms, and let warm air flow up from the masonry storage floor of the sun room.

Accent walls of solid board paneling add visual warmth and texture to the rooms. Western cedar bevel siding adds beauty and individuality to the exterior. Exterior walls are of 2x6 construction.

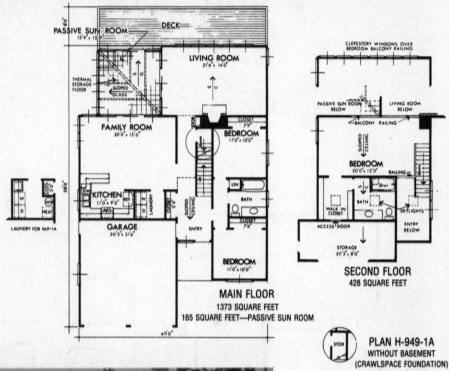

MAIN FLOOR
1373 SQUARE FEET
165 SQUARE FEET—PASSIVE SUN ROOM

SECOND FLOOR
428 SQUARE FEET

PLAN H-949-1A
WITHOUT BASEMENT
(CRAWLSPACE FOUNDATION)

PLAN H-949-1B
DAYLIGHT BASEMENT

PLAN H-949-1
STANDARD BASEMENT

First floor:	1,373 sq. ft.
Passive sun room:	165 sq. ft.
Second floor:	428 sq. ft.
Total living area:	1,966 sq. ft.

(Not counting basement or garage)

Blueprint Price Code B

Plans H-949-1, -1A & -1B

Compact Three-Bedroom Home

- A stylish blend of traditional and contemporary architecture emanates from this compact, three-bedroom home.
- Two bedrooms and an adjoining bath occupy one corner of the main level, segregated from the living areas by a central hallway.
- Large living and dining area has sloped ceilings, wood stove, and access to side deck.
- Master suite occupies entire 516 sq. ft. second floor, features sloped ceilings, and overlooks the living room below.

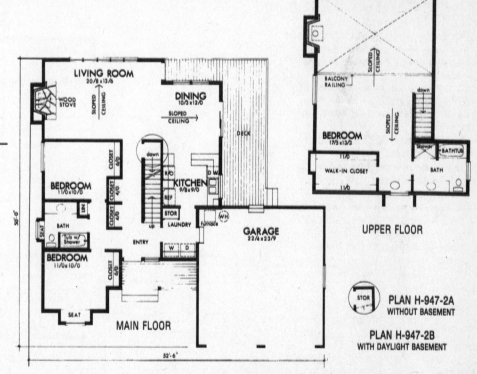

UPPER FLOOR

MAIN FLOOR

PLAN H-947-2A
WITHOUT BASEMENT

PLAN H-947-2B
WITH DAYLIGHT BASEMENT

Plans H-947-2A & -2B		
Bedrooms: 3		**Baths:** 2
Space:		
Upper floor:		516 sq. ft.
Main floor:		1,162 sq. ft.
Total living area:		1,678 sq. ft.
Basement:		approx. 1,162 sq. ft.
Garage:		530 sq. ft.

Exterior Wall Framing:	2x6
Foundation options:	
Daylight basement (Plan H-947-2B).	
Crawlspace (Plan H-947-2A).	
(Foundation & framing conversion	
diagram available — see order form.)	
Blueprint Price Code:	B

(Prices and details on pp. 12-15.)

TO ORDER THIS BLUEPRINT,
CALL TOLL-FREE 1-800-547-5570

Plans H-947-2A & -2B

Rustic Home Offers Comfort, Economy

- Rustic and compact, this home offers economy of construction and looks at home in any setting.
- The homey front porch, multi-paned windows, shutters and horizontal siding combine to create a rustic exterior.
- An L-shaped kitchen is open to the dining room and also to the living room to create a Great Room feel to the floor plan.
- The living room includes a raised-hearth fireplace.
- Main floor master suite features a large walk-in closet and a double vanity in the master bath.
- An open two-story high foyer leads to the second floor, which includes two bedrooms with walk-in closets and a full bath with two linen closets.

Plan C-8339

Bedrooms: 3	Baths: 2
Space:	
Upper floor:	660 sq.ft.
Main floor:	1,100 sq.ft.
Total living area:	1,760 sq.ft.
Basement:	Approx. 1,100 sq.ft.
Garage:	Included in basement.
Exterior Wall Framing:	2x4
Foundation options: Standard basement only. (Foundation & framing conversion diagram available — see order form.)	
Blueprint Price Code:	B

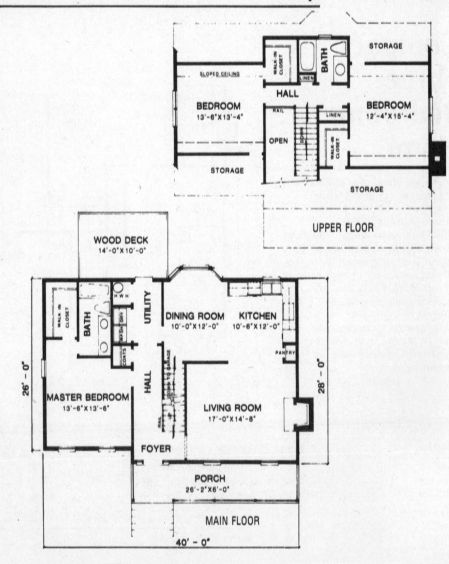

Plan C-8339